THE

EARLY RELIGION OF ISRAEL

VOLUME II.

THE

EARLY RELIGION OF ISRAEL

AS SET FORTH BY BIBLICAL WRITERS AND BY MODERN CRITICAL HISTORIANS

BY

JAMES ROBERTSON, D.D.

PROFESSOR OF ORIENTAL LANGUAGES IN THE UNIVERSITY
OF GLASGOW

VOLUME II.

NEW YORK

THOMAS WHITTAKER

2 AND 3 BIBLE HOUSE

CONTENTS.

VOLUME II.

CHAPTER XI.

THE JAHAVEH RELIGION.

The Jahaveh religion characteristic of Israel—The points to be examined in this chapter: I. Its origin; II. Its specific initial significance—I. Origin sought for in (1) Indo-Germanic; (2) Assyro-Babylonian; (3) Egyptian; (4) Kenite; and (5) Canaanite language or religion—Conclusion that it is distinctively Israelite—II. Significance—Etymological considerations—Critical derivation, "Thunderer"—Biblical derivation—Historical considerations in its favour—Importance of determining the initial signification of the name—If it is of Israelite origin, and introduced under definite historical circumstances, it must have a specific signification—The other explanation is open to the following objections: (1) There is no evidence that Jahaveh was a tribal God; (2) No reason is given for the substitution of the name Jahaveh for El; (3) Stade's proofs are a confusion of early and late, and give no intelligible account of the initial significance of the pre-prophetic conception of Jahaveh—Conclusion that higher qualities were there from the first.

THE thing that distinguished Israel in early times from the surrounding nations, and in later times, was their contribution to the religious good of the world, was the possession of the Jahaveh religion. Even if we admit that, as is maintained, Jahaveh was only to them what the gods of the nations around them were to their worshippers, they had this, at least, as a distinctive mark; and it was from it as a germ that the purer religion of the prophets was developed. Even if, in pre-prophetic times, the national religion was of a low type, at the bottom of it lay the belief that Jahaveh was Israel's God; nay, even if they thought it no sin to employ the names of heathen deities in forming proper names and so forth, they were all the time professors of the Jahaveh religion, and the most that can be said is, that they bestowed on Jahaveh Himself those names that other nations applied to their gods. I have advanced considerations to show that the positions referred to as to the low character of the pre-prophetic religion are not by any means established. But I insist upon this point now, that even if they were established, the great problem has still to be solved. Two points, mentioned in a former chapter,[1] still remain to be demonstrated: (1) We must be shown the origin of the Jahaveh religion, and it must be seen to have such distinctive marks as will make it characteristic of Israel, and bind them together at the most critical period of their history; and then (2) the process of development must be pointed out by which, in well-marked historical stadia, it rose to the religion which is described as ethic monotheism. Briefly put, we must have an explanation of the Jahaveh religion at both extremities of its development, at its start and at its final development; and it is incumbent on those who refuse to take the Biblical account of the matter to present us with another that will stand the test of historical criticism. They must show us (*a*) the source of the Jahaveh religion; (*b*) its specific initial significance; and (*c*) its historical development from

[1] Chapter vi. p. 166.

the lower to the higher stage. A consideration of the first two of these three points will be the subject of this chapter.

I. In regard to the origin of the Jahaveh religion, as in regard to other distinctive features of the history, investigations have been pursued in various directions with the view of discovering, if possible, some point of contact with and dependence upon other nations with which Israel was brought into connection; and different investigators have thought that they have discovered either the actual name Jahaveh, or the idea which it expresses, in the languages and religious conceptions of different peoples. Inquiries of this kind are perfectly legitimate, and often lead to most instructive results. The issue of them, however, must be carefully noted. When, for example, Wellhausen says that Nabiism passed over from the Phœnicians to Israel at a certain time, that is not a final explanation of Israelite prophetism. Even if the fact were as he asserts—and it depends very much on his assertion—there still remains to be explained how the " passing over " took place at such a time, and the more difficult fact that it passed over into so different a phenomenon; and for both these circumstances we have to fall back upon some predisposing cause, and some inherent capability in Israel. Similarly, should it be proved that the name Jahaveh, or the idea denoted by the name, is found among some other people, we are no nearer the solution of the problem. First of all, we are driven a step farther back in our search for its origin, and have to explain whence that other people got it; and

secondly, we have to account for Israel's adopting it;
and lastly, we have to explain why it became, in
their hands, quite a new thing.

The investigations that have been made in the directions indicated are interesting and exhaustive.
The name, or the idea which it expresses, has been
in turn sought for in (1) Indo-Germanic; (2) in
Assyro-Babylonian; (3) Egyptian; (4) Kenite; and
(5) Canaanite language or religion.   We must briefly consider the arguments advanced for these various
views.

(1.) An Indo-Germanic source of the name has
been sought by some scholars.   Thus Von Bohlen,[1]
referring to the varying forms, Jave, Jaho, and Jao
(Iαω), under which the name appears in writings of
the Jews, Samaritans, and Christian fathers, says
that "in this shape it is clearly connected with the
names of the Deity in many other languages"—Greek,
Latin, and Sanscrit—and that the original form would
have been Jah.   This opinion has been pronounced
by J. G. Müller[2] as "not lightly to be set aside."
The idea is that the Indo-Germanic root *div* = shine,
which lies at the basis of Jovis or Diovis, is to be
recognised as also underlying the Hebrew tetragrammaton, which originally may have sounded Javo,
Jevo, Jove, or Jeva.   But the connection of the Indo-
Germanic root with the Hebrew vocable cannot be
made out so easily as is thus done.   And there are
two special difficulties in the way of such a theory,—

[1] Introduction to the Book of Genesis, Heywood's Translation (1855),
vol. i. p. 151 f. Compare Vatke, Bibl. Theol., p. 672.

[2] Die Semiten in ihrem Verhältniss zu Chamiten u. Japhethiten
(1872), p. 163 f.

(*a*) that if Jahaveh is originally an Indo-Germanic word corresponding to a root *div*, which is widely diffused in these languages, it does not appear to have passed over in this sense into the Semitic languages generally, but only to have been appropriated for a special name by a small and comparatively insignificant branch of them; and *(b)* more particularly, there is already in the Hebrew language, not to speak of other branches of Semitic, a common root, *hawa*, from which the name can be derived by an exact analogy with other proper names, like Isaac, Jacob, and so forth.

Hitzig[1] sought in another way to derive the name, or rather the idea, from an Aryan source. The Armenian name of God is Astuads (Astovads)—*i.e.*, *astvat*, "the becoming one"; and Hitzig supposed that Moses—to whom he ascribes the introduction of Jahaveh as a divine name—reflecting on the truth and depth of the thought contained in this designation of the Deity, adopted it in a translated form as the name of the God whose religion he taught. What gives a colour of support to this explanation is, that some of the earliest traditions of the Hebrews seem to come from or to be connected with Armenia and the north-east generally. [2] There remains the difficulty, however, of explaining how Moses, in the land of Egypt, should have had a knowledge of the Armenian language, and should

---

[1] Bibl. Theol. d. Alten Test., p. 37 f.

[2] Dillmann, in a paper, "Ueber die Herkunft der urgeschichtlichen Sagen der Hebräer" (Sitzungsberichte der Akad. d. Wissenschaften zu Berlin, 27 April 1882), contends that many of these traditions not only have their counterparts in Babylonian beliefs, but are the common property of other Eastern peoples.

have turned to that quarter for an idea to denote
his God. If there is any truth in the theory at all,
it would rather lead to a pre-Mosaic origin of the idea.
And if the early Armenians expressed the idea they
attached to God by a word denoting Being or Becoming, it is possible to conceive that the family of
Abraham, travelling from Babylon by that way, may
have reached the same notion; and that thus the
idea, kept as a primitive tradition down to the time
of Moses, found expression in the tetragrammaton
which was its translation.

(2.) Turning now to another quarter, Friedrich
Delitzsch[1] has lately maintained that the name Jehovah is of Assyro-Babylonian origin. The divine
name Jau, he says, the Hebrews had in common with
at least the Philistines, and probably with the Canaanites generally; and it was in fact to distinguish
their own God from the Jau of the other peoples that
the name was modified to the Hebrew form, in the
sense of the "becoming one." But, he proceeds,
this Canaanite name Jah (like most other Canaanite
divine names) has its root in the Babylonian pan-
theon, answering to Ja-u (corresponding to Ilu), the
supreme God of the oldest Babylonian system. The
name, however, is the creation of the non-Semitic
people of Babylon, though it came to the Canaanites
through the Semitic Babylonians. The original Ac-
cadian form of the name was *i*, which the Semitic
Babylonians transformed into Jau, in which form it
reached the Canaanites; so that, instead of forms
like Jah, Jahu, being abbreviations of the longer

---

[1] Wo lag das Paradies? (1881), p. 158 ff.

Jahaveh, the longer form was produced by successive modification from the primary monosyllabic *i*. As to this opinion, it is just as conceivable, to say the least, that the full name Jahaveh became contracted into Jahu, Jau, Jo, or Jah, as that the converse process took place. We have a parallel example to illustrate the contracting process,[1] but the lengthening process, especially as described by Delitzsch, seems highly artificial; and, in point of fact, another competent authority,[2] in examining the question whether the name Jahaveh can be traced to Accadian-Sumerian origin, denies that deities of the names Jau and *i* were ever recognised at all in those regions.

In another way it has been attempted to prove that this name came from the same quarter. It is supposed that Canaanite immigrants who wandered out from the region of the Erythræan Sea[3] and came in contact with Semitic peoples, brought this name with them, and that it was adopted into Semitic. In support of this view it is pointed out that Toi, king of Hamath, in David's time sent his son, named Joram, to salute David (2 Sam. viii. 9), and that the name of this son contains the tetragrammaton in an abbreviated form, just as certain names of Hebrew personages do. There are other isolated cases found on the cuneiform inscriptions; but seeing that they occur at a period when the religion of Jahaveh was

---

[1] As has been pointed out, there is a complete analogy in the form yishtahaveh (יִשְׁתַּחֲוֶה) regularly contracted into yishtāhu (יִשְׁתָּחוּ).

[2] Friedrich Philippi in Ztschr. für Volkerpsychologie u. Sprachwissenschaft (1883), pp. 175-190.

[3] In proof of such wandering, see König's Hist. Krit. Lehrgebäude der Heb. Sprache, vol. i. (1881) p. 14 f. The proof, he maintains, is not invalidated by Budde, Die Biblische Urgeschichte (1883), p. 329 ff.

long the acknowledged religion of the Hebrews, it is
perhaps safer to regard these as isolated instances
of what was not uncommon—a non-Semitic people
adopting the name of a Semitic god into the circle of
their deities.   This is the view taken by Baudissin,[1]
and also by Schrader, whose cautious remarks, in
favour of a concurrent derivation of the name Jahve
by the Hebrews and Assyrians, are worth referring
to.[2]

(3).   Let us turn now to Egypt and see whether
any light can be derived from that quarter.   And
here we have, (*a*) first the attempts to trace the
name itself, as by Röth,[3] who identifies Jahaveh with,
or makes it a modification of, the Egyptian Joh, the
moon-god.   He does not explain, however, how it
was that the name of a god especially associated
with the moon should have been bestowed on a deity
of whose connection with the moon we have no trace;
and it is very probable that we have here nothing
more than a fortuitous coincidence of two names
which never had any connection in the minds of those
who employed them.   (*b*) On the other hand, not a
few have thought that the *idea* expressed by the name
is to be found in Egyptian sources, and may have been
borrowed in Hebrew form by Israel in Egypt.   (*a*)
Plutarch mentions an inscription on the temple of
Isis at Sais, in which a deity is described in terms re-
sembling the " I am that I am " denoted by Jahaveh

---

[1] Der Ursprung des Gottes namens Iαω, in his Studien, vol. i. p. 223.

[2] The Cuneiform Inscriptions and the Old Test., Eng. transl., vol.
i. p. 23 ff.

[3] Geschichte unserer Abendländischen Philosophie, Erster Band,
2te Auflage (1862), Note 175, p. 143.

(Exod. iii. 14); but the ideas conveyed by the two do not, when examined, correspond in the way that it is alleged.[1] *(β)* Others, again, find in the name Jahaveh a Hebrew reproduction (I am that I am) of the Egyptian *nuk pu nuk.*[2] But on this subject we should hear what is said by so competent an authority as Le Page Renouf:[3]

"It is quite true that in several places of the Book of the Dead the three words *nuk pu nuk* are to be found; it is true that *nuk* is the pronoun I, and that the demonstrative *pu* often serves to connect the subject and predicate of a sentence. But the context of the words requires to be examined before we can be sure that we have just an entire sentence before us, especially as *pu* generally comes at the end of a sentence Now if we look at the passages of the Book of the Dead where these words occur, we shall see at once that they do not contain any mysterious doctrine about the divine nature. In one of these passages the deceased says, 'It is I who know the ways of Nu.' In another place he says, 'I am the ancient one in the country [or fields]; it is I who am Osiris, who shut up his father Seb and his mother Nut on that day of the great slaughter.' "

These attempts to derive the name or the idea from Egypt are therefore very precarious.

(4.) Once more, the idea has been put forth that the national God of Israel was first of all the tribal God of the Kenites, with whom Israel came in contact in the wilderness, and to whose family Moses is represented as being related by marriage (Exod. ii. 16; Judges i. 16, iv. 11). This supposition, advanced

---

[1] König, Hauptprobleme, p. 31, to whom I am indebted for much of the material and many suggestions in this chapter.

[2] So Wahrmund, Babylonierthum, Israelitenthum, Christenthum, p. 219.

[3] Hibbert Lecture for 1879, p. 244 f.

by Ghillany,[1] has been taken up and advocated by
Tiele,[2] and also by Stade.[3] The only shadow of
proof I can find for this view as put forth by Stade
is, that Moses must have borrowed the name of his
deity from some one; and as Jethro was a priest and
Moses was in close association with him, the name
was simply carried over, and thus marks the contin-
uation of an older faith. Of actual proof that this
was so, we have none; and even if we had, we should
simply have to go in search of an older source. No
proof is given that Jahaveh was the tribal God of
the Kenites, nor is any explanation given why the
Hebrews, if they had no tribal god before, should
have adopted this deity, or, if they had, why they
made the exchange at this particular time. It may be
urged, moreover, against this supposition, that the
Kenites, though both in the wilderness and in
Canaan seen in close friendship with Israel, are always a small body, and occupy somewhat the position of pious sojourners or proselytes; and it seems
contrary to the usual way in which even the critical
writers explain events, that the larger people should
have adopted the god of the smaller tribe.

(5.) Most of the views that have already been
mentioned have this in common, that they place the
adoption of the Jahaveh religion by the Hebrews at
some period anterior to their entrance into Canaan.

[1] Theologische Briefe an die Gebildeten der deutschen Nation von
Richard von der Alm (1862), vol. i. pp. 216, 480. Through Ghillany
writes under this pseudonym, the tone of this work, like that which
finds expression in his ' Menschenopfer der Hebräer, ' is unmistakable.
The deity of the Kenites, he says, was the sun—worshipped, however,
not as a living bull as in Egypt, but in the form of a metallic image.

[2] Vergelijkende Geschied. van de Egypt. en Mesopot. Godsdien-
sten, p. 559; Kompendium, § 52.

[3] Geschichte des Volkes Israel, vol. i. p. 130 f.

We have now, however, to look at another explanation, which regards the name of Jahaveh as one
gradually adopted with other parts of religious belief and practice from the Canaanites in Palestine.[1]
As, however, this view has been successfully at-
tacked by writers of the same general school of criticism, it may be sufficient to refer to what these latter
have advanced in the way of refutation. The objections urged by Kuenen against Land[2] deserve special
emphasis. He argues as follows: (*a*) It cannot be
denied—Land himself admits it—that, in the struggles that took place between the Canaanites and the
Israelites, there was involved a contest between the
gods of the two peoples; and since at the close of the
contest the Israelites and their God were victorious,
it cannot be supposed that the deity who thus
asserted his superiority was originally of Canaanite
origin. Further, (*b*) not only have we, he contends,
in the names Jochebed (Moses' mother), Joshua
(Moses' contemporary), and Jonathan (Moses' grandson)—in all which the name Jo or Jeho enters as an
element—an indication that the name was known to
the Israelites independently of and prior to their
contact with Canaanites; but also the song of Deborah, in which Jahaveh is represented as coming
from Seir, furnishes a plain proof that the God of the
Israelites was conceived as having His original home
outside of Palestine. Lastly, (*c*) he argues rightly

[1] This view was independently put forward by Colenso (Pentateuch, Part II. chap. viii.), who afterwards discovered (Part VII. chap. xix.) that he had been anticipated by Hartmann, Von Bohlen, and Von der Alm. It has also been advocated by Dozy (De Israeliten te Mecca, Germ. transl., 1864, p. 39), Land (Theol. Tijdschr., 1868, pp. 156-170), and Goldziher (Mythology among the Hebrews, Eng. tr., pp. 272, 290).

[2] Relig. of Israel, vol. i. pp. 398-403,

that the view under consideration deviates from the whole tenor of Israelite tradition, which gives no support to the supposition that Jahaveh was a God of Canaanite origin. " I will not," he says, " assert that the latter [*i.e.*, the Canaanite origin of the name] must be rejected on this account alone, but I do assert that it is only on strong grounds that it can be accepted. In other words, it must be clearly and irrefragably proved that Jahaveh was really a god of the Canaanites. The evidence with which this is attested must be of such a nature as to leave no room for reasonable suspicion of Israelite or Old Testament influence. But such proof as this is not furnished." [1] The principle which Kuenen here lays down is of wide application,—viz., that the clear testimony of the religious consciousness of Israel— in other words, a persistent tradition—is only to be set aside on the most undoubted positive proof. Kuenen himself is far from observing his own canon, and Wellhausen openly contradicts it; [2] although by rejecting it we cut ourselves away from any firm ground of historical criticism.

Among the writers who seek to derive the name of Jahaveh from a Canaanite source reference may be made to Von Bohlen, [3] who would place the introduction of the name as late as the time of David and Solomon. Some of his arguments are of little force, and he has found few supporters of his view; but there is one argument he employs which, though not

[1] In spite of Land's rejoinder in Theol. Tijdschr., iii. Bd., 1869, pp. 347-362. Kuenen's position may be held as proved. So Baudissin has on this point taken Kuenen's side, Studien, vol. i. pp. 213-218.

[2] Hist. of Israel, pp. 318, 319.

[3] Introduction to Genesis, Heywood's transl., vol. i. p. 153 f.

valid for his purpose, directs our attention to a fact which is worth noting. He remarks that proper names compounded with the more primitive name of God, El, such as Israel, Samuel, disappear from history more and more from David's time, and that names compounded with Jeho first appear in David's reign or about his time. Now it is a fact that this element does not appear widely in proper names before the time of Samuel. We have the names of Joash, father of Gideon (Judges vi. 11), Jotham, Gideon's son (Judges ix. 5, 7), and Jonathan, grandson of Moses (Judges xviii. 30). Besides these, we have two names before the time of Samuel—viz., Joshua, the companion of Moses, whose name is said to have been changed from Hoshea (Num. xiii. 16), and Jochebed, the mother of Moses (Exod. vi. 20). In view of these it becomes no longer a question as to the introduction of the name Jeho or Jahaveh in the time of David, but how we are to explain its existence in the name of Joshua, Moses' contemporary, or, allowing that to be an altered name, in the name of the mother of Moses. It is known that whereas the Jahavist writer in Genesis freely uses the name Jahaveh in reference to times antecedent to that of Moses, the Elohistic writer retains faithfully the distinction of the periods; but the name of the mother of Moses would lead us to conclude that even before the time when the God of Israel proclaimed His sacred name to Moses at the bush, the name itself had been known beforehand in a narrower circle, or at least in the family of Moses himself. And this view is adopted by many of the best interpreters.[1] On this subject Kuenen says, "Moses can scarcely be supposed to have *invented* the name 'Jahaveh'; in all probability it was already in use, among however limited a circle, before he employed it to indicate El Shaddai, the God of the sons of Israel;"[2] and to the same effect Wellhausen[3] says that Jahaveh was before Moses a designation for El, and that he was originally a god in the family of Moses or in the tribe of Joseph.

On a review of this whole inquiry, therefore, we need not wonder that Kuenen[4] comes to the conclusion that the name is of Israelitish origin. It may be observed in passing that it is somewhat remarkable that the attempt should always be made to derive the religious conceptions of the Hebrews from non-Hebrew sources, without supposing that an influence in the opposite direction may have been exerted, from the Hebrews to their non-Hebrew neighbours. It is no doubt the case that the tradition places the native place of Abraham in Chaldæa, and it is natural to suppose that the progenitors of the Israelites were affected by the thoughts of the time and country from which they came, just as the nation was sensibly affected by contact with Egyptians and Canaanites. It must be remembered, however, that the tradition ascribes Abraham's departure from his native land to religious impulse, and Renan has dwelt upon the circumstance that religious conceptions remain more pure and elevated among

[1] A list of writers who take this view is given by König, Hauptprobleme, p. 27.

[2] Relig. of Israel, vol. i. p. 279 f.   [3] Hist. of Israel, p. 433.

[4] Relig. of Israel, vol. i. p. 398.

simple nomads than among civilised dwellers in cities.[1] The exhaustive inquiry, however, that has been made by scholars, has its justification in the conclusion to which it comes, that there is no outside source from which it can be shown that the religion of Jahaveh was derived. The use of the name is, at least, as old as the time of Moses; and whether to any extent (which in any case must have been limited) it was known before his time, he has the distinction of having impressed it upon the consciousness of the people of his time in a special way as the designation of their national God, under the aspect in which He was distinctively made known to them, and by them to be exclusively reverenced. The unanimous voice of Israelite tradition is that the declaration, "I am Jahaveh thy God," was made through Moses. There is not the least hint in the recollections of the people that the name was proclaimed by any other person. Between Moses and Samuel there was no time at which we can conceive it to have been introduced; and the time of Samuel itself is but a time of revival and reformation, after which it was not unnatural that the name of the covenant God, to whom the people's heart had again turned, should appear, as has been pointed out, more extensively in the formation of proper names.

In opposition to all attempts at deriving the name or conception from a foreign source, and as showing how it was regarded throughout by the people of Israel as a distinctive possession of the nation, there

[1] Hist. d'Israel, vol. i. chap. iii.

stands the hard fact that in Scripture Jahaveh is ever the God of Israel alone. According to the views of the Hebrew writers, the non-Israelite has no part or right to Jahaveh, but knows only the general name of Elohim, God, or that of his own native deity.[1] In the mouth of such a one the name Jahaveh would denote a strange god—*i.e.*, the god of the people of Israel (cf. 1 Kings xx. 23 with v. 28). So when a Hebrew speaks to a non-Israelite, he is represented as using the name Elohim, and so also when a non-Israelite addresses a Hebrew. And in such cases it is noticeable that the name Elohim is sometimes construed with a plural verb (cf. 1 Sam. iv. 8), the narrator thereby assuming for the time the standpoint of the non-Hebrew speaker or hearer.

This hard fact is not to be set aside by any vague etymological arguments. Even if it were shown to be certain, or even probable, that the name or the conception of Jahaveh was got from some non-Israelite quarter at some time or another in history, it would remain beyond dispute that, on the one hand, the name thus borrowed disappeared from the language and thoughts of the people from which it was derived; and on the other, that it came very soon to be regarded as the exclusive and distinguishing possession of the people who borrowed it—a supposition which, considering the attributes with which Jahaveh was endowed, and the readiness of polytheistic nations to retain the names of any number

[1] This is well brought out by Tuch in his Comm. to Genesis, second edition. p. xxxii. He refers to these and other passages : Judges i. 7, vii. 14; 1 Sam. iv. 7, 8; Jonah iii. 3, where with verses 5, 8, 9, 10, compare 1 Sam. xxx. 15, xxii. 3.

of gods, especially such as had vindicated themselves as powerful, is not to be entertained.

II. We come now to inquire whether we can determine what precisely was the idea attached to this name among its earliest possessors, so as to discover, if possible, wherein the inner potency of the Jahaveh religion consisted. The introduction of a new name we would expect to be accompanied with a new reference, a new attitude, a new mode of regarding the deity; and we naturally ask whether the name itself does not furnish its own explanation.

Those who seek to prove that the religion of Israel was originally a nature religion, in which the powers of nature were deified, explain the name Jahaveh in keeping with this view. Thus Daumer [1] connects the verb from which it is derived with the idea of destroying, and makes Jahaveh "the Destroyer," an idea which suits his notion that Jahaveh and Moloch were originally names for the same deity. The more common view of those who similarly seek the source of the name and idea in nature religion, is that the verb from which the name is derived means to "come down," "fall down," and then in its transitive form "to send down" or "cast down"; according to which Jahaveh would be a *Jupiter tonans*, the Being who casts the thunderbolt, or the lightning, to the earth. In support of this view, we are pointed to the fact that the verb in Arabic (*hawa*), which, letter for letter, corresponds to the Hebrew verb, has the sense of gliding freely, and particularly of gliding or falling down. This sense, it is said, actually

[1] Feuer und Molochdienst, p. 11.

attaches to the Hebrew verb itself in one place at least (Job xxxvii. 6), "He saith to the snow, Fall thou on the earth."

The Biblical derivation of the word, as is well known, is from the verb in the sense "to be" or "become." It may be that from such a primary and material sense as that of "falling," the verb in Hebrew came to have the more abstract and secondary meaning of becoming—viz., to "*fall* out," "happen," "come to pass," as in Gen. vii. 6, "the flood was upon the earth."[1] This is certain, that the sense "to fall" can at most be only detected as adhering to the Hebrew verb, which has, however, appropriated to itself the one signification of becoming. In other words, from the earliest time at which we know the language, this verb was the usual one employed to express the idea of "being," not, however, in the abstract sense of "existence," but in the sense of "becoming"; there was no other verb in the language with that signification; the meaning of "falling," if it originally belonged to it, had almost disappeared; and another verb altogether was employed to express that idea.

We can quite easily comprehend how a verb "to fall," and then "to send down," could, among a polytheistic people, or even a monotheistic people at a primative stage of culture, furnish the starting-point for a name of the deity. He would then be the Being who "sends down" rain, or thunder, or

---

[1] For the idea of being and becoming, the Hebrew uses almost exclusively *kayah* הָיָה, *hawah* הָוָה being found in that sense only in poetic archaic passages; as in Gen. xxvii. 29, where Jacob is blessed by Isaac, "Be lord over thy brethren," also Isa. xvi. 4, the oracle on Moab. Later writers are influenced by Aramaic.

whatever it might be. The name would stand on the same level, or, I should say, a lower one, than such names as *El*, or *Shaddai*, the "strong one," or *Baal*, *Adon*, "lord," or *Molech*, "ruler"; for any one of these gives a fuller significance to the Being so named. Against this origin of the name among the Hebrews, however, we have, besides the fact that there is no proof whatever of the Hebrews adopting a god of that name from Arabic tribes as Stade will have it, or of their attaching such an idea to the name of their national god, the stronger fact just alluded to, that the verb had appropriated to itself the sense of *be, become*, which would be transitively to *cause*. That is to say, assuming that such a name was formed or introduced at some historic time, at some time when the language contained the roots or stems it now possesses, the mere utterance of the name would call up in the mind of the hearer the idea of being, becoming, causing. And this is very much the same as saying that the person who introduced it wished to convey by it that meaning, since he could not but have seen that it would suggest such an idea. To attach to the name the other and more physical signification, would necessitate some proof that the name is of much older origin than the time of Moses, older than the language in the form in which we have it; and that—if the primary meaning of descender or sender down attached to it— there must have been a constant effort in the mind to retain this antiquarian idea, and to exclude another which was soon suggested and *which was more exalted*. For it is a point of the greatest significance here, that the other names of God found among the Hebrews and their neighbours are connected with stems which are in the language and have a precise and intelligible meaning. On this line of reasoning, then, I should conclude, that from the time that the verb to be, to become, was a regular constituent element of the language, the name Jahaveh must of necessity, if it was later than the verb, have partaken of that signification. Either the name Jahaveh was directly formed from an existent verb "to be"; or it was formed from a verb having the meaning to descend, which meaning, however, was, if not obliterated, yet certainly overshadowed, at the earliest known stage of the language, by another sense.

Of course this argument proceeds on the assumption that those who used the name, or at least the thoughtful part of the nation when they used it, attached to it *some* signification, which is surely very likely, and in analogy with such names as Moloch and Baal, which could not but keep in the mind the ideas of kingship or lordship. It would surely be an extraordinary supposition that the Hebrews had got hold of a non-Hebrew name for their deity which they used for a time without attaching to it any sense at all, and then read into it a meaning suggested by its resemblance to a common verb in the language. It is not certainly to be concluded that the bare etymological meaning and no more would always adhere to a word; but if this name Jahaveh starts from the idea of being, or must have suggested that idea at its first use, the expansion of the conception in the minds of thinking persons would be in the line of the primary meaning.

Now, as we have already seen, the name was introduced at what the tradition makes a pretty advanced stage in the development of the religion. By the time of Moses the whole patriarchal phase of it had run its course; and, according to the Biblical account, the earlier conception of the deity had been expressed by the terms El and Shaddai, embodying the simpler ideas of strength, power. Stade himself tells us that in the pre-Mosaic religion, the name *El* was used to denote the native spirit or spirits, and the name *Elohim* is certainly old. And just as the abstract idea of being, or transitively the idea of causing, is one that comes comparatively late in consciousness, or at least does not come at the primitive stage, so the introduction of the name of Jahaveh, " He who will be," or " who will cause to be," marks a point of advance in the conception of the national God. It is therefore fitly placed in the time of Moses; for it cannot be denied that, as the whole consciousness of Israel looked back to the period of the exodus as a new era in their national life, so the belief that Jahaveh was their God from Egypt onwards, as it is expressed by Hosea, was deeply rooted in the nation's mind and heart.

It seems to me that the frank recognition of this fact, so firmly embedded in the national life and literature, would go far to explain the striking phenomena which criticism has brought into clear light; and, on the other hand, that the refusal to accept it frankly has led modern writers to the precarious shifts and extravagant positions which mark the course of their disquisitions. They look for development, but they will not look for it at the right place. Instead of accepting the fact, that in the patriarchal period there was already a knowledge of God, at least on a level with, and presumably higher than, that of the polytheistic nations around Israel, they insist on finding the transition from the barest animal religion going on in a period after that stage had, for the enlightened part of the nation, passed away. Instead of accepting the fact that the name Jahaveh denotes a high stage achieved, they insist on starting with that name as embodying the most primary conceptions; and in tracing the development of the conception in the hands of the prophets, they neglect the clue given to the development in the possession of the name itself. I take my stand upon the assumption that this name must have had some meaning, some suggestion, to the thinking portion of the people, and must have, to an appreciable extent, controlled the conceptions of God which were raised in the mind by the mention of the name. There were other names—El, Elohim, Shaddai, Elyon, Baal, Molech—all of which may have been used to denote deity; but each and all of them have a specific meaning attached to them, and Jahaveh must have also had its meaning, a specific meaning; and being a special proper name, must have been intended to denote all the others put together, nay, more than all the others combined, else there would have been no reason for the introduction of a new name. The question is, What *was* that meaning? If the name meant merely "the one that sends down rain" or "thunderer," I submit that that does not go beyond El or Shaddai, and would not therefore entitle Jahaveh to be selected as the highest name that the best could bestow on God. There is the verb "to become" lying patent as a verb with which to connect a name which comes to supplement or to comprehend all the other names. And the name is put at the very period when the nation's consciousness of a destiny before it is represented as appearing. All this cannot be fortuitous, nor is it likely to have occurred as a happy thought to the early writers who have left us these traditions. The conclusion seems well justified, that, with the use of the name Jahaveh, the idea seized the mind of Moses and his successors that the God they worshipped was one of ever-developing potency, an ever self-manifesting, ever actively-defending God, whose character was not so much denoted by a quality as by a constant activity, or rather (judged by the analogy of similar personal names) by a person ever active; that in fact, as a nation does not die, so their national God would ever be with them. The name comes in at a definite historical crisis in the nation's life, and was meant to indicate that the deity so named was concerned, not merely with natural phenomena, but with national and historical events.

Let us try to think of Moses proclaiming to his people a new name that they had never heard before, or heard only as the name of the sender of the lightning, and his saying to Israel—and with effect— "this Thunderer is to be your only God for all time

coming." The question would naturally arise,
"Who is Jahaveh that *we* should serve Him? We
know what is meant by a 'Strong One,' a 'Lord,' a
'Master,' a 'Most High One' (for kindred nations
had called their gods by such names as far back as
we have knowledge, and why should the Hebrews
be placed beneath them in intelligence?). But who
is the sender of rain or of thunder any more to us
than the deity we already worship? What is He to
us, or what are we to Him in particular, that we
should be thus wedded together?" The only answer
that he could conceivably have given to such most
obvious questions is, that Jahaveh had done something for them to claim their regard. People do not
set up gods for nothing. What then had Jahaveh
done for them? Wellhausen comes to our aid (though
Stade refuses to go so far), and tells us that the
people had experienced His power in the deliverance from Egypt.[1] This is a reasonable account to
give; but it only raises another question, "Who
was this that interfered on behalf of a nation of
slaves in Egypt, and why did He interfere?" And
the only answer that all these questions admit of is
just the Biblical answer, "The God of our fathers
hath appeared to me:" in other words, there is a
linking on of the deliverance of the present to the
recollections of the past; the God of Abraham is not
dead, but alive and acting on behalf of Abraham's
seed; and in commemoration of the new deliverance,

[1] Wellhausen, Hist. of Israel, pp. 429-433; cf. here Kuenen, Relig.
of Israel, vol. i. p. 276 ff. Stade will not even admit that the Israelites,
in any appreciable sense, ever sojourned in Egypt. "If any Hebrew
clan dwelt in Egypt," he says, "no one knows its name."—Geschichte,
vol. i. p. 129.

and to mark a new era, He receives or adopts a
new name, distinctive from mere appellations of
deity generally, and the God of pre-Mosaic times is
the same God in fuller manifestation still. Moses,
says Prof. A. B. Davidson, "stamped an impress
upon the people of Israel which was never effaced,
and planted seeds in the mind of the nation which
the crop of thorns that sprang up after his death
could not altogether choke. Of course, even he did
not create a nation or a religious consciousness in
the sense of making it out of nothing. When he appealed to the people in Egypt in the name of Jehovah their God, he did not conjure with an abstrac-
tion or a novelty. The people had some knowledge
of Jehovah, some faith in Him, or His name would
not have awakened them to religious or national
life. In matters like this we never can get at the
beginning. The patriarchal age, with its knowledge
of God, is not altogether a shadow, otherwise the
history of the exodus would be a riddle. Moses
found materials, but he passed a new fire through
them, and welded them into a unity; he breathed a
spirit into the people, which animated it for all time
to come; and this spirit can have been no other than
the spirit that animated himself." [1]

The importance of dwelling on this question of the
meaning attached to the name of Israel's national
God in its initial conception and at its first use will
be self-evident. It brings to a point the sharp contrast between the Biblical account of the matter and
the views presented by writers of the modern criti-

[1] Expositor, third series, vol. v. p. 42.

cal school.   We may say, in a general way, that the
various aspects of the pre-prophetic religion, as we
have seen them put forward in the preceding chapters, have this in common, that they represent
the Jahaveh of pre-prophetic times as a being rather
of might than of moral greatness, a nature-God rather
than a God of nature, the only national God of Israel
indeed, yet, except in this particular, very little if
anything different from the gods of the surrounding
nations even in the estimation of His own worshippers.   Such representations of Jahaveh are the natural development of the initial conception with
which these writers start.   Wellhausen says[1] that
" no essential distinction was felt to exist between
Jehovah and El, any more than between Asshur
and El; " and Stade tells us that El denotes a superhuman being, though not sharply separated from nature in which he operates.   Each place had its El,
and the collective Elim or Elohim was the sum of
these, or the expression in a plural of majesty, of the
power of these superhuman beings.[2]   According to the
view of these writers, then, the name Jahaveh, given
originally to a family or tribal god, either of the family of Moses or tribe of Joseph, as Wellhausen[3] supposes, or of the tribe of the Kenites as Stade thinks,
implied no more than El; only, having become current within a powerful circle, it " was on that account all the more fitted to become the designation
of a national God."

But if there is any force at all in the considera-

[1] Hist. of Israel, p. 433.   [2] Stade, Geschichte, vol. i. p. 428.

[3] Hist. of Israel, p. 433.

tions that have been put forward, that this name
Jahaveh is not of foreign but of Israelitish origin,
that as a separate and new name it must have indicated something more than other names already existing, and that in its derivation or immediate suggestion it had the sense of "becoming," then we
must demand for the initial stage of the Jahaveh religion a much higher level than the critical school allows. In addition to this general remark, there are
the following points again to be insisted on:—

(1.) There is absolutely no proof that Jahaveh was
originally the name of a family or tribal god in the
sense understood by these writers. Even if the name
of the mother of Moses be taken as an indication that
the name was known in the circle of his family, there
is no proof that it denoted no more than El or a
superhuman nature-spirit.

(2.) And then no reason is assigned for the name
Jahaveh superseding El or the Elim, if, according
to the hypothesis, it signified no more than these
names. Dillmann remarks[1] that wherever an actual
change in the religion of a people takes place, there
is ever a historical consciousness of the fact preserved among them. The assertion that this name
was a special name of El, which had become current
in a powerful circle, and on that account was all the
more fitted to become the designation of a national
god, is, in the first place, destitute of historical
proof, and, in the second place, most improbable. If
the introduction of the name was connected with
some striking event, such as the exodus, we should

[1] Ursprung der Alttestl. Religion, p. 6, quoted by Baudissin, Jahve et
Moloch, p. 77.

expect the name to mark an advance—as the Biblical writers represent—on the conception; but according to the modern view, Jahaveh still remains a nature-God: although a national God, His attributes are almost entirely physical.

(3.) In the next place, though the proofs from Scripture which Stade, for example, advances in support of his picture of the character of the pre-prophetic Jahaveh, are selected and manipulated in the extraordinary fashion to which reference has already been made,[1] yet it is exceedingly difficult to form a conception of the character he seeks to delineate. He roams at will over Genesis, the historical books, and even the prophets, finding in later productions proofs of a low tone, and in the earlier books proofs of a high tone of religious thought, till it is absolutely impossible to make out what the initial conception of Jahaveh, in his theory, could have been. An example may be taken from his treatment of the story of Elijah. At one time, in the midst of his argument to prove that Jahaveh's power was confined to His own land, he tells[2] us that Elijah, who fights valiantly in the land of Israel against the worship of Baal, yet goes and lives with a widow at Sarepta, who must have been a Baal-worshipper, and eats her food, which would be consecrated by offering to Baal—touches for which there is absolutely no warrant, and which make the character of the "prophet of fire," as drawn by the narrator, simply incomprehensible. Presently he tells us that in this same story of Elijah the belief finds expression that

---

[1] In chap. viii. p. 205.   [2] Stade, Geschichte, vol. i. p. 430.

Jahaveh accompanies His worshippers in their wanderings, for He performs miracles at Sarepta at the prophet's request, and sends him back to his own land.[1] This same belief, he says, is expressed in the promise to be with Jacob (Gen. xxviii. 15, J.), in His being with Joseph in Egypt (Gen. xxxix. 2, J.), and in His going down to Egypt with Jacob (Gen. xlvi. 3 f., J. and E.) And in order to prove the same thing he refers to a passage as late as Isaiah xix., where the prophet speaks of Jahaveh riding on a swift cloud and coming to Egypt, and the idols being moved at his presence. Similarly he proceeds in speaking of Jahaveh's power. The conceptions of all-mightiness and omniscience, we are told, are not yet reached. That He was not regarded as knowing *all* things is seen from the patriarchal stories, which speak, for example, of God going down to Sodom to see whether its condition was such as the cry represented it.[2] Still the same God knows Sarah's thoughts, and the belief in the oracle shows that He was regarded as having a knowledge of secrets such as children ascribe to God. His power came in the same way to be represented by the religious sentiment as adequate to anything, as appears in the saying, "Is anything too hard for Jahaveh?" (Gen. xviii. 14); and in that other saying, "There is no restraint to Jahaveh to save by many or by few" (1 Sam. xiv. 6). So He performs wonders, shakes the earth, overthrows cities, punishes His land with famine and plague, and slays men without any apparent disease. One other ex-

[1] Ibid., p. 431. [2] Stade, Geschichte, vol, i. p. 432.

ample may be given of Stade's reasoning. The
preponderance of the idea of might in the conception
of God, he says, combined with the fact that in a
primitive age the difference between evil and misfortune was not apprehended, hindered men from
regarding Jahaveh as a Being who always acted for
moral ends. Traces of a higher conception are not
indeed wanting in the pre-prophetic age. Jahaveh,
as the defender of His people and of the land, is the
guardian of moral customs, the avenger of broken
covenants, and so far as concerns the relations of
one Israelite to another, His will is the expression
of moral and just rule.[1] Thus He avenges a broken
oath, and fulfils the prayer of the unjustly oppressed.
Especially is He the avenger of innocent blood,
which cries to Him from the ground (Gen. iv. 10,
xlii. 22, E.) So, as He is the God of the land, He
maintains law and order in it, punishing—*e.g.*, Sodom
and Gomorrah—for breaking it. By such advances
as these the idea of holiness was enlarged and purified in later times. But in earlier times these ideas
did not extend to the general course of events, and
to the relation of Israelites to non-Israelites and the
surrounding world. In such matters moral conceptions are so little apparent, that God is the author
even of evil. Men had not reached the belief in a
world in which imperfection was necessarily involved, and of evil left for a time even for the sake
of the good. Accordingly, when we would say God
permits this or that, the ancient Israelite said straight
out that Jahaveh did it.[2] Evil and misfortune are

[1] Ibid., p. 434.   [2] Stade, Geschichte, vol. 1. p. 435.

expressed by one word, *ra';* and Amos says (iii. 6), "Is there evil in the city, and Jahaveh has not done it?" And not only outward calamities, but the evil passions and inner impulses of men, are ascribed to Jahaveh; and, as among heathen nations, He is believed to make people mad, or leads them on to do things which will bring down His own wrath. Thus the schism of the kingdoms, the greatest misfortune to Israel, was from Jahaveh (1 Kings xii. 15). So He sends a lying spirit among the prophets of Ahab, that the king may be led to go confidently against Ramoth-Gilead, and only the prophet Micah remains unmoved (1 Kings xxii. 20 ff.) So He sends an evil spirit between Abimelech and the Shechemites. And that this is not merely or in all cases a punishment for former transgression, is proved by the remarkable passage (1 Sam. xxvi. 19) in which David says to Saul, "If Jahaveh hath stirred thee up against me, let him accept an offering; but if it be men let them be accursed of Jahaveh."

This kind of reasoning may be carried out indefinitely, but though it may make a big book, it does not amount to a strong argument. Stade does not or will not see that by thus heaping together texts referring to different periods within or beyond the prophetic period indiscriminately, he is destroying the position he holds that the prophetic religion is an advance on the pre-prophetic. And when he finds in such a writer as Amos, or even Isaiah, instances of the lower type of conception, what becomes of the position that higher types found in

Genesis, *e.g.*, are "signs of advance" or "breaking down" of narrow views? What we want to know is the alleged initial stage at which the national God was no more than *El*, a nature-God; and instead of this we get this mixing up of early and late which is quite unintelligible. The truth is, the difficulty he finds in reconciling the contradictory or conflicting statements of contemporaneous authorities arises simply from the fact that the "higher" or moral conception is present from the first. In opposition to all this kind of reasoning I would take my stand upon the reasonable principle, that in writings belonging practically to the same period the lower expressions are to be controlled by the higher, and that one statement in plain terms should outweigh any amount of metaphorical or figurative language. The Hebrew writers employ the boldest anthropomorphisms, for example; but as Stade himself says, this was a necessity for people unaccustomed to philosophical speculation: it is more, it is a necessity of religious language. Nor are they afraid to employ the most simple and child-like expressions; but there is ever the absence of gross conceptions, and ever and anon the utterance of the most exalted ideas, showing what the essential character of Jahaveh, in their opinion, was. Side by side with the boldest anthropomorphisms are found the most spiritual expressions, and the same writers who speak of Jahaveh as having a local seat ascribe to Him control over all the nations of the world. In view of all this it is sheer trifling to explain the one set of expressions as remnants of a belief in a nature-God, and the other as signs of a breaking down of narrow views. The Hebrew writers, from the earliest times at which we have access to their words, are on a higher plane of thought than the modern critics will allow; and just because they are so firmly fixed there, they do not hesitate to employ the boldest pictorial or meta· phorical language to express their thoughts.

CHAPTER XII.

ETHIC MONOTHEISM.

The great objection to the modern account of the Jahaveh religion—I. Necessity of postulating moral elements in Jahaveh's character, and how their origin is explained by Stade—Distinctive features in the Jahaveh religion as stated by him—Jealousy, and sole reverence—Examination of this: (1) Are these really distinctive? (2) If they are really so, the theory is at fault, for no sufficient explanation of their origin is given—II. Transition to ethic monotheism—Distinction of monolatry and monotheism—Proofs of monolatry—Jephthah—First Commandment—Naming of gods of the nations—Kuenen's argument examined—Popular conception of power nourished by political events—Agreement of prophets with popular idea in fundamental principles—Rise beyond this on the appearance of the Assyrian power—Appeal again to earliest writing prophets, in whom monotheism is not nascent, but fully developed—The prophets claimed to be the true interpreters of the fundamental principles of the religion—The attribute of grace or love which is made central by Hosea, gives the explanation of the origin of the popular and the prophetic views.

THE difficulties in the way of accepting the modern account are seen to be greatest when we inquire what it was that distinguished the Jahaveh religion from the religions of neighbouring nations. We are told *ad nauseam* the points in which it resembled them; one feature after another is toned down to the level of nature or national religion. Yet the pre-prophetic religion must have had something distinctive to mark out the Israelites from their neighbours, and give them the pride in their national faith which they possessed. It must have contained, moreover, some germ which by way of development enabled it to rise to the so-called ethic monotheism of the prophets. We must now examine the modern theory as to these elements.

I. Stade, in drawing his picture of the pre-prophetic Jahaveh as a national deity evolved from a nature-God, is bound, as we have seen, to put in here and there features of a more elevated and moral character. All that he can say as to the origin of these higher conceptions is, that they arise not from mental reflection, but from religious feeling and impulse. In this way, for example, "the feeling arises" that Jahaveh, although the God of the land of Israel only, will accompany His worshipper into a foreign country; and also, "the confidence arises" that He will be more powerful than the gods of the heathen, just as Israel itself, when in captivity, bursts its bonds. These two ideas blend into the conviction that Jahaveh, brought willingly or by force into a strange land, will there show His power by inflicting evil on the heathen gods, as happened to Dagon at Gath, and as is indicated in the passage of Isaiah to which reference has already been made. And, more particularly, he strives to find, amid all the features that are common to Jahaveh and the heathen gods, some distinctive characteristics which will insure the Jahaveh religion having an independent existence and a possible development. In this connection he lays particular stress on two things:—

(1.) While the early Israelite conceptions of Jahaveh's power and holiness are in strict analogy with the heathen conception of their gods, there is one element, he says, which distinguishes the religion of Israel. The anger of Jahaveh takes the form of jealousy of the worship of any other God; which worship He avenges and punishes. And this idea, which attains its full development in the teaching of the prophets, is an element of the Mosaic religion. On Stade's theory the power of Jahaveh is first of all thought of as a terrifying attribute, for He is the God of the storm, and the idea is not for some time reached that divine might must be exercised on the side of good. His holiness also is merely majesty jealous of its honour, and insisting on due reverence, so that the bounds between Him and man are not to be trespassed with impunity. Instances illustrating this are found in the judgments that befell the people of Beth-shemesh and Uzzah, for looking into or touching the ark, the symbol of His presence; and the idea is found as late as Isaiah (viii. 14), who speaks of a sanctuary as an object of terror.[1] This representation of Jahaveh, however, assumes a milder form and kindlier aspect from the fact that He is Israel's God, and will defend His own people. But it is to be noted that, while He is true and faithful to His own, the counterpart of His faithful-

[1] Stade, Geschichte, vol. 1. p. 434.

ness to Israel is His anger against Israel's foes. This is seen chiefly in war. The oldest monument of Hebrew poetry, the song of Deborah, represents Him as coming from Sinai to discomfit the army of Sisera, and Meroz is cursed because it did not come to the help of the Lord against the mighty.[1] A trace of the same idea is found in the title of the 'Book of the Wars of Jahaveh,' and in Abigail's speaking of David fighting Jahaveh's battles. So the ark, according to the oldest views, was taken into the battle, and Jahaveh was the "Lord of hosts."

(2.) Another fundamental point of difference between the pre-prophetic religion of Israel and heathen systems, according to Stade, is this:[2] Whereas in Greece, Rome, and Egypt, the worship of ancestors and reverence for founders of tribes remained alongside the worship of the gods—the latter remaining at the head of what came to be a family, consisting of gods, half-gods, and heroes, so that the inferior gods really came to receive the greater homage from the mass of the people—this development never took place in Israel. They have no mythology, and the reason is that Jahaveh did not admit the worship either of ancestors or of heavenly bodies along with His own. His worship is directly opposed to such, and so gradually eliminated it. And we have neither the slightest trace in Israel of Jahaveh being regarded as a *primus inter pares*, nor of His having a consort as Baal had in Astarte.

[1] Geschichte, vol. i. p. 437. [2] Ibid., p. 438 f.

This distinguishing feature of the Jahaveh religion, Stade concludes, cannot be traced to any peculiarity in the Semitic race, for other members of the Semitic family exhibit polytheism exactly like that of Greece. It can only be explained on the supposition that from the moment Israel received the Jahaveh religion His character was differently apprehended from that of the polytheistic gods. But when we expect him to tell us what the element in Jahaveh's *character* was which thus distinguished Him, this is what he tells us: The distinguishing thought which made this religion of Jahaveh different from these can only have been that Jahaveh was the only God of Israel, and therefore His worship excluded that of all other gods. Had not this idea been firmly held from the beginning, considering the temptations that lay on every side, from the time the tribes entered Canaan, to polytheistic views, the result could not have been the view of Jahaveh's unity that came to prevail. It goes back for initiation to the founder of the religion. This much is due to the work and the thought of Moses.[1]

These statements of Stade deserve to be well weighed. They suggest two questions:—

(1.) Are the points which he marks out as distinctive of the Jahaveh religion actual points of difference from other Semitic religions as these are understood by himself? He and other writers of his school are never tired of telling us that Jahaveh was the God of Israel or of Canaan, just as Chemosh was the god of Moab. And Kuenen says plainly[2]

---

[1] Geschichte, vol. i. p. 439.　　　　[2] National Religions, p. 118.

that though Jahaveh was believed by Israel to be mightier than the gods of other nations, there was nothing in this to distinguish the Israelite religion, for this was the belief of the Moabite with regard to Camosh (Chemosh), and of the Ammonite with regard to Malcám (Moloch). As to the national god being able to follow his worshipper and defend him in a strange land, the inscription of Salmsézab, referred to by Renan, is urged in proof that this was a common belief. As to its being a distinction that Jahaveh was at the first declared to be the sole deity to be reverenced in Israel, the neighbouring nations also had each their national and exclusive god. If Stade should reply that these nations admitted the recognition and worship of other gods alongside their national god, why, this is the very thing that he and his school say the Israelites all did up to the time of the prophets. It is they also who point to the obscure passage in the book of Kings to prove that the god of the Moabites was stirred up by the horrible sacrifice of the king's first-born to defend his own people; so that the jealousy of one national god against another, which Stade makes a distinctive mark of the Jahaveh religion, is, on his own principle, a common belief.

(2.) If these points *are* really distinctive of the Jahaveh religion in any significant sense, then what becomes of the whole position of Stade and his school, that the Jahaveh religion was at first a mere nature-worship? On this ground it is not a question of showing how pre-prophetic Jahavism was purified and exalted by the prophets; it is a question of ex-

plaining this *initial* distinctiveness which runs back
to Mosaic times. How can Stade explain the manner in which a mere nature-god was adopted by
Israel, and made from the beginning the sole object
of worship? When he says that the character of
Jahaveh was from the first differently apprehended
from that of the heathen gods, this is just what the
Biblical writers say. But when he goes on to say
that the distinguishing thing was that this God
alone was to be Israel's God, he is giving no adequate explanation. The question is, Why was Jahaveh regarded as Israel's God to the exclusion of all
others? and Stade answers, Because from the first
He was so regarded. Surely it was something in
His character, something that He did or was believed
to have done, that gave Him this pre-eminence.
But Stade, held fast in his naturalistic theory, cannot admit this, and so lands himself in helpless confusion. The distinctive elements of the Jahaveh
religion, as he puts them, are not distinctive at all;
or if they are, they are distinctive in a much higher
sense than he ascribes to them.

II. The modern theory, it seems to me, thus
breaks down utterly at this the initial point; and I
do not think it can establish itself any more successfully in explaining the development at the other end
—*i.e.*, in accounting for the alleged transition from
belief in a merely national god to the " ethic monotheism," as it is called, of the prophets. On this
subject writers of the modern critical school[1] draw
an intelligible distinction between monolatry and

---

[1] Stade, Geschichte, vol. i. pp. 428 ff., 507.

monotheism—*i.e.*, the worship of one God, and the belief that there *is* only one God.[1] The ancient Israelites, says Stade, were theoretically polytheists, but practically monotheists: they believed in the existence of Chemosh, the god of Moab; of Milkom (Moloch), the god of the Ammonites; and Baalzebub, the god of the Ekronites, and others, just as they believed in the existence of Jahaveh, their own God. The distinction which they drew was not between God and idols, or between God and no-gods, but between Jahaveh and the "gods of the nations." This explains the expression "the God of the Hebrews" (Exod. iii. 18, &c.), and the other expression "Jahaveh the God of Israel" (Judges xi. 21, &c.), and even the mode of speaking of the God of Abraham, Isaac, and Jacob. The idea of a universe, he says, was beyond the comprehension of a people who knew only the countries round about Canaan; and the passages that represent God as the Creator of all things are the product of later times. Such passages as Amos v. 8, 9, which are from an *early* book, are inconvenient for this theory, and accordingly are set aside as disturbing the progress of the discourse, and probably not genuine.[2] But this is a trifle.

The argument at first sight seems forcible, but on examination it will be found not to sustain the position which it is used to support. No doubt the Biblical writers continually speak of the gods of the nations by name, as if they believed in their existence and operation. So does Milton in his 'Paradise

---

[1] See Note XXI.

[2] Kuenen, National Relig., p. 113. Comp. above, chap. vi. p. 146.

Lost.' The passage (Judges xi. 24) in which Jephthah says to Moab, "Wilt not thou possess that
which Chemosh thy god giveth thee to possess?"
seems to be quite decisive on this point; and so it
has been referred to constantly from Vatke [1] to Wellhausen [2] to prove that originally "Israel is a people
just like other people, nor is even his relationship to
Jehovah otherwise conceived of than is, for example,
that of Moab to Chemosh." But, as Dr. Davidson
has pointed out,[3] Wellhausen invalidates his own argument when in another place [4] he makes this whole
passage an interpolation based on Numbers xxi. 29,
which would bring it well down in the age of the
canonical prophets. Indeed, as Davidson points
out, there is a passage of Jeremiah (xlviii. 7) which
would prove that even he believed in the godhead of
Chemosh,—a proof that such a mode of reasoning
has no force.

So, too, the language of the Decalogue, "Thou
shalt have no other gods before me," may seem at
first sight to imply that the *existence* of other gods
was taken for granted, only that Jahaveh alone was
to be worshipped by Israel. On this I cannot do
better than quote the thoughtful words of Dr.
Davidson:—

"To our minds such a statement as this, that Israel shall have
no God but Jehovah, immediately suggests the inquiry, whether
there be any other god but Him. But such questions might not
present themselves to minds of a different cast from ours and in
early times, for our minds are quickened by all the speculations

---

[1] Bibl. Theol., p. 258.　　　　　　[2] Hist. of Israel, p. 235.
[3] Expositor, third series, vol. v. p. 49.
[4] See Bleek's Einleitung, 4te Aufl., p. 195.

about God which have filled the centuries from the days of
Moses to our own. We may not have evidence that the mind
of Israel in the earliest time put these general and abstract
questions to itself. But we are certainly entirely precluded from
inferring from the form of the first commandment that the
existence of other gods was admitted, only that Israel should
have none of them. For if we consider the moral element of
the Code, we find the commandments all taking the same negative form; but who will argue that when Moses said to Israel,
Thou shalt not kill, he made murder unlawful merely in Israel,
without feeling that it was unlawful wherever men existed?" [1]

The truth is, we have here to do with an instance
of the imperfection of language and the freaks the
human mind plays in the use of names. How was
an Israelite to speak of the heathen gods unless by
using their names? And as soon as we give a thing
a name, it has a certain existence for us. St. Paul
tells us how hard it was for Christians in his day,
accustomed to the names of heathen gods, to grasp
the fact that "an idol is nothing in the world;" [2]
and even at the present day, I doubt very much
whether the majority of people who speak of Jupiter
and Apollo consciously carry in their minds the
conviction that these are mere names of what never
had existence. [3] The early preachers of Christianity
in pagan countries had the utmost difficulty in root-
ing out the belief in heathen gods. So long as the
names lingered, the unsophisticated mind assigned

---

[1] Expositor, *l.c.*, p. 44.   [2] 1 Cor. viii. 4-7.

[3] An amusing instance of the facility with which the name takes the
place of the thing is furnished by Voltaire. In the Latin Bible the
witch of Endor is called Pythonissa (in the LXX. Ἐγγαστρίμυθος);
and Voltaire argued that since the name Python could not have been
known to the Hebrews in the days of Saul, this history cannot have
been earlier than the time of Alexander, when the Greeks traded with
the Hebrews. One wonders how many of Voltaire's readers perceived
his mistake.

to the *numen* an actual existence; and hence, perhaps, we may explain how the missionaries and
their converts turned these pagan objects of worship
into demons or evil spirits. We need not wonder,
in the face of this psychological phenomenon, if the
simple-minded Hebrews use language that may be
drawn into a wrong sense. If they asked themselves
at all what they meant by such language, the common people would be perhaps as perplexed as, *e.g.*,
an ordinary person would be if asked to explain
what Allah, or Moloch, or Asshur is in his mind.
The modern Jew would not admit that his nation's
God is the Allah of the Mohammedan; but are we to
say that the Jew is not yet a monotheist?[1] I believe
it may safely be asserted that there is not a single
passage in the Old Testament which can be taken to
prove that the leaders of religious thought—prophets and prophetic men—ever regarded Jahaveh
as on a level with the gods of the nations, as no
more to Israel, no more in the world, than Chemosh
or Milcom or Baal to their worshippers. Nay, there
is one passage, in an early writing too, which ought
to be decisive of this matter. Elijah, on Carmel,
is represented as using language in regard to the
Phœnician Baal (1 Kings xviii. 27) which, if it is
taken as a mockery of the conceptions of the Baal-
worshippers, is in striking. contrast with even the
boldest anthropomorphisms applied by Israelites to
their God, and, in any case, shows that this prophet
had got very nearly to, if he had not actually appre-

[1] Do not we continue to speak of the God of the Christian, although
we believe that there is none other?

hended, the truth that "an idol is nothing in the world." This may not be monotheism in an abstract philosophical sense—for religion was to Israel not a product of thought but an instinct—yet it is infinitely more than the bare monolatry of which modern writers speak.

We come now to consider the arguments by which it is sought to be proved how, from a circumscribed national monolatry, in which Jahaveh was regarded as the only God of Israel, there was reached the "ethic monotheism" of the prophets, in which He is viewed as the God of the whole earth, the only God. Here we take for our guide Kuenen, who has devoted a special work [1] to the subject.

In the popular conception, says Kuenen (p. 118), Jahaveh was a great and mighty God, mightier than the gods of other nations. And this popular conception was stimulated and supported by political events. "When David waged the wars of Yahweh with a strong hand (1 Sam. xviii. 17; xxv. 28), and when victory crowned his arms, he made Yahweh Himself rise in the popular estimation, Solomon's glory shone upon the deity to whom he had consecrated the temple in his capital." In this popular conception of their national deity, the attribute of *might* was the principal element. The people no doubt ascribed to their God moral attributes (as is proved by the priestly Torah), but these were only some among many of His attributes, and in the popular conception the stage of an ethical *character* had not been reached (p. 115). Jahaveh as a very

[1] Hibbert Lecture for 1882, National Religions and Universal Religions.

mighty One, and Jahaveh inseparably bound to
Israel His people, these were the fundamental ideas
of the popular religion. In proof of this, Kuenen
appeals to the historical books of "the Old Testament—whose authors certainly stood higher in this
respect than the great masses." In these books
"the idea comes into the foreground more than once,
that Jahaveh had to uphold His own honour, and
therefore *could not* neglect to protect and bless His
people. Thus, in the conception of the people,
Yahweh's might, or, if you prefer to put it so,
Yahweh's obligation to display His might, must
often have overbalanced both His wrath against
Israel's trespasses and the demands of His righteousness" (p. 115 f.)

With this popular view the prophets so far agreed,
although on essential points they differed from it.
As to the agreement, I quote Kuenen's words (p. 105):[1]
"*Yahweh Israel's God, and Israel Yahweh's people!*
It surely needs no proof that the canonical prophets
endorse this fundamental conception of the popular
religion, that not one of them ever thinks of deny-
ing it. The whole of their preaching takes this as
its starting-point, and leads back to it as its goal.
On this latter point I wish to place the utmost emphasis." He then goes on to show that though the
prophets looked forward to the extinction of the
national life of Israel, and the captivity of the
people into a strange land, yet in their mind this
was to be followed, sooner or later, by a restoration.
This is indeed to be accompanied by a transforma-

[1] See also Kuenen's Religion of Israel (Eng. trans.), vol. i. p. 219 ff.

tion in the people themselves. "But however great the change may be—though the wolf lie down with the lamb and the sucking child play by the adder's hole; nay, though there be new heavens and a new earth, yet the relation between Jahaveh and Israel remains the same" (p. 106 f.) So that the canonical prophets of the eighth and succeeding centuries are not only the legitimate successors of Elijah and Elisha, but it would be a contradicting of these prophets themselves were we to begin by loosening the tie that unites them to the Israelite nation.

"We are indeed doing the prophets ill service if we conceal the fundamental thought of all their preaching. In this respect, *Iliacos intra muros peccatur et extra.* Rationalists have branded as 'particularism,' and supranaturalists have done their best to explain away or evaporate, what is really nothing less than *the very essence of the Israelitish religion*, to which even the greatest prophets could not be untrue without sacrificing that religion itself" (p. 109 f.)

And now, having seen to what extent the prophets agreed with the popular religious conceptions of their time, we have to consider in what respects, according to Kuenen, they differed from them. For there is no doubt that in essential points they stood opposed to the religious opinions of their day, and held views that brought them into sharp antagonism with not only the common people, but even the official heads of the nation. "The prophets," says Kuenan (p. 73), "while admitting the national worship of Jahaveh as a fact, nevertheless condemn it from time to time in the strongest terms. It answers in no degree to their ideal."

" The images of Yahweh which adorned most of the bamoth as well as the temples at Dan and Beth-el, imply that the ideas men had of Him were crude and material in the extreme. Of the religious solemnities we know little, but enough to assert with confidence that they embodied anything but spiritual conceptions. Wanton licence on the one hand, and the terror-stricken attempt to propitiate the deity with human sacrifices on the other, were the two extremes into which the worshippers of Yahweh appear by no means exceptionally to have fallen. No one will undertake to defend all this, especially as at that very time there was already another and a higher standard in ancient Israel opposed to the lower, and judging it" (p. 75 f.)

What then was this "ideal," this "higher standard," in ancient Israel which the prophets had got hold of? The true prophet, we are told (p. 112), was, as Jeremiah characterises him (Jer. xxviii. 8, 9), a prophet of evil. And why? Because he was "the preacher of repentance, the representative of Yahweh's strict moral demands amongst a people that but too ill conforms to them." That is to say, holiness is now no longer one attribute among many others, as it was in the popular conception: "in the consciousness of the prophets, the central place was taken, not by the might but by the holiness of Yahweh. Thereby the conception of God was carried up into another and a higher sphere (p. 119)." And "as soon as an ethical *character* [as distinguished from merely a moral attribute among others] was ascribed to Yahweh, He *must* act in accordance with it. The Holy One, the Righteous One, might renounce His people, but He could not renounce Himself" (p. 115 f.)

"This profoundly ethical conception of Yahweh's

being," Kuenen proceeds to reason (p. 114), "could not fail to bring the prophets into conflict with the religious convictions of their people." For whereas the latter had emphasised the attribute of might, and relied upon the fact that Yahweh and Israel were inseparable, so that He was bound to help them, even at the expense of His holiness, the prophets put it differently—that, being above all things holy, He was bound to assert His holiness even at the expense of His people. Thus, when the people, as troubles gathered on the political horizon, thought they could appease their God and secure His favour by more numerous and costly sacrifices and multiplied vows (p. 115), reckoning with certainty (Micah iii. 11) upon the help of the God who was in their midst, or when in straits they cast about for new help, lavishing even sacrifices of their own children (p. 122), the prophets denounced such confidence as vain, and saw in the very troubles that came upon the nation the righteous hand of Yahweh Himself, asserting not only His might, but pre-eminently His holiness against an ungodly nation. Thus the two modes of viewing political events and national experience were diametrically opposed. The one, the popular view, based its faith on earthly prosperity and success. "But," says Kuenen (p. 118 f.), "it lies in the nature of the case that a faith reared upon such foundations was subject to many shocks, and under given circumstances might easily collapse. Born of the sense of national dignity, growing with its growth and strengthening with its strength, it must likewise suffer under the blows that fell upon it, must pine and ultimately die when, with the independence of the nation, national self-consciousness disappeared." The other, the prophetic view, making Yahweh's holiness His central attribute, and ascribing to Him an *ethical character*, was not dependent on the fluctuations of political events. "When others," says Wellhausen, "saw only the ruin of everything that is holiest, they saw the triumph of Jehovah over delusion and error;" to which Kuenen adds (p. 124):—

"What was thus revealed to their spirit was no less than the august idea of the *moral government of the world*—crude as yet, and with manifold admixture of error, but pure in principle. The prophets had no conception of the mutual connection of the powers and operations of nature. They never dreamed of the possibility of carrying them back to a single cause or deducing them from it. But what they did see, on the field within their view, was the realisation of a single plan—everything, not only the tumult of the peoples, but all nature likewise, subservient to the working out of one great purpose. The name "ethical monotheism" describes better than any other the characteristics of their point of view, for it not only expresses the character of the one God whom they worshipped, but also indicates the fountain whence their faith in Him welled up."

Thus then, though the prophets were regarded by their contemporaries as speaking nothing less than blasphemy (p. 117) when they declared that Jerusalem should be destroyed and its people carried into captivity, and though in effect they were the destroyers of the old national religion, yet they were led by the contemplation of political events, and by the working out of their own ethical conceptions, to lay the foundations of a religion of world-wide applica-

tion and significance. They still held to the in-
separability of Jahaveh and Israel; but in their
glowing descriptions of the blessings of the coming
age, they represented Israel as no longer the special
object of God's care and recipient of His favours,
but as the organ and instrument of blessings to the
whole world. Thus anticipations which, in the
popular conception, were limited, became transformed. "Many of the descriptions of Israel's
restoration, and of the *rôle* which the heathen will
take therein, have none but literary and æsthetic
claims on our admiration" (p. 126); whereas, on
the other hand, it lay in the nature of the case that
ethical monotheism, even in the period of its genesis,
must give a fresh turn to expectations with regard
to Yahweh and the peoples. In its full development, of course, this idea of universalism took its
highest flight of all, as is seen most conspicuously
in the exalted ideas and comprehensive views of the
prophets which culminate in the glowing anticipations of the second Isaiah (p. 128).

There is much truth and much suggestiveness in
what Kuenen here puts forward. What he says
throws much light both on the relation of the
prophets to the "popular religion," and also on the
gradual progress in the conceptions of the prophets
themselves. In speaking of the "popular religion,"
we must, with Kuenen, admit that "all sincere religion is true religion, and must secure its beneficent
result;" that "not in vain did men thank Yahweh
for the blessing of harvest, perform their work with
eyes fixed upon Him, trust in His help under afflic-

tions, and turn to Him for succour in times of peril "
(p. 76). And in regard to the prophetic religion,
we frankly admit that the course of political events
taught the prophets much, and that through outward events and the germination of the inner conception which they entertained, they reached purer
and more comprehensive views as time went on.
But all this does not reach the point we wish to
attain. What we wish to know is the best and
highest that any in the nation had reached at the
earliest times at which we can catch a view of the
Jahaveh religion, and how much of that survived as
a national inheritance. We wish to know whether
the popular religion and the prophetic had not a
common starting-point, one source from which they
sprang and then separated; we want to know
whether this prophetic ideal is not derived from the
pre-prophetic times; and if it is not, we wish a
definite explanation of its origin and its development out of the lower conceptions to which it stood
opposed. And this I think Kuenen with all his
ingenuity has not furnished.

1. In the first place, when Kuenen sets down as
the very essence of the Israelitish religion the fundamental article on which people and prophets
agreed, *Yahweh Israel's God, and Israel Yahweh's
people,* he only states in his own way what the
Biblical writers one and all insist on, and what the
Hebrew historians represent in various fashions as
an election or choice of Israel by Jahaveh, or a
covenant relation between the two. It is but just
to Kuenen to draw attention to the fact that he

ascribes to Moses this amount at least of influence on Israel, in saying that "the consciousness that a peculiar and intimate relation existed between the God in whose name Moses came forward and the tribes of Israel, never died out." He would not call this a covenant in the Biblical sense,[1] and he insists that the conviction went no further than this brief acknowledgment, since Moses failed in impressing on the people his own ideas of God's moral nature. "In one word," he says, "whatever distinguished Moses from his nation remained his personal possession and that of a few kindred spirits. . . . Under Moses' influence Israel took a step forward, but it was only one step."[2] In view, however, of Kuenen's clear recognition of the one fundamental piece of common ground occupied by prophets and people, we are entitled to ask him what was the common conviction from which both started, seeing that both in their respective modes held so tenaciously to it. There must have been some objective fact in the history that gave a start to this common conception, or some point of time at which this relationship was pressed home on the consciousness of the nation, to give it this firm, incontrovertible position with people and prophet alike. And if the conception is synchronous with the adoption of the Jahaveh religion—if, that is to say, as

[1] Smend (Moses apud Prophetas, p. 19) says distinctly, "That a covenant was once on Mount Sinai concluded by Moses, is affirmed from of old by the most certain and unanimous tradition." Wellhausen, however, perceiving that the admission of a covenant entered into under definite historical conditions would shatter his system, says that the word for a covenant between Jehovah and His people is not to be found in the older prophets (Hist. of Israel, p. 417 f.) See Note XXII. Cf. below, p. 338.

[2] Relig. of Israel, vol. i. p. 294.

Stade has concluded, from the moment that Jahaveh was accepted as the God of Israel, the impression that He and none but He was to be their god— then we go back to the time of Moses for the common fountain of this conviction. That is to say, at a historical time and under some historical conditions, the whole nation became possessed of the idea that Jahaveh and His people were inseparably joined to one another. And then the question arises, What were those historical conditions? and which of the two shall we take as the better interpreters of what that relation was—the mass of the unthinking and careless people, or the *élite* of the nation's religious men? Surely an idea held so tenaciously by all classes in common must rest upon something more definite and positive than the mere choice by a nation, or by their leader for them, of some "Thunderer." Kuenen himself is obliged to admit that, even in the popular conception, the idea of holiness was present from the very first, though not as a central attribute. If, then, the conception of holiness was there from the first, are not the prophets more likely than the common people to have preserved, to have inherited from the best of their predecessors, from their spiritual teachers, the *place* of that attribute in Jahaveh's character? The attribute of might never disap-peared from the conception which the prophets had, nor can a time be pointed to when the attribute of might existed apart from that of holiness. Since Kuenen and his school feel themselves constrained to postulate a moral attribute from the very first, it is much more reasonable to believe that the thinking and more religious part of the nation would assign to the moral a higher and more central place than to the physical. In brief, the *character* of Jahaveh was moral in its initial conception.

2. In the second place, I think his reasoning is quite insufficient to show that mere political events produced either the popular or the prophetic conceptions. No doubt these nourished the one idea or the other, or stimulated it to greater developments; but something deeper, in the one case and the other, must be assumed, before we can understand either set of phenomena. The *popular* idea, he says, was stimulated and supported by political events, so that David's wars and Solomon's magnificence reflected a glory upon the national God in the popular estimation;[1] and that is no doubt true in a sense. But it is not so easy to follow him when he goes on to say that the popular conception, born of the sense of national dignity, was bound to suffer under the blows that fell upon it, and ultimately to die, when, with the independence of the nation, national self-consciousness disappeared (p. 119). We are confronted by historical facts that are irreconcilable with this sweeping assertion. If the popular conception was "born of the sense of national dignity," and had no firmer foundation, it would have disappeared long before the time of the Assyrian invasions. There were times in the nation's history when the national fortunes were at the very lowest point, such

[1] National Religions, p. 118. Compare also Wellhausen, Hist. of Israel, p. 20.

as the times succeeding Joshua, and the period immediately preceding the appearance of Samuel.   If
outward reverse had been able to break up the feeling of national consciousness, it was at such times
that the thing would have happened.   But it did
not; and in fact it is just at times of deepest
depression that the religious life of Israel makes
new departures.   Wellhausen, *e.g.*, places the rise
of Nabiism in the time when Israel was held down
hardest by the Philistines.   On Kuenen's own principles, therefore, we are bound to assume that (since
a faith born of mere national dignity cannot stand
such shocks) the popular faith had something else to
sustain it.   The popular faith must at these earlier
times have had a confidence resting on something
else than a mere belief in the arbitrary might
of Jahaveh.   We conclude, therefore, that what
Kuenen calls the prophetic belief must have been in
existence from such an early period—was indeed
pre-prophetic; that in fact pre-prophetic and prophetic are identical, both resting on some historical experience.

Even more inadequate, in my opinion, is his attempt to prove that the *prophetic* belief was brought
about by political events.   Kuenen seems to be so
well satisfied with Wellhausen's statement of the case
here,[1] that he contents himself with repeating his
words almost *verbatim*.   The passage is as follows:—

" Until the time of Amos there had subsisted in Palestine
and Syria a number of petty kingdoms and nationalities, which

---

[1] Wellhausen, Hist. of Israel, p. 472. Kuenen, National Religions, pp.
120-125,

had their friendships and enmities with one another, but paid no heed to anything outside their own immediate environment, and revolved, each in its own axis, careless of the outside world,[1] until suddenly the Assyrians burst in upon them. They commenced the work which was carried on by the Babylonians, Persians, and Greeks, and completed by the Romans. They introduced a new factor, the conception of the world—the world, of course, in the historical sense of that expression. In presence of that conception, the petty nationalities lost their centre of gravity, brute force dispelled their illusions, they flung their gods to the moles and to the bats (Isa. ii.) The prophets of Israel alone did not allow themselves to be taken by surprise by what had occurred, or to be plunged in despair; they solved by anticipation the grim problem which history set before them. They absorbed into their religion that conception of the world which was destroying the religions of the nations, even before it had been fully grasped by the secular consciousness. Where others saw only the ruin of everything that is holiest, they saw the triumph of Jehovah over delusion and error."

I humbly think that the language here used is badly chosen at the very point where we want the utmost clearness. If the words are to be taken literally, it is little wonder that the nationalities lost their centre of gravity, or even their gravity itself, over the performance here ascribed to a "conception." A "conception" of the world was introduced by the Assyrians; at its presence the petty nationalities lost their centre of gravity; the prophets of Israel alone did not allow themselves to be taken by surprise; they "absorbed" into their religion that conception, "even before it had been fully grasped by the secular consciousness,"—and the thing was done. Let us, however, try to get behind the phrases and understand the thing that is supposed to have actually happened.

[1] See Note XXIII.

The Assyrians appeared upon the narrow stage on which Israel and other little nationalities moved. With their appearance arose the conception of the world in the usual historical sense—*i.e.*, I suppose the petty nationalities came to understand that there was a world much larger than their own circumscribed territory, and agencies at work superior to those with which they were familiar.   If the most of the petty nations threw their idols to the moles and to the bats, it would be because they were convinced that these, their own gods, were of no avail to resist the stronger power, which, under the patronage of foreign gods, was trampling down petty nationalities like their own.   The "conception," therefore, which is not a thing floating in the air, but a product of reflection, arose in the minds of Israel's neighbours as well as in the minds of the prophets. This is all plain enough; but when we come to the vital point, Why did the prophets of Israel take a different view? we have no explanation of the fact. We are simply told they "absorbed the conception into their own religion, even before it had been fully grasped by the secular consciousness." That is to say, before even the secular consciousness had fully grasped the fact that there were greater powers outside their narrow confines than their local national gods, the prophets at once started to declare that it was their own national God that was controlling these forces—at once they leaped from the idea of a local national deity to that of a deity controlling the world; or, at all events, they saw a divine plan, a Providence in all these things, which so staggered others. Then, I suppose, it was that the shifting took place in the conception of the attributes of Jahaveh, and He came to be conceived as One with not only moral attributes, but with ethical character. I cannot see that the thing is made any clearer, or that the development is made out. What we want to know is, What enabled the prophets alone to read the signs of the times as they did? Their teaching, in face of the events, is a clear proof that from the first utterance of it they had a higher idea of their God to start with. The solution of the political problem was indeed ready before the problem presented itself, just because the idea of a God whose character was ethical was a much older idea. The earliest writing prophets knew of a God different from the gods of the nations around them; and they themselves speak of such a God as revealing Himself to prophets before them. Even the writer or writers of the patriarchal stories, and the writer of the accounts of Elijah, at a time when there was no threatening of a collapse of the State from foreign invasion, have pure ethical conceptions of Jahaveh, and regard Him as controlling the destinies of the world. The conception of Jahaveh as a Ruler of the world is much older than the time in which Kuenen and his school would place it; and it is in vain that we ask the outward events of the history to give an explanation of that religious consciousness which, from the earliest times, underlies all these events.

3. But in the third place, let us leave abstract inquiries into what must have happened, and this subtle following of the movement of a conception: let us

come to actual facts. If it be true that the appearance of the Assyrians gave the first impulse to this wider view, the view is so far removed from what is called the pre-prophetic conception that we ought to see it growing under our eyes. At the Assyrian period, we have the contemporary writings of Amos and Hosea; and from them onwards, we have the writings of other prophets who lived through the trying times of the Assyrian invasions, and down to the Babylonian captivity. Amos speaks only in the vaguest terms of the great Assyrian power; Isaiah saw it in the land; Jeremiah witnessed the final collapse of Israelite independence. We ought to be able to trace the gradual expansion of the prophetic view, from its first stage to its last. Now what do we find? We find indeed an advance from Amos to Jeremiah as to the *conditions* on which the relation of Jahaveh to Israel rests, and in regard to the relation of the Jahaveh religion to the outside world; but within the range of written prophecy we do not find the development of the idea of Jahaveh Himself. In regard to the conception that He controls the whole world, there is no difference in the teaching of Amos and Jeremiah. I know that Wellhausen and Stade would reject all passages in Amos[1] which express such high views of Jahaveh's character, on the ground that they disturb the connection. Robertson Smith,[2] though he does not reject them, says mildly that they are not necessary for the understanding of the context; and he refers, apparently

[1] Such passages as Amos iv. 13, v. 8 ff., ix. 1-7. See chap. vi. p. 146.

[2] Prophets of Israel, p. 398 f.

with favour, to Wellhausen's explanation of their presence in the text—that they are *lyrical intermezzi*, like those that are found so frequently in the Deutero-Isaiah. *Lyrical intermezzi* forsooth! Any one with the least sympathy with the writers will recognise in them the outpourings of hearts that were full of the noblest conceptions of the God whom they celebrate, and will perceive that they come in most fitly to emphasise the context.

On this point Kuenen has to defend himself, and he explains at length [1] his position as compared with that of Baudissin and contrasted with that of H. Schultz. His explanation amounts to this, that, if the prophets of the eighth century use expressions concerning Jahaveh's supremacy over the heathen world as well as Israel, and concerning the gods of the heathen, which practically amount to a denial of the existence of the latter, this shows that they belong to a period of transition or of *nascent monotheism.* Traces of this are still to be found distinctly in Deuteronomy itself.[2] This nascent monotheism in the prophets of the eighth century Kuenen describes as "a repeated overstepping of the line between monolatry and the recognition of one only God." He says: "I recognise monotheism *de facto* in these strong expressions of the prophets, and only deny that they had acquired it as a permanent possession. Now and then they rise to the recognition of the sole existence of Jahaveh, and the denial of "the other gods"; "but generally they do not get

[1] National Religions, note vii. p. 317 ff.
[2] Theol. Review, 1874, pp. 347-351.

beyond the monolatry in which they, or at any rate
the earlier ones among them, had been brought up."
He maintains, however, in opposition to Schultz,
that "the still older monotheism of the period before the prophets has no existence."

Now, if we examine this so-called nascent monotheism, which is admitted to be *de facto* monotheism,
we find it full-grown at its birth.   Amos, the earliest writing prophet, utters it in clear tones, as a
familiar and admitted truth, in saying that Jahaveh
had brought the Philistines from Caphtor and the
Syrians from Kir, as he had brought Israel from
Egypt, and in ever representing righteousness as the
basis of the divine character.   A being whose character is ethical, and whose rule unerringly controls
the destinies of all nations alike (Amos ix. 7), is infinitely more than a national god, such as heathen
nations conceived their deities; and in no case does
Amos give any countenance to the so-called monolatry, as if the monotheism he taught was held
loosely in his hands.   But what are we to think of
Kuenen's position that this *nascent* monotheism is
also still to be found a century *after* Amos in the
book of Deuteronomy?   It is there *de facto* in Amos;
still a century later it is only nascent; whereas in
Elijah, a century before Amos, it has no existence,
although in another connection both are declared to
be equally organs of the Jahaveh religion.   And we
are to accept all this on the " I recognise " and " I
maintain " of Dr. Kuenen.   In regard to the ethical
character of Jahaveh, Amos and Hosea were just as
bold and firm in chiding the sins of their contempo-

raries as Isaiah, who on this theory is supposed to have attained a conception of holiness which was only nascent in these earlier prophets; and the prophets that follow Isaiah are not more emphatic in the same strain, and yet they do not, like Isaiah, call Jahaveh the Holy One of Israel. In fact, this explanation of the rise of pure monotheism is artificial in the extreme, and the "ethic monotheism" is merely a pretentious phrase. The same truth that Amos proclaimed finds expression in the words put in the mouth of Abraham by the Jehovistic narrator, "Shall not the Judge of all the world do right?" (Gen. xviii. 25); it was *de facto* held by Elijah and the seven thousand who like him would not bow the knee to Baal; it was held also by Samuel when he set up the stone Ebenezer, saying, Hitherto Jahaveh hath helped us: [1] and these men could not have asserted it, one after the other, so emphatically as they did, in times of deepest national depression, unless it had been deeply impressed on the hearts of the best of the nation from the early times at which the Biblical writers assume it.

4. Lastly, let us come back to Kuenen's emphasised assertion that the prophets agreed with the people in the tenacity with which they clung to the belief that Jahaveh and Israel were inseparable. The point is not disputed; but surely such a conviction must have been based upon something definite and positive, and it is most reasonable to assume that that something was believed to be *inherent in*

[1] König, Hauptprobleme, p. 44 f.

the nature of Jahaveh Himself. If the nation believed that He would never give them up, however
far they fell from Him; if the prophets believed that
He would never give them up, and even would have
a special favour for them when He became the God
of all the families of mankind,—there must have
been in the minds of all a belief of some quality
strong enough to bind Jahaveh in this inseparable
manner to His own people. Neither ' might,' nor
holiness in its terrifying aspect, will explain this.
Now such a quality or character we do find ascribed
to Him by the earliest prophets, although it is a
quality to which I think Kuenen makes no reference.
It is an attribute, without taking account of which
we can neither understand the Old nor the New
Testament. I call it, without hesitation, the quality
of *grace.* In various ways the belief in it comes
out; by various names the shades of its signification
are expressed; but this variety only shows how
central, to use Kuenen's own word, this attribute
was in the conception. And I am not to reason
from abstract principles here, or from the whole
tenor of Biblical teaching. I take as witness one of
the earliest of the writing prophets, who lived at
the very time Kuenen's supposed development should
have been taking place, and it is marvellous to me
that Kuenen and other writers could have passed by
a witness whose testimony is so precise. The whole
of Hosea's book turns upon that idea,—God had
loved Israel in the time of the nation's youth; and
the touching story (or figure) of the wayward wife,
going her own evil course, yet not rejected,—just

because her husband had loved her at first,—and
finally brought back, and by the power of love taught
to love her husband,—all this is *applied* for us by
the prophet himself to the history of Israel.[1] Here
is another attribute than either might or holiness—
and it is here at the very dawn of written prophecy,
and placed by the prophet at the dawn of the national history—an attribute which surely raises the
character of Jahaveh to a higher level, and casts
light upon the apparent contradictions which Kuenen
has exhibited. Jahaveh was, above all things,
"faithful." He had done great things for Israel
(Amos ii. 9-11) in the past out of mere grace, not
because they had deserved it. The prophet Amos
also, though he dwells more on the righteousness of
Jahaveh, does not leave out of account the divine
love and mercy. These attributes are implied in the
great things that had been done for the nation in the
past, and emphatically taught in the 7th chapter in
the repeated visions of the prophet, in which the
Lord " repents " of the evil about to be inflicted on
His people: " It shall not be, saith Jahaveh." We
get thus, instead of mere reasonings as to how conceptions arise, positive historical facts as the means
of producing the idea which was held so tenaciously
to the last. If the people perverted this doctrine,
and sinned that grace might abound; if they pre-
sumed that, because Jahaveh could not deny Himself, therefore they might sin and repent,—this is no
more than thousands have done in the times of the

[1] This is the substance, under any interpretation, of chapters i. to iii.
See also chapter xi. 8 ff., " How shall I give thee up, Ephraim? "

Gospel. But their tenacity to the belief that *He would* not forsake them can hardly be explained without such a belief underlying it. Even their redoubled zeal in the matter of vows and offerings, taken in connection with this belief in Jahaveh's faithfulness, is not without its significance,—not as showing that they believed these would turn the faithful One from His purpose, but as showing that they recognised them as the outward expression of *their* faithfulness, or promise of faithfulness, on their part. At all events, this unconquerable conviction, which the prophets held in a purer, and the people in a more corrupted form, guarantees the conclusion that both alike recognised in the character of Jahaveh an attribute which had a more personal relation to them than either the attribute of might or that of holiness, an attribute which Hosea simply calls *love;* which will explain, on the one side, His forgiveness of offences, and on the other His unalterable care and regard. And therefore we are entitled to conclude that this *fundamental* conception of Jahaveh underlying the views of people and prophets together, was substantially that embodied in the declaration of His character, which is by the Biblical writers placed as far back as the time of Moses (Exod. xxxiv. 6, 7, R.V.): "Jahaveh, Jahaveh, a God full of compassion and gracious, slow to anger and plenteous in mercy and truth; keeping mercy for thousands, forgiving iniquity and transgression and sin; and that will by no means clear the guilty; visiting the iniquity of the fathers upon the children, and upon the children's children, upon the third and upon the fourth generation." It seems to me that if we place at the outset such a conception of Jahaveh, which is two-sided, and capable of expansion in two different lines, we can account for the development of the popular idea equally with that of the prophets from one common source; that we can give some explanation of the clearness with which the very earliest of the writing prophets represent the character of the national God, and also the persistency with which the people held to their view to the last. We obtain, in a word, development from a definite starting-point, whereas on Kuenen's view we neither find a reasonable meeting-point for the two divergent tendencies, nor can follow the steps in the development of either the one or the other.

"The principles which we see operating from the earliest times," says Professor A. B. Davidson, " are the principles wielded by the prophets. They are few but comprehensive. They form the essence of the moral law—consisting of two principles and a fact,—namely, that Jehovah was Israel's God alone; and that His being was ethical, demanding a moral life among those who served Him as His people: and these two principles elevated into a high emotional unity in the consciousness of redemption just experienced." [1]

---

[1] Expositor, third series, vol. v. p. 43.

CHAPTER XIII.

AUTHORITATIVE INSTITUTIONS—THEIR EARLY DATE.

Connection of this with the preceding—Reasons for postponing consideration of forms, (1) because practice is not a sure index of profession, and (2) because external forms, even when authorised, are not sufficient index of the truth of which they are signs—Mode of procedure as before—Three things to be distinguished, Law, Codification of Law, Writing of Law-books, on all of which the Biblical theory allows a latitude of view—Points at which the Biblical and the modern view are at variance—The conclusions of the modern theory, (1) Law not of Mosaic origin, (2) Codes so inconsistent that they must be of different dates—Position similar to that before assumed—Presumption that Moses gave definite laws—The Covenant, how signalised—Proofs from prophetical writers; from Psalms; from admitted historical books—Conclusion that a Norm or Law, outside of prophets and superior to them, was acknowledged—What was it?

Up to this point the object of our inquiry has been to determine, as far as possible, what the religion of Israel was, in its essential and internal elements, at the earliest period to which we have access. We have examined the testimony given by the earliest admitted written sources to the nature of the religion at the date to which they belong, and have endeavoured to estimate the value of this class of witnesses for the determination of the religion of an antecedent and early time. Without relying on disputed books, we have found that those which are admitted confirm in many ways the statements of those which are not primarily taken into account. The earliest writing prophets, though not appealing to the authority of books, appeal to admitted and undeniable facts which are asserted in these books; and our conclusion has been, that whereas the modern theory is obliged to overstrain those admitted facts of history and experience which have a show of being in its favour, and to underrate those which seem to oppose it, the Biblical theory is confirmed in the main, and that the religion of Israel had, at a much earlier stage than the modern critical writers admit, the purer and more ethical character which they would relegate to a later time.

We come now to consider whether in outward form also and positive institutions the religion of Israel had not, before the time of the earliest writing prophets, or before the time at which modern critical writers place such an organisation, a more defined shape and authoritative arrangement than the modern historians allow. The two things are closely connected. Religious belief and practice always act and react upon one another. According to the Biblical view, as there was an early revelation of spiritual truth, so there was an early institution of law and religious observance. On the modern view also the two things are intimately related. Wellhausen says,[1] " All writers of the

[1] Hist. of Israel, p. 27.

Chaldæan period associate monotheism in the closest way with unity of worship;" and it is a fundamental element of his theory that the process of centralisation and spiritualisation which marks the development of the law and worship went on under prophetic influence and *pari passu* with the development of prophetic thought and teaching.[1]

It might seem at first sight that it would have been more proper to begin with outward observances, which are so obvious and give so tangible a representation of a people's religious belief; and then to reason from them to the essential character of the religion. There are, however, these two considerations to be taken into account. (1) In the first place, outward observance is not always, nor indeed generally, a faithful indication of religious profession; and when we are in search, as we are in this case, of a religion which claims to have been positively given with definite fundamental principles as well as formal institutions, it would be unfair to rest either upon the moral practice or the religious usages of a people making profession of such a religion. Forms may be perverted, obscured, or corrupted, and the life of the people is pretty certain to fall short of their faith. We might, for example, from the mere observance of facts and phenomena gather what was the "state of religion," as we use the phrase, in any given age of the Christian Church, but we would not be safe, from the mere contemplation of any age, in drawing a conclusion as to the essential

[1] Hist. of Israel; cf. p. 26 with 47, 81, 103.

character of Christianity. To argue from custom or observance in religion to the requirements and essence of religion would, in the case before us, be begging the question, which is virtually as to whether or not there was an ideal or positive religion to start with. By examining, as we have done, first of all the writings of the prophets, we gain some guiding light on this the fundamental point. And (2) in the second place, outward rites and ceremonies, in a special manner, do not furnish a sufficient indication of the truth of which they are symbols or concomitants. In such rites there has often been a carrying over and adaptation of old customary observances, which are in this transference invested with a new meaning. Many of the observances of Christendom are of this description; even the sacraments of the New Testament rest, as symbolic ordinances, upon earlier usages, although in the Gospel they are invested with new meaning. So also it is well known that some of the observances that are now characteristic of Islam were adopted and adapted from pre-existing Arabian usages. In any of these cases, to argue from the forms, without knowing what they were meant to signify, would be manifestly and grossly unfair. It would be similar to the false reasoning, which we have had occasion to notice already, from the primary or etymological signification of a word, without taking note of the sense in which, at a given time and in a particular context, it is employed. And it is necessary now to enter this *caveat*, because, as we shall have occasion to notice, this mode of reasoning is not a little relied on in the treatment of this subject. Certain observances of the Israelite religion, which are represented by the Biblical writers as commemorative or symbolical of national religious facts, have the outward forms of old observances or popular customs, and several of them are connected with the cycle of the natural year; and the conclusion is drawn, that down to a very recent period the sacred festivals signified nothing more than the bare outward form expressed. Hence the necessity of determining, first of all, as we have endeavoured to do, whether in religious conceptions and beliefs Israel had not at a much earlier period passed beyond the elements of a mere naturalistic faith. Hence also the necessity of caution in reasoning from the mere outward concomitants and expressions of religion to the essence of the thing signified.

No doubt a certain prepossession, on the one side or the other, arising out of the preceding inquiry, attends us as we enter on this part of the subject. If we admit the conclusion that the religion of Israel was gradually evolved or developed from an animistic stage, we shall scarcely expect to find in the pre-prophetic period institutions of a high moral significance; but if, on the contrary, we are satisfied that the religion was in its earlier and fundamental stage of a more ethical and exalted character, it will not surprise us to find, in the period referred to, a set of religious institutions in keeping with and expressing the higher class of conceptions. We shall, however, endeavour to consider this part of the subject independently of any conclusions already reached; and in doing so, to follow the same method of procedure as before. From the known and admitted we shall seek to make our way to the unknown or disputed; endeavouring from clear indications of the records which are unquestioned to make out the state of religious ordinances of their time, and the testimony which they may give to a greater antiquity. And here again what is primarily to be determined is, not the date of certain books in which the formal statement and prescription of outward observances are contained, but the existence of the institutions, or the knowledge of the prescriptions at the time and on the part of the writers whose dates are known. If we shall find that the witnesses who are available testify to the existence of laws and ordinances such as are found in the documents whose date is unknown, there is a strong presumption that these ordinances are the things we are in search of; and even if the documents in which they are embodied should be of late composition, they will to us still retain substantially their historical value.

In the inquiry now before us there are three things which are easily distinguishable, and which ought to be kept distinct in our minds. These are, (*a*) the origin of laws and observances, (*b*) the codification of laws, or the formal ratification of observances, and (*c*) the composition of the books in which we find the laws finally embodied or the ordinances described. Laws and institutions may grow out of custom, or they may be matter of formal enactment; but in either case they may exist for a longer or shorter time without being embodied in written pre-

scriptions. Again, the writing down of such prescriptions may be a gradual process, and result in
the formation of more than one code; but even after
laws are codified and institutions enacted, all experience proves that they may undergo modification.
Finally, the writing of a book or books, in which
codes or collections of laws and prescriptions of observances are strung upon a historical thread, may
quite conceivably be a work later than the formation
of separate codes, and much later than the origina-
tion of the laws or ordinances.

A full investigation into all these subjects would
take us very far afield; but we are kept within
limitations by the nature of our present inquiry,
and also by the circumstances of the case. We are
not called upon, for example, to go into the abstract
question of the origin of law and institutions, any
more than in the former part of our inquiry we had
to investigate the origin of religion. The Biblical
writers maintain that from a certain historical
period onwards—viz., from the time of Moses—
Israel had a certain body of positive institutions
(just as they assert that from Abraham's time they
had a pure faith); and that these institutions are
embodied in certain law-books which are preserved
to us. Our inquiry is therefore limited to a certain
time, and concentrated upon certain subjects. It is
also important to observe that, on all the three
points just indicated, in so far as they are elements
of the inquiry into the history of the religion of
Israel, various views may be held, and that the
Biblical theory, within certain limitations, leaves

room for great latitude of view on details. (*a*)
Religious observances, such as sacrifice, are spoken
of as matters of course, and existing before there
was formal legislation in regard to them. Even the
so-called Grundschrift or Priestly Code does not
exclude sacrifices from the patriarchal age, nor
represent them as originating in the time of Moses.
Nor is there anything either in history or in the
nature of the case to make it improbable that usage
at a certain point was stamped with the authority
of law. (*b*) Further, if we take the statements of
the law-books themselves, we are led to the conclusion that the laws therein contained were written
down at different times. Moses is said to have
written this and that, and in regard to many more,
it is not said who wrote them at all. In regard to
the collections of laws in particular—while it is said
that Moses wrote the laws of the book of the
Covenant and the Deuteronomic Code—it is not
said that he wrote the Levitical laws, nor are we
told who wrote them. (*c*) And finally, the books of
the Pentateuch, as composite productions, containing both law and history, are anonymous compositions, and may have assumed their present form
after the laws had existed for a time as a separate
code or codes. It is greatly to be lamented that so
much has been made of the mere question of the
authorship of these books containing the laws.
Although other books, which are also anonymous,
are accepted as materials for history, although the
books of the Pentateuch, with supreme indifference,
say nothing about their authorship, it has been

tacitly assumed that their whole value stands or falls with their Mosaic or non-Mosaic authorship. A broad distinction is evident between the questions, By whose instrumentality or authority was law given? and, By whose hands were books written which contain the law? The essential question is not as to the early or late date of the books of the Pentateuch, but as to the relation in which the legislation of the Pentateuch stands to the whole development of the history.

On this deeper question of the origin and religious meaning of the laws and institutions the two theories are as much opposed as we have seen them elsewhere. For just as, in the matter of religious conception and belief, the earlier phase is toned down by the modern historians to a naturalistic level, so in the matter of law the element of early positive enactment is minimised to the lowest possible degree. Custom and usage are made to account for the origin of a great part of the laws; for ages the nation is supposed to have been without authoritative law; and the actual amount of influence exerted by Moses is so explained away as to be almost inappreciable. On the other hand, though the Hebrew writers do not say anything as to who wrote the law-books, they assert positively that the law laid down in these books is Mosaic. Moreover, the theories being opposed as to the character of the Mosaic religion, their interpretation of the institutions will vary. To a deity who might be worshipped anywhere, who was circumscribed in the place of his abode, and who was merely a storm or sun or fire god, a kind of service might be appropriate that would be without proper significance in the worship of a deity who was in his central attributes holy, and in his nature spiritual. The Mosaic or pre-prophetic religion will determine the significance (if not the outward form) of the Mosaic or pre-prophetic institutions.

It is clear that to determine the point in dispute, we must appeal, if possible, to some independent testimony outside the laws themselves or the books in which they are contained; and that the value we shall attach to these legislative books will depend on the conclusions to be drawn from such independent sources. The only use that can be made of the laws themselves in the controversy, is to compare them with one another and with the prophetical and historical literature whose authority is admitted. Such a comparison has in fact been the task of criticism. As a result, the modern historians claim to have proved, (1) that the history of the time succeeding Moses, and down to a comparatively late period, does not show that the laws claiming to be Mosaic were in force, but shows, on the contrary, that the practice of the best men of the nation was inconsistent with them; from which the inference is drawn, that these laws were not up to that time in existence; and (2) that the laws themselves which are called Mosaic, when examined and compared, are so inconsistent with one another that they cannot all have been in force at the same time; particularly there are three codes discernible, which indicate three distinct modes of observance, and must have belonged to three historical periods, widely separated, which periods can be determined by comparing the requirements of the respective codes with the practice prevailing at different times in the history. In short, gradual growth by development is to be made to explain the origin of institutions, just as it explained the origin of religious conceptions; and this growth is to be exhibited within the field in which we have the means of testing conclusions by historical documents. Accordingly, just as we had to inquire into the elements of the Mosaic religion of Jahaveh, and trace the connection of the pre-prophetic with the prophetic religion, so here we have to inquire into the origin of the laws, and the consistency of the codes which are contained in the Pentateuch, in order to determine whether, or to what extent, they may be held to be, or proved not to be, Mosaic. In the present chapter we confine ourselves to the inquiry whether there is any presumptive or any positive proof that Moses gave to Israel such a positive legislation as the law-books exhibit.

It occurs at once as a striking thing that the uniform tradition is, that Moses gave laws and ordinances to Israel. And that it is not a blind ascription of everything to some great ancestor, may be gathered from the fact that there are ordinances and customs which are not traced to him. The Sabbath is made as old as the creation; circumcision is a mark of the covenant with Abraham; sacrifices are pre-Mosaic; and the abstaining from the sinew that shrank is traced to the time of Jacob. The body of laws, however, that formed the constitution of Israel as a people, is invariably referred to Moses. There must be some historical basis for the mere fact that all the three successive codes, as they are called, dating, as is alleged, from periods separated from one another by centuries,[1] are ascribed to Moses; whereas another alleged code, found in the book of Ezekiel, never obtained authoritative recognition. The persistence with which it is represented that law, moral and ceremonial, came from Moses, and the acceptance of the laws by the whole people as of Mosaic origin, proves at least that it was a deeply seated belief in the nation that the great leader had given some formal legal constitution to his people. It seems to me that it is trifling with a great subject to say, in the same breath, that Moses could scarcely have been even the author of the whole of the Decalogue, and also that he "was regarded as the great lawgiver, and all laws which God was considered to have sanctioned were placed under his name, that being the regular and only method of conferring authority upon new enactments."[2] The testimony of a nation is not to be so lightly set aside: it is the work of criticism to explain and account for tradition, not to give it the lie. And all the circumstances of the time make it abundantly probable that the tradition rests upon some good foundation.

Moses and his people came out of a country that had been long civilised, and in which ritual and

---

[1] The separate codes will be more particularly described in the next chapter.

[2] Allan Menzies, National Religion, p. 17 f.

legislation were particularly attended to. They came into a land which, as we now know, possessed civilisation and education before they appeared in it, and they not only secured a footing, but gained supremacy and maintained it, believing all the time that they were divinely guided. Now, if the tribes whom Moses led had any unity at all, if they did not wander aimlessly into Canaan, if they had the least feeling of the necessity of adhering closely together in the face of the inhabitants whom they dispossessed,[1] such a unity and cohesion would be produced or fostered by the possession of definite laws or customs, marking them off from their neighbours, and binding them together into one. Mere common belief, especially of the elementary kind which modern writers allow to them, would not have sufficed to separate them from the Canaanite inhabitants in such a way as to ensure their ultimate supremacy; a common tradition must be put into practical shape and active operation by common observances. Even if the work of Moses was merely the consolidation of common observances prevailing prior to the Mosaic age, these must have been stamped with special authority, supplemented by special institutions, and raised to the dignity of definite ordinance, if there is any truth at all in the unanimous ascription of law to Moses. Moreover, if ever there was a crisis in the history of Israel at which the setting up of formal institutions, the laying down of formal rules for national guidance, was naturally to be expected, it was at this stage. It is

---

[1] See Note XXIV.

strange indeed that critical historians of Israel
should postulate the putting forth of "legislative
programmes" at various later points in Israel's
history, and should be so unwilling to admit the
same for the time of Moses.   For just as individuals
in their early life, when moved by a high purpose,
sketch out for themselves careers and lay down
rules of conduct and principles of action, it was
surely the most natural thing in the world for the
great leader of Israel to trace out a programme of
conduct, and hedge it round with precautionary
measures, at a time when his nation was to pass
from a nomadic to a more settled life, and when
they were liable to be led away by various temptations from the simplicity of their primitive faith.
Any one who can recall his plans and resolutions
formed in early life, or who has perchance preserved juvenile journals or memoranda, will admit
that in such circumstances there is a natural tendency to run into minute details, which the exigencies of actual life afterwards modify or even render
impracticable.   The First Book of Discipline, drawn
up by Knox and his associates at the Reformation
in Scotland, is a striking historical instance of such
a programme.[1]   So that, if in the post-Mosaic
history of Israel we find little mention of many of
the enactments ascribed to Moses and the early
Mosaic time, this need not surprise us when we bear
in mind the totally new environments of life of the
people, and the common frailties of human nature.

[1] Story's Church of Scotland, Past and Present.   See particularly vol.
ii. p. 437, *foot.*

How much more may be implied in the undoubted fact that the succeeding books take little account of the detailed legislation of the Pentateuch, we need not here consider. Enough has been said to prove in a general way that a certain amount of legislation must be ascribed to Moses. If his name stands for any fact at all in the history of Israel, if in any conceivable way he made an abiding impression upon his people, it was by producing, or by cementing an already existing intimate relation between their consciousness and the national God. This relation the Biblical writers call a covenant.[1] Critical writers can hardly avoid using the expression, and are bound to admit the fact, by whatever name it may be called. They tell us that the compact amounted to this, "Israel was to be Jahaveh's people, and Jahaveh Israel's God." Is it conceivable that at a period such as that in which this compact is placed, at a time when the nation needed outward props and helps, a time when forms of worship and observance were the most natural and unavoidable, even a bare covenant like this should have been unaccompanied with any ceremonial to keep it alive in the national consciousness, and impress its significance upon their lives? Can we believe that Moses taught the people that the God whom they could not see was "just and righteous," that by being just and righteous they could best please Him, that, in a word, "Moses set up the great principle that the true sphere of religion is common life,"[2] and yet that he left a people

[1] See Note XXII., and compare above, p. 313.
[2] Allan Menzies, National Religion, p. 24.

such as they were without any ordinances of worship, and without any laws for the guidance of their daily life? A people, too, who at that very time, and in the power of their faith, were asserting their individuality! A "peculiar" people, as such a covenant necessarily made them, must have distinctive outward marks; a "holy" nation, on the very lowest ideas of holiness, must be separated from what is unclean; a "holy" deity, still on the most elementary conception of the term, must be fenced off by some restrictions, must be reverenced by some sacred ceremonial. The very idea of a covenant, if it does not even imply sacrifice, is intimately associated with it (Ps. l. 5). Whether the ceremonies were adaptations of old customs or new institutions, if such a definite thing as a covenant stands at the threshold of the national history, then to deny to Moses the organisation of Israel on the basis of definite observances, not only of a moral but also of a ceremonial character, is altogether an excess of arbitrariness, and leaves the unvarying tradition of later time without any adequate explanation or support.

But more precise and direct proof may be drawn from the prophetical and other accepted literature of the time to which we are confining ourselves. We may not have, indeed, unequivocal "references" to the books of the Law, or to the codes in which certain laws are contained; nor do we find full accounts of the observances of the minute ceremonial and liturgical prescriptions of the Pentateuch. It has been too much the habit of apologetic writers to look for positive citations of the books of the Pentateuch, or to argue from the use of certain expressions in prophetical or historical books that the legislative books in which such or similar expressions also occur were then in existence and were thus consciously referred to.[1] But critical writers have gone to the other extreme in arguing that where a law or ordinance is not mentioned by historical or prophetical authors, it was not known to them, and therefore had no existence in their day. We shall have to test the value of this argument in the sequel; in the meantime we have to look at the testimony borne by the prophetical and other books on this subject.

From the whole tone of the prophetical literature we may argue in a general way that there was in the times of the earliest writing prophets a universal recognition of a well-known *norm* or rule of conduct as possessed by the nation, though sadly dishonoured so far as concerns its observance. The attitude of reproof taken up by the prophets, and the absence of gainsaying on the part of the people whom they addressed, prove the recognition of some authoritative norm lying at the threshold of the nation's history, according to the principles laid down by St. Paul (Rom. iii. 20), that through the law is the knowledge of sin, and (v. 13) that sin is not imputed where there is no law.[2] An argument of this kind is not indeed sufficient to establish the Mosaic origin of all the legislation of the Pentateuch; it may not

---

[1] See before, chapter v. p. 108.

[2] So De Wette reasoned in a Review of Vatke in Theol. Stud. u. Krit. for 1837, p. 1003.

even necessarily lead to the conclusion that formal codes were in existence at all; but it warrants the conclusion, not merely that guidance was given to the people, from time to time as occasion required, by prophetic or priestly men, but that some standard of obedience and religious observance was acknowledged as set up for permanent appeal and authority.

But we can go much further than this. The manner in which the earliest prophets refer to such an authority—if language is to retain its ordinary meaning at all—implies principles of action embodied in concrete recognised laws. When Amos threatens Judah, "because they have rejected the law of the Lord, and have not kept His statutes" (Amos ii. 4), whether he is thinking of books or not, he is certainly thinking of certain standing principles objectively regarded as regulative of moral and religious life. Law or Torah may conceivably have been at first, as the critics assert, no more than instruction conveyed from time to time by prophet or priest; and this matter we shall consider in the next chapter. But the conjunction of the word "statutes" leaves no room for doubt that the prophet referred to an objective and concrete norm. Torah *may* be teaching, but statutes are determinate things, not given once and then forgotten, but set up as a standing rule. Moreover, the sins for which Israel in the sequel of the same chapter is reproved, though all of a moral kind, are just such sins as are condemned in the moral parts of the Pentateuchal codes. This prophet has no doubt, and his hearers

dare not deny, that the oppression of the poor, the
retaining of pledges,[1] the perversion of justice, and
the like, are violations of rules which every one admitted to be binding upon the nation. It is particularly to be noticed that the sins for which Israel
and Judah are threatened are more precise and
special than those breaches of the most elementary
laws of humanity against which the prophetic reproofs of other nations, Damascus, Philistia, Tyre,
Edom, Ammon, and Moab, are directed; and that it
is precisely in Judah, where "law" and "statutes"
would be best known and most universally acknowledged, that their violation is singled out for repro-
bation.[2]

The case is similar with the prophet Hosea.
"They have wandered from me," he says (vii. 13):
"they have transgressed my covenant and trespassed against my law" (viii. 1). The sins for
which he reproves the men of Israel of his time are
just such sins as the moral laws of the Mosaic legislation condemn;[3] and we have in one passage a
clear indication that written law, and that of considerable compass, was known and acknowledged in
his days. The passage (Hosea viii. 12), much as it
has been commented upon, and sought to be explained away in this connection, cannot be taken to
give any other sense that is at all reasonable.
Whether we read, with the Revised Version, "though

---

[1] Amos ii. 8. Comp. Exod. xxii. 26.

[2] I do not press the allusions in Amos iv. 4, 5, although an argument
might be drawn for the recognition of ritual laws, which are there represented as exaggerated or perverted.—See Bredenkamp, Gesetz u. Propheten, p. 82.

[3] See the whole of Hosea iv.

I write for him my law in ten thousand precepts," or, with the margin, " I wrote for him the ten thousand things of my law "—whether, that is to say, we take the words as positive or hypothetical, as referring to the past, or to the present or future—the prophet indicates a thing that his hearers would regard as either done, or natural to be done, and that thing is the writing of law in a copious manner, and the writing done directly by divine authority.

The manner in which Wellhausen gets rid of this passage is exceedingly characteristic. He says: [1]—

" In another passage (viz., this) we read, ' Ephraim has built for himself many altars, to sin; the altars are there for him, to sin. How many soever my instructions (*torothái*) may be, they are counted those of a stranger.' This text has had the unmerited misfortune of having been forced to do service as a proof that Hosea knew of copious writings similar in contents to our Pentateuch. All that can be drawn from the contrast, ' instead of following my instructions they offer sacrifice ' (for that is the meaning of the passage), is that the prophet had never once dreamed of the possibility of cultus being made the subject of Jehovah's directions."

Here, to begin with, Wellhausen omits in his citation the significant word "write," a proceeding which, looking to the question involved, is, at the least, not ingenuous; for the word so rendered cannot be toned down to the general sense of "prescribe." And then, if all that the passage means is what he says, "instead of following my instructions they offer sacrifice," is it not a very remarkable way of saying it, and does not the mention of " writing," in this subsidiary fashion, prove all the more strongly

[1] Hist. of Israel, p. 57,

that written instructions (*torothái*, and where are such to be found if not in some code or other?) were familiar and well known? Not in this fashion does Wellhausen pass by significant words in a verse when these can be turned to the support of his theory. The fact that "writing" occurs to the prophet where he does not base his main argument upon it, is the strong point; and thus, occurring in the connection in which it stands, this single passage suffices to establish the existence of written law of considerable compass at the time of Hosea. And as if to assure us that ritual ordinance was as well known as moral precept, and as if to anticipate Wellhausen's remark that "the prophet never once dreamed of the possibility of cultus being made the subject of Jehovah's direction," the prophet goes on in the following verse to say, "As for the sacrifices of *mine* offerings, they sacrifice flesh and eat it." The occurrence of the single suffixal *mine* here, as in Isaiah i. 12, "to tread *my* courts," in a passage in which that prophet is by modern critics maintained to deny the divine authority of all sacrificial service, are much more convincing proofs to the contrary than formal statements would have been. Both these prophets rebuke the performance of sacrifice as it went on in their day, and we need not wonder at the sharpness of the rebukes. But at the same time, both of them, in claiming Temple and offerings as belonging rightly to Jahaveh, tacitly confirm the supposition, which is most natural in itself, that Israel up to their time had a law of worship which was undisputed, and that the Temple, set apart to the outward service of the national God, was provided with an authoritative order and ritual.[1]

These indications in the earliest writing prophets are entirely against the supposition that it was through the influence of the prophets that the codes of law came into existence, as they are against the idea that law was regarded by them as a thing still in flux, and given out from time to time by either prophet or priest as occasion demanded. Any references that are found to laws or ordinances in the prophetical writings are always of the nature of references to things existing and well known in their times. If, in a few passages, the law or laws are spoken of as having been given by prophetic mediation, it will be found that the references (as in Ezra ix. 10, 11) will apply to Moses, who is regarded as a prophet and the leader of the prophets.[2] In any case, the law or norm is regarded as a thing antecedent to the prophets, and having a divine sanction and authority apart from themselves.

Passing beyond the prophetical books—and we have only glanced at the earliest of these—we might find the same conclusion confirmed in a very striking way by an examination of the Psalms, in which God's law, statutes, and commandments are referred to in such a manner as to suggest positive, well-understood things as the guides of religious conduct, the comfort of a religious life. Here, however, the dates and authorship of the compositions are so much disputed, that, with the limitations we have imposed on our inquiry, we must content ourselves

[1] See Note XXV. [2] Deut. xviii. 15; Hosea xii. 13.

with a brief reference.　　When all has been done that modern criticism can do to relegate the bulk of the Psalms to a late period, and make the Psalter the book of praise of the post-exilian synagogue, there still remain, even in the accepted pre-exilian Psalms, certain expressions which cannot be explained away. Even so thorough-going a critic as Hitzig accepted the latter part of Psalm xix., with its praise of the law, as Davidic, although Cheyne [1] has recently pronounced it to be late.　　But if any part of the Psalter is to be ascribed to David at all, it is the 18th Psalm; and, not to speak of other references it contains to God's "ways" and His "word," it is not easy to see what precise meaning can be attached to v. 22, "For all His judgments were before me, and I did not put away His statutes from me," if there was no body of positive religious principles of action existent in his day.　　The "uncritical" English reader should, however, be reminded here that it is not on linguistic considerations, but on the grounds of a higher criticism—*i.e.*, of a theory of the religious development—that so many of the Psalms are assigned to a late date.

Let us next consider what conclusion is to be drawn from the undisputed portions of the books of Judges and Samuel.　　Though they do not give us much information as to legal observances, and are usually claimed as proving that the Deuteronomic and Levitical codes were unknown at the periods to which they refer, there are certain indications in

---

[1] The Book of Psalms; or, The Praises of Israel.　A new translation with commentary (1888).

them pointing unmistakably to the conclusion that there was a recognised order of some kind in those days. It is self-evident that the Tabernacle at Shiloh could not have existed, nor have formed the centre of worship, without some recognised ritual. Even should it be proved that the practices of Eli's sons mentioned in the book of Samuel were inconsistent with the requirements of the Levitical code, this is no more than might have been expected from such men. The wonder would be if the practices of men such as they are depicted were in keeping with any conceivable authoritative rule at all. The point, however, now insisted on is, that the Shiloh worship must have been invested with authority; and therefore that the idea of authoritative law for ceremonial was familiar by that time. And so the sacrifices offered by Samuel, even should it be proved that his manner of performing them contradicts the requirements of the codes, imply a recognised and authoritative law or rule of sacrifice. They are offered to Jahaveh and in connection with the national recognition of Him, and must therefore have been regarded as sanctioned and accepted by Him. In other words, at that time there was some received legislation. So in the period of the Judges there are indications that the people were acquainted with some standard of authority, and accustomed to conceptions involving national obligations.

There is, for example, the incidental mention of the ark in Judges xx. 27, 28. It is true this occurs in a portion of the book which is pronounced to be late. But even if we had not this mention at all, we come upon the ark again at the opening of the book of Samuel, where it is the centre of the worship for the time; and we should be bound to explain whence it came, and how it had acquired this dignity. The very brevity of the allusion however, in Judges, is proof that the writer looked upon the ark as a national institution; and if the statement has any historic value at all, it proves the possession by Israel of some outward bond of religious life. In other words, they were not at this time merely a number of isolated tribes, related in some loose way to one another, and owning one common tribal god; but they had, previous to this time, been accustomed to regard themselves as one people, and, as a mark of their unity, had some form of outward worship. We must therefore go back to the time preceding the Judges for some account of this feature of their religious life; and no Biblical writer gives the least hint of the existence of anything like it in the early patriarchal age. The reference to Phinehas, the son of Eleazar, the son of Aaron, who ministers at the ark, indicating a hereditary priesthood in the family of Aaron, of course does not suit the modern theory. It is simply called by Wellhausen[1] "a gloss which forms a very awkward interruption." Much more to his purpose is the statement (in xviii. 30) that Jonathan, the son of Gershom, the son of Moses, became a priest to the Danites, as a proof that there was no regular Aaronic priesthood—although it is added in the next verse that "Micah's graven image" was at Dan "all the time that the house of God was

---

[1] Hist. of Israel, p. 237.

in Shiloh." At all events we have here, in these two incidental allusions, sufficient to carry us back to a period antecedent to the Judges for an explanation of the religious position of the people at that time. The ark of God, a priesthood, whether hereditary or not, a house of God at Shiloh—all these imply much more than they express. The priest must have a function, the house of God some ritual, an ark some history. These things could not have been borrowed from the Canaanites the moment the conquest was secured. Even such matters as the distinction of clean and unclean animals, the prohibition of certain foods, and the treatment of lepers, which may, and probably do, go back to pre-Mosaic times, imply regulation, ceremony, and, in many cases, the offering of sacrifices. All these, however, are just the things that would be taken under the sanction of the covenant, which was to set apart a holy people, and made matters of prescription by a legislative founder like Moses. For it is always to be remembered that by this time certainly the Israelite tribes were in possession of the Jahaveh religion. These outward arrangements, whatever their origin, were associated with their worship of Him as their only God; and as that religion, on any explanation of it, was the characteristic mark separating them from their neighbours, it is surely most extraordinary to suppose that the outward concomitants of the religion should present no difference from the worship of the peoples around them.

Again, it is maintained by Wellhausen and his school that the tribe of Levi was originally a

secular tribe like the others, and associated with
the kindred tribe of Simeon, whose fate it shared in
being dispersed in Israel; and it is maintained that
the Levitical guild was a growth of much later time,
when priestly development had far advanced.   Now
the story of Micah in the book of Judges is much relied on by the critics for the state of religion [1] at
this early period.   In that story (chap. xvii.) a
young man of the family of Judah, who was a Levite,
departs from Bethlehem-Judah to sojourn where he
could find a place, and comes to Micah, who hires
him to be his priest.   It is added: "Then said
Micah, Now know I that the Lord will do me good,
seeing I have a Levite to my priest."   And again,
in the 19th chapter, which is allowed to contain
archaic matter, we find a certain Levite sojourning
on the farther side of the hill-country of Ephraim.
Now it might be said, these are simply members of
the extinct tribe of Levi.   But it does seem remarkable that in both cases they should be seen sojourning—moving about, in fact—as the Levites, according to the legal requirement, might be expected to
do.   And more remarkable is the fact that they are
specially called Levites—though why the tribal
designation is kept up when the tribe is absorbed is
not clear; and most remarkable of all that Micah,
steeped to the lips in superstition, should believe
that good was sure to come to him because he had
a Levite for a priest.   On the theory of the Old
Testament writers, the fact, notwithstanding all the
surrounding superstition, is easily explained.   There

[1] See chapter ix. p. 231.

was a tribe of Levi without territory, with a priestly or *quasi*-priestly function, the members of which were held in repute on that account. On the new theory, we meet with a feature of the life of that rude age that calls for an explanation, and fails to find it. To my mind such an incidental notice is a very strong corroboration of the history which declares that a tribe of Levi was set apart for sacred functions; and considering the age in which the events occurred, a more convincing proof of the accuracy of the book than an elaborate attempt to show that all the requirements of the Levitical law were in force. The discovery of a fact like this, in the darkness and ignorance of those times, sends us back to a time antecedent to the Judges for the proper basis of the religious constitution of Israel.

The references we thus find in undoubtedly early compositions, though not perhaps numerous, yet just because they are incidental and indirect, establish a very strong presumption that the pre-prophetic religion was backed up by a well-recognised system of positive enactments, and account for the persistent ascription of code after code to Moses. There are other considerations, pointing in the same direction, which should not be left out of account. There is, *e.g.*, the remarkable fact that, during the whole of the regal period, we never hear of the kings making laws, while there is a constant reference to law, in some sense or other, as an authoritative thing in the nation. The solitary instance that is recorded (1 Sam. xxx. 25) only proves the rule. Again, there is the undisputed fact that a recognised priesthood existed in Israel from very early times. It is hardly conceivable that such an order should have existed without formal regulation and prescribed functions; and as the critical historians refer to priestly circles the very earliest collection of laws, contained in the book of the Covenant, and admit that the priests always appealed to the authority of Moses, the inference does not seem unwarranted that a priestly law, of some extent and of a definite description, formed part of the constitution given to Israel by the great lawgiver.

It is, it must be confessed, somewhat remarkable that so little is said of Moses by the earlier prophets, though some have overstated the matter, and have drawn from it a conclusion which is quite unwarranted. Ghillany,[1] *e.g.*, mentions it as a circumstance hitherto unnoticed, that the name of Moses, except in the post-exilic Malachi (iv. 4) and Daniel (ix. 11, 13), does not occur in any of the prophets; or at least he had not discovered the name anywhere else in the prophets—not even in Ezekiel. Elsewhere [2] he says that Moses, so renowned among the Jews after the captivity, is only named five times altogether in the whole prophetical literature, and that of all the prophets who lived before B.C. 622, the year in which the so-called Mosaic law was found in the Temple, not one mentions Moses as a lawgiver or appeals to his authority. Only in one of the prophets before that period (Micah vi. 4) is there found an exception; and this passage is declared to

---

[1] Die Menschenopfer der alten Hebräer, p. 27.
[2] Theologische Briefe von Richard von der Alm, vol. i. p. 179 ff.

be an interpolation. It is clear, however, that Hosea, though he does not name him, directly refers to Moses when he says that by a "prophet" the Lord brought Israel out of Egypt (xii. 13). Jeremiah also must have had Moses in mind when he said, "Since the day that your fathers came forth out of the land of Egypt unto this day, I have even sent unto you all my servants the prophets, daily rising up early and sending them" (Jer. vii. 25, &c.) Moreover, in Isa. lxiii. 11, Moses is expressly named. The inference, however, from such texts, is rather against than in favour of the modern theory.[1] So precarious is the argument from silence, that one is almost tempted to maintain the paradox that the things which are least mentioned were the most familiar. The historical fact stands undoubted, that, from first to last, legislation was ascribed to Moses; and if the critics should succeed in making out from this silence that the earlier prophets knew little or nothing of Moses, then it is all the more difficult to explain how a person so unknown and undistinguished should have had invariably the immense work of legislation ascribed to him. Much rather should we say that the work of Moses was so familiar to the national mind that there was no need to mention him by name; a mere reference to Egypt or Sinai was to the popular mind more than a verbal mention. We know how in other Scriptures, which are not from the hands of prophets, the highest place is assigned to Moses as an organ of divine revelation

[1] König, Hauptprobleme, p. 16; Delitzsch, Comm. on Genesis, Eng. trans., vol. i. p. 11 f.

(Exod. xxxiii. 11; Num. xii. 6-8; Deut. xxxiv. 10). Such passages are surer indications than express mention of his name, that Moses was in the estimation and recollection of the nation "the most exalted figure in all primitive history";[1] and account satisfactorily for the constant ascription to him of the legislation. Still we come back to what is better than verbal references, the underlying assumption in the earlier prophets and extra-legislative literature, that there was an objective and undisputed norm, to whose authority prophets, priests, and people alike acknowledged submission. The question, therefore, which now presses itself upon us for solution is, What was the law or norm which is thus referred to?

[1] Ranke, Universal History, translated by Prothero, p. 31.

CHAPTER XIV.

AUTHORITATIVE INSTITUTIONS—THEIR RELIGIOUS BASIS.

Brief summary of leading positions of the modern school— Examination of main points: (1) Oral law before written law; references to law of priests and prophets; theory of law orally given from time to time down to reign of Josiah shown to be untenable: (2) Origin of feasts and worship according to the theory—Natural and agricultural basis, centralisation, fixity, historical reference— The theory criticised: (a) the mere joyousness of a nature feast made too much of; the basket of fruits; (b) exaggerated importance of idea of centralisation; (c) failure to show transition from agricultural to religious feasts, and to explain the historical reference—The Passover a glaring instance.

IN the preceding chapter we have seen reasons for ascribing to Moses a definite and authoritative system of law. If the references of the prophetical and other books have been rightly interpreted, we should expect to find somewhere a code or codes of laws regulating the life and worship of Jahaveh's people; and as we know of no other laws than those contained in the law-books, there is a primary presumption that these are the laws in question. If not, the question is, Where are the laws, or what has become of them? or, put otherwise, What are the laws which these books contain?

The account the modern theory gives of the matter is something to the following effect: Moses neither wrote nor ordained an elaborate body of laws. Law (Torah) was at first and for a long time an oral system of instruction, which at definite and comparatively late periods was codified for special purposes. Nor are the religious rites and ceremonies that claim to have been given by Moses of Mosaic origin, but survivals of old customary observances, principally connected with the agricultural year, and transformed at a late time into ceremonies of a more national and religious nature. This view, it is claimed, is not only consistent with the statements of the prophets, but is the only one in harmony with the history. To the main points here stated we now turn our attention.

(1.) In the first place, we are told there was an oral law before there was a written law. The priests had as their function to teach the people; the prophets also were teachers; but the law or teaching communicated by both was an oral thing, given forth as occasion demanded, at the request of individuals who came to the priests for direction, or spontaneously by the prophets when they were moved to give their testimony. The priestly Torah was a more regular thing; the prophetic, sporadic and occasional; and there was this difference, that the priest rested upon tradition, whereas the prophet spoke by his own authority, or rather in the name of God directly. "The priests derived their Torah

from Moses; they claimed only to preserve and guard
what Moses had left (Deut. xxxiii. 4, 9 *seq.*) He
counted as their ancestor (xxxiii. 8; Judges xviii.
30); his father-in-law is the priest of Midian at
Mount Sinai, as Jehovah also is derived in a certain sense from the older deity of Sinai."[1] When
priests and prophets are mentioned together, "the
priests take precedence of the prophets. . . . For
this reason, that they take their stand so entirely
on the tradition and depend on it, their claim to
have Moses for their father, the beginner and founder
of their tradition, is in itself the better founded of
the two."[2] "The prophets have notoriously no
father (1 Sam. x. 12). . . . We have thus on the
one side the tradition of a class, which suffices for
the occasions of ordinary life; and on the other, the
inspiration of awakened individuals, stirred up by
occasions which are more than ordinary."[3] The
priestly Torah was chiefly confined to law and
morals, though the priests "also gave ritual instruction (*e.g.*, regarding cleanness and unclean-
ness)." In pre-exilian antiquity, however, "the
priests' own praxis [at the altar] never constituted
the contents of the Torah," which "always consisted of instructions to the laity."[4]

That the word Torah is applied to oral instruction, and means originally, like the corresponding
words $\delta\iota\delta\alpha\chi\dot{\eta}$ and *doctrina*, simply teaching, need
not be disputed. It seems to have the primary idea
of *throwing out* the hand in the gesture of guidance

[1] Wellhausen, Hist. of Israel, p. 396.   [2] Ibid., p. 397.
[3] Ibid., p. 398.   [4] Ibid., p. 59, note.

or *direction*[1] (which would perhaps be a better rendering), and it is found in this general sense in Prov. i. 8, iii. 1, iv. 2: "The instruction of thy father, and the law of thy mother;" "my law." So that any advice, for the purpose of guidance (for that is always implied), is naturally denoted by it; and the guidance or instruction of priests or prophets, who were the religious guides or instructors of the people, is, as a matter of course, denoted by one common word, Torah. Examples of the use of the word to express *prophetic* teaching are found in Isaiah, who says: "Hear the word of the Lord, ye rulers of Sodom; attend to the law of our God, ye people of Gomorrah" (i. 10), where he is clearly referring to his own teaching; and even if we suppose a reference to a written law, it could only be to the substance and not the letter of it that he directed attention. So when he says, "Bind up the testimony, seal the law among my disciples" (viii. 16), though he is speaking of something objective, positive, and authoritative, it is most natural to see a reference to what he had just said or was about to say. Probably also a general sense should be given to the word in xxx. 9, "This is a rebellious people, lying children, children that will not hear the law of the Lord." Again we have mention of a specific *priestly* Torah in the

[1] There seems, however, no reason to conclude that Torah, from a verb "to throw," originally referred to the casting down of some kind of dice, as, *e.g.*, Urim and Thummim, to determine a course of action, as Wellhausen (Hist. of Israel, p. 394) supposes. There is no instance of decision by the Urim and Thummim being called Torah; and Wellhausen himself strenuously maintains an oral Torah by the prophets, which could not have been of this description. Stade, of course, traces back the oracle and the use of the lot to fetishistic and animistic practices, and the priest to the soothsayer. The prophet who, at a later time, contended with the mechanical priestcraft, was also a survival of the primitive "seer."—Geschichte, vol. i. pp. 468-476.

Blessing of Moses, one of the oldest pieces of Hebrew literature, where it is said of the tribe of Levi, "They shall teach Jacob Thy judgments, and Israel Thy law: they shall put incense before Thee, and whole burnt offerings upon Thine altar" (Deut. xxxiii. 10). Whatever else we may learn from the verse, the function of the Levite to teach is clearly stated, and this means a course of instruction or acts of instruction to the people. That a distinction was drawn between the teaching of the priests and that of the prophets, we may also conclude from such a passage as Micah iii. 11, "The heads thereof judge for reward, and the priests thereof teach for hire, and the prophets divine for money." A similar distinction, showing the existence of a priestly law, is found in Jeremiah, "The law shall not perish from the priest, nor counsel from the wise, nor the word from the prophet" (xviii. 18); in Lamentations (ii. 9), "Her king and her princes are among the nations where law is not; yea, her prophets find no vision from the Lord;" and in Ezekiel, "The law shall perish from the priest, and counsel from the ancients" (vii. 26); "her priests have violated my law, and profaned mine holy things," &c. (xxii. 26). In other passages, again, "law" seems to be used as synonymous with "the word of the Lord," generally to express the whole of the truth of revelation, as in Isaiah ii. 3, v. 24, xlii. 4; Micah iv. 2; and perhaps Amos ii. 4, and Hosea viii. 1.

While, however, these distinctions are noticeable, the inferences drawn from them are not at all warrantable. The general use of the word to denote divine revelation of truth as a whole implies a unity in that truth, and to this extent it is true that even the priestly Torah was mainly, or we should rather say, fundamentally, of a moral character; although we have seen in the last chapter good reason for concluding that the prophets knew of and recognised a ritual law as well. But the main point now in hand is the alleged long existence of oral apart from and antecedent to written Torah; and it may be maintained, even on the ground of the passages just cited, that the inference is too bold. Let us make the supposition demanded by Wellhausen, that the priests had the practice of giving oral decisions as occasion arose. Still, the question arises, Did the priests decide individual cases according to their individual judgment? and if not, what precisely were the guiding principles on which they acted? It is hardly conceivable that such instruction, if regularly given, up to a comparatively late time, should not have assumed, in practice, some concrete expression. The sentences uttered on various and recurring occasions must, at all events, have been regarded as self-consistent, and of concordant tenor, before they could be spoken of under this comprehensive term of Torah or instruction. Then we have to note particularly how it is admitted that the oral priestly Torah, which is thus assumed, always claims for itself, not only high antiquity, but Mosaic sanction. And, since even the priestly Torah is represented as a unity, we are led to inquire whether there was not some positive guide in the form of typical decisions which would account for so firm a tradition, and give some kind of uniformity to the oral sentences. If an oral teaching by the prophets did not prevent them from writing down their discourses, why should the priests, who had a teaching of a much more detailed and technical kind to convey, not have had a written Torah for their guidance? Wellhausen feels the force of this, for he says it might be supposed that, even if Deuteronomy and the Levitical Code are late, the Jehovistic legislation contained in the book of the Covenant (Exod. xx.-xxiii., xxxiv.) "might be regarded as the document which formed the starting-point of the religious history of Israel. And this position is in fact generally claimed for it." [1] It belongs, however, he says, to a period much later than the active oral Torah of the priests, and he reduces the Mosaic elements in it to the barest minimum, scarcely even admitting the Mosaic origin of the Decalogue.

So that the alleged oral Torah, on the hypothesis, rests upon nothing but immemorial custom, each decision as it was given constituting a Torah or law to meet the case in hand. That this was the way the law arose, and not by the promulgation of a set of statutes, is said to be indicated by a chapter in Exodus (xviii.), which represents Moses himself as sitting hearing cases in person, and deciding each case on its own merits. But this very chapter, so much relied upon, seems itself to draw the distinction between legislation and administration. Moses is represented as discharging both functions; but the chapter tells how he was advised to separate them.

[1] Hist. of Israel, p. 392.

He set over the people able men, who were to judge the people in small matters, reserving the "great matters" for his own decision. If the critics are prepared to take this chapter as a plain historical statement, then we get a positive starting-point for Mosaic law, and that, too, of a pretty comprehensive compass. For if the decisions on great matters were given by Moses, we have Mosaic legislation, since his sentences were given (presumably) on new cases or were regulations of older usages; and the small matters doubtless were controlled by precedents set by him. There is no reason to assume that such decisions as were given by Moses and his assessors remained unwritten, or in flux, till the time to which the book of the Covenant is brought down; and it is to be noted how care was taken, by the appointment of capable judges and by the *teaching* of the "statutes," that uniformity and consistency should be maintained. Unless, indeed, there was some guiding rule, the decisions could not have remained consistent with themselves, and could never have assumed a shape in which, collectively, they would have acquired respect. So in the passage already cited from the Blessing of Moses, where it is described as the function of Levi to teach the people the law, there is presumably something definite and positive to be taught; just as the second half of the verse speaks of the offerings which they had to present on the altar. Wellhausen's position, so confidently assumed, that the "teaching is only thought of as the action of the teacher"—if the teaching is to have any consistency at all—seems to me only conceivable on the supposition of a guidance of the teacher, an inspiration, in fact, of a kind that I fancy Wellhausen would be the last to admit. It is, besides, flatly contradicted by such a passage as Hosea iv. 6, where the priest is reproached (according to the common interpretation which applies the passage to the priestly class) for having forgotten the law of God, as indeed by all the passages which reprove the priests for unfaithfulness. If everything taught by the priest was Torah, with no guiding norm, such reproofs were out of place. Yet it is to be observed that the prophets, whatever they may say about the priests as a class, always speak of their Torah as a thing of unquestioned authority; and they were not the men to speak thus of the haphazard decisions on "law and morals" given by a class which was too often both lawless and immoral. Looking at it from any possible point of view, in the face of this persistent ascription of law to Moses, we are bound to assume something positive and plain, of such a character that a priesthood, often ignorant and corrupt, would be guided to give forth sentences that prophetic men could speak of with respect. To say nothing of the intricate cases of ceremonial cleanness and defilement, which Wellhausen admits constituted an element of the Torah, there were also "law and morals," as he tells us, and there must have been countless cases of casuistry and jurisprudence calling for decision at the mouth of these men, from whom there was no appeal; and the whole, when collected, forms, we are to suppose, the legislation on these subjects which afterwards became systematised into codes. Moreover, there were the matters relating to the right performance of priestly functions and the proper observance of sacred ceremonies. Wellhausen indeed says positively—although on no positive evidence—that "the priests' own praxis [at the altar] never constituted, in pre-exilian antiquity, the contents of the Torah."[1] Yet, considering the punctilious observance that must have been required in such services, and the jealousy of a priestly class to maintain forms in their rigour, one would have expected that just in matters of this kind the Torah, whether oral or written, would be most definite. Although there was no need for the priests to instruct the laity in these matters, they were of such a kind as would suggest the writing of them down in longer or shorter collections to aid the memory of the priests themselves, to guide the partially initiated, and to secure accurate preservation. Many of the laws of Leviticus, in fact, to an ordinary reader, have the appearance of "memoranda" which might be ready at hand for instruction in such functions. The insistence on the authority of law, combined with the reproof of the priesthood, can thus have but one meaning—viz., that the priests were in possession of an ancient authoritative norm, according to which even ignorant men with technical training could have no excuse for going astray.

The priests' function, indeed, was to give instruction to the people, but the fact that they did so orally is no proof that there was no written or ob-

[1] Hist. of Israel, p. 59, note.

jective standard by which they taught. Nay, we
have positive proof to the contrary. Both in Haggai (ii. 11) and in Malachi (ii. 7), by whose time
certainly the law was codified and recognised, there
is mention of the oral teaching of the priests. And
if oral instruction was necessary at that time, though
co-existent with a written law, we are not bound to
conclude when Micah, for example, speaks of the
priests of his time teaching for hire (Micah iii. 11),
that they drew upon a tradition which was entirely
in their own possession. We have still Christian
pastors and teachers, although the Scriptures are in
every one's hands, and expounders of the law would
be more necessary in ages when printing was unknown and books rare. Indeed, if at a late time,
when the law was fully codified, there was need of
oral exposition, much more would oral instruction
require a definite basis at the earlier periods when
priests and people were so tempted to fall into corruption. Yet during even the worst times the
prophets have no doubt of the purity and fixity of
the priestly Torah. In speaking of the instruction
of the priests, they regard it as a thing superior to
and binding upon the class and the people. "Sentences," "judgments," "statutes" could have had
no coherency apart from a standard. It need not
of course be concluded, that wherever "law" occurs
there is a reference to the Pentateuch as a whole, or
to any *book* whatever in the modern sense. But the
alternative is not, as seems to be hastily assumed,
that there was no concrete law nor written code of
guidance—nothing, in short, but oral law, still in

process of being delivered. Such a supposition is in itself hardly conceivable, considering the conditions of the nation and the long period over which this oral law is said to extend; nor is it supported by an unforced exegesis of the prophetic utterances.

(2.) We have next to consider the assertion that the ceremonies and observances of the religion of Israel were not matters of divine authoritative appointment at first, but were the growth of custom.

" In the early days," says Wellhausen, " worship arose out of the midst of ordinary life, and was in most intimate and manifold connection with it. A sacrifice was a meal—a fact showing how remote was the idea of antithesis between spiritual earnestness and secular joyousness. . . . Year after year the return of vintage, corn-harvest, and sheep-shearing brought together the members of the household to eat and to drink in the presence of Jehovah; and besides these, there were less regularly recurring events which were celebrated in one circle after another. . . . The occasion arising out of daily life is thus inseparable from the holy action, and is what gives it meaning and character; an end corresponding to the situation always underlies it." [1]

And this is the case even in regard to the more distinctively national feasts:—

" It cannot be doubted, generally speaking and on the whole, that not only in the Jehovistic but also in the Deuteronomic legislation [2] the festivals rest upon agriculture, the basis at once of life and of religion. The soil, the fruitful soil, is the object of religion; it takes the place alike of heaven and of hell. Jehovah gives the land and its produce. He receives the best of what it yields as an expression of thankfulness, the tithes in

---

[1] Hist. of Israel, p. 76.

[2] These two stages of legislation, as will appear in the sequel, are placed by the critical school, the former in the earlier writing period, and the latter about 621 B.C.

recognition of his seignorial right. The relation between Himself and His people first arose from His having given them the land in fee; it continues to be maintained, inasmuch as good weather and fertility come from Him."[1]

So that the great feasts, which were the prominent features of the worship, are ultimately traceable to the Canaanites, just like Nabiism, which was a chief characteristic of the religion. For—

"Agriculture was learned by the Hebrews from the Canaanites, in whose land they settled, and in commingling with whom they, during the period of the Judges, made the transition to a sedentary life. Before the metamorphosis of shepherds into peasants was effected, they could not possibly have had feasts which related to agriculture. It would have been strange if they had not taken them also over from the Canaanites. The latter owed the land and its fruits to Baal, and for this they paid him the due tribute; the Israelites stood in the same relation to Jehovah. Materially and in itself the act was neither heathenish nor Israelite; its character either way was determined by its destination. There was therefore nothing against a transference of the feasts from Baal to Jehovah; on the contrary, the transference was a profession of faith that the land and its produce, and thus all that lay at the foundations of the national existence, were due not to the heathen deity, but to the God of Israel."[2]

The transition from this simpler and more naturalistic phase of worship to distinctively religious and non-secular observance took place, according to the theory, in connection with and in consequence of the movement for centralisation of worship, that culminated in the introduction of the Deuteronomic Code and the reform in the time of Josiah. The view is, that up to that time the worship at the Bamoth or

[1] Hist. of Israel, p. 91 f.　　　　　[2] Ibid., p. 93 f.

high places up and down the land[1] was the **regular**
and normal thing, and that the reform of Josiah
abolished these local sanctuaries, and concentrated
the worship at the one sanctuary at Jerusalem, thus
severing the connection between the old joyous religious worship and the daily life (p. 77). "Deuteronomy indeed does not contemplate such a result,"
and, as we have already seen, the assertion is that
still in the Deuteronomic legislation the festivals
rest upon agriculture. The transition was only fully
effected in the Priestly Code (which dates at the
earliest from the time of Ezra).

"Human life has its root in local environment, and so also
had the ancient cultus; in being transplanted from its natural
soil it was deprived of its natural nourishment. A separation
between it and the daily life was inevitable, and Deuteronomy
itself paved the way for this result by permitting profane slaugh-
tering. A man lived in Hebron, but sacrificed in Jerusalem;
life and worship fell apart. The consequences which lie dormant
in the Deuteronomic law are fully developed in the Priestly
Code" (ibid., p. 77).

And then as to the distinctively historical references which the feasts eventually attained, Wellhausen says:—

"It is in Deuteronomy that one detects the first very perceptible traces of a historical dress being given to the religion and
the worship, but this process is still confined within modest
limits. The historical event to which recurrence is always
made is the bringing up of Israel out of Egypt, and this is significant in so far as the bringing up out of Egypt coincides with
the leading into Canaan, that is, with the giving of the land, so
that the historical motive again resolves itself into the natural.

---

[1] See before, chap. viii. p. 199 ff.

In this way it can be said that not merely the Easter festival but all festivals are dependent upon the introduction of Israel into Canaan, and this is what we actually find very clearly in the prayer (Deut. xxvi.) with which at the Feast of Tabernacles the share of the festal gifts falling to the priest is offered to the Deity " (ibid., p. 92).

It is, however, as has been said, in the Priestly Code that the development is fully carried out, and

" the feasts entirely lose their peculiar characteristics, the occasions by which they are inspired and distinguished : by the monotonous sameness of the unvarying burnt-offering and sin-offering of the community as a whole, they are all put on the same even level, deprived of their natural spontaneity, and degraded into mere ' exercises of religion.' Only some very slight traces continue to bear witness to, we might rather say to betray, what was the point from which the development started— namely, the rites of the barley-sheaf, the loaves of bread, and the booths (Levit. xxiii.) But these are mere rites, petrified remains of the old custom " (ibid., p. 100).

There is a certain coherence and roundness about this theory that make it very specious; but unfortunately it is supported by little positive proof, and it fails, besides, to give an adequate account of well-established facts.

(*a*) In the first place, no one can object to the statement that "religious worship was a natural thing in Hebrew antiquity; it was the blossom of life, the heights and depths of which it was its business to transfigure and glorify " (p. 77). But just because it was so, we should have expected the worship to pass beyond the ordinary level of the soil to those " heights and depths " which had been reached in connection with the early national history. It is

simply inconceivable that a people who were ever
erecting pillars and offering sacrifices to commemo-
rate deliverances or celebrate victories, who associated ever so many places with events in their religious history, and who had, from the time of Moses,
passed through an unparalleled experience, should
still, in the time of Hosea or later, have practised
merely a worship whose sole motives were "thresh-
ing-floor and wine-press, corn and wine," and "vo-
ciferous joy, merry shoutings its expression " (p. 98).
By the time of Hosea, Israel had lived through a
very considerable part of its national and political
existence, and by the days of Josiah that life had
wellnigh run its course. Yet Wellhausen would
have us believe that, even as late as the time of
Josiah, the first perceptible trace is visible of a historical reference in the worship, and that, in the
time of Hosea,

"the blessing of the land is the end of religion, and that quite
generally—alike of the false heathenish and of the true Israelitish.   It has for its basis no historical acts of salvation, but nature simply, which, however, is regarded only as God's domain
and as man's field of labour, and is in no manner deified.   The
land is Jehovah's house,[1] wherein He lodges, and entertains the
nation; in the land and through the land it is that Israel first
becomes the people of Jehovah. . . . In accordance with this,
worship consists simply of the thanksgiving due for the gifts of
the soil, the vassalage payable to the superior who has given
the land and its fruits " (p. 97).

In opposition to this low and narrow view of the
conceptions of that time, we can point to the fact

---

[1] Hosea viii. 1, ix. 15.

before considered,[1] that Hosea dates the intimate
union between Jahaveh and His people from the
exodus and the desert life, before the land had become "Jehovah's house." In the very passages
which Wellhausen here cites, a distinction is drawn
between the Baalim (unlawful lovers) and Jahaveh
(the rightful husband), as if to prove that it was *not*
"through the land that Israel first became the people of Jehovah." No doubt an agricultural people,
if they would offer anything to their God, must offer
what they had,—the fruits of the land; but does a
Christian who gives his money for missions, let us
say, recognise no blessing that God has bestowed
upon him but silver and gold? No doubt Hosea and
all the prophets, early and late, connect the fertility
of the land and material prosperity with the blessing
of Jahaveh and the fidelity of His people, as many
people still do.[2] But the thing to be noted is that
Hosea, appealing to the consciousness of the men of
his time, reminds them of God's doings for them as
a people in the early days. His very reproof, in
the connection appealed to, is one against unfaithfulness to Him who had betrothed Israel to Himself
before they came into Canaan; and "I refuse to believe" (to adopt one of Wellhausen's modes of rea-

[1] See chap. v. p. 110.

[2] Wellhausen's own opinion is frankly stated in another place. In
speaking of Samuel's words, "God forbid that I should cease to pray
for you and teach you the good way" (1 Sam. xii. 23), he makes the comment: "They do not need to trouble themselves about means for ward-
ing off the attacks of their enemies; if they fast and pray, and give up
their sins, Jehovah hurls back the foe with His thunder and lightning,
and so long as they are pious He will not allow their land to be invaded.
All the expenses are then naturally superfluous by which a people usually safeguards its own existence. That this view is unhistorical is
self-evident. . . . It is the offspring of exilic or post-exilic Judaism."—
Hist. of Israel, p. 255.

soning [1]) that a prophet with views so advanced as
Hosea saw no more in worship than an acknowledgment of vassalage, payable to the superior of the
land, whoever he might be. Yet not only in the
days of Hosea, but two centuries later, Wellhausen
would have us believe that Israel was in this condition, for "it is in Deuteronomy that one detects the
first very perceptible traces [2] of a historical dress
being given to the religion and the worship." That
it is, however, "confined within modest limits," he
tries to prove from the prayer or hymn which was
uttered at the presentation of fruits. He quotes the
prayer at length, but if it has any meaning at all,
every clause of it contradicts the conclusion built
upon it:—

"A wandering Aramæan was my father; and he went down
to Egypt, and sojourned there a few men strong, and became
there a nation, great, mighty, and populous. And the Egyptians evil entreated them, and oppressed them, and laid upon
them hard bondage.   Then called we upon Jehovah, the God of
our fathers, and He heard our voice, and looked on our affliction, and our labour, and our oppression. And Jehovah brought
us forth out of Egypt with a mighty hand, and with an out-
stretched arm, and with great terribleness, and with signs, and
with wonders; *and brought us unto this place, and gave us
this land, a land where milk and honey flow.   And now, be-
hold, I have brought the best of the fruits of the land, which
Thou, O Lord, hast given me*" (Deut. xxvi.)

Wellhausen emphasises the words put in italics, and
concludes triumphantly (p. 92), "Observe here how
the act of salvation whereby Israel was founded is-

---

[1] Hist. of Israel, p. 51.

[2] Compare Kuenen's account of " nascent monotheism " at the same
period.   See above, chap. xii. p. 320.

sues in the gift of a fruitful land." We all knew
that, as we also knew that the only gift which Israel
could offer in return was the produce of the land.
But what of all the other blessings, of a *national
and religious kind,* which are heaped up, clause by
clause, as if the suppliant would stir up his soul, and
all that was within him, to forget not all the benefits
bestowed upon the nation? "*He* went down. . . .
The Egyptians evil entreated *them.* . . . He heard
our voice and brought *us* forth." If the author of
this prayer had not a clear recognition of the unity
of the nation from the time of the patriarchs, and of
the national blessings from first to last which they
had received, then language has no meaning. It
seems to me that this little basket of fruit, like Gideon's cake of barley-bread, upsets the whole array
of Wellhausen's well-marshalled argument of feasts
taken over from the Canaanites, and tribute offered
indifferently to Baal or Jahaveh, as lord paramount
of the land, not to speak of "the soil, the fruitful
soil, taking the place alike of heaven and hell." As
to the references to agricultural matters in even the
earliest code, the book of the Covenant, which are
made so much of to prove that this legislation could
have had no existence till Israel came into Palestine,
it is enough to say that it is taken for granted that
Moses had no knowledge of agricultural situations,
and that he had no idea he was leading his people
into a country like Palestine, or no forethought to
give them guidance for their ordinary life in it; for
none of which have critical writers any authority.[1]

[1] See Note XXIV.

(*b*) Again, an influence altogether exaggerated is ascribed to the centralisation of worship. This, indeed, is Wellhausen's strong point, on which he rests his whole theory. "My whole position," he says, "is contained in my first chapter [entitled, The Place of Worship]; there I have placed in a clear light that which is of such importance for Israelite history— namely, the part taken by the prophetical party in the great metamorphosis of the worship, which by no means came about of itself."[1] Speaking of Hosea and Amos, he says:—

"The language held by these men was one hitherto unheard of, when they declared that Gilgal, and Bethel, and Beersheba, Jehovah's favourite seats, were an abomination to Him; that the gifts and offerings with which He was honoured there kindled His wrath instead of appeasing it; that Israel was destined to be buried under the ruins of His temples, where protection and refuge were sought (Amos ix.) . . . That the holy places should be abolished, but the cultus itself remain as before the main concern of religion, only limited to a single locality, was by no means their wish. But at the same time, in point of fact, it came about as an incidental result of their teaching that the high place of Jerusalem ultimately abolished all the other Bamoth. External circumstances, it must be added, contributed most essentially towards the result" (p. 23 f.)

He then goes on to explain (p. 24) how the downfall of the kingdom of Samaria left the way clear for the sanctuary at Jerusalem to assume importance. Still, although Hezekiah is said to have even in his time made an attempt to abolish the Bamoth (p. 25),[2] it was not till about a century after the destruction of Samaria that men ventured "to draw the practi-

[1] Hist. of Israel, p. 368. [2] See below, p. 450.

cal conclusion from the belief in the unique character of the temple at Jerusalem " (p. 26). This was done, not "from a mere desire to be logical, but with a view to further reforms;" and so prophets and priests combined to prepare the Code of Deuteronomy, which was officially and for the first time to authorise the Jerusalem Temple as the place of worship.

"The turning-point in the history of the sacrificial system was the reformation of Josiah; what we find in the Priestly Code is the matured result of that event " (p. 76).

"The spiritualisation of the worship is seen in the Priestly Code as advancing *pari passu* with its centralisation. It receives, so to speak, an *abstract* religious character; it separates itself, in the first instance, from daily life, and then absorbs the latter by becoming, strictly speaking, its proper business" (p. 81).

Of the alleged influence of the prophets in bringing about centralisation of worship and codification of the law, and also of the alleged discrepancy of the three Codes, we shall have to speak at length in the sequel. In the meantime, attention must be drawn to this effect of centralisation on the spirit and heartiness of the worship. Wellhausen's idea is, that "to celebrate the vintage festival among one's native hills, and to celebrate it at Jerusalem, were two very different things;" that "it was not the same thing to appear by one's self at home before Jehovah, and to lose one's self in a large congregation at the common seat of worship " (p. 77); and hence that the old joyousness of the feasts was destroyed by the celebration at the Temple at Jerusalem. Now, admitting for a moment that this cen-

tralisation took place in the way he explains, it simply is not the fact that the joyous feature disappeared. Delitzsch has shown [1] that in the period of
the second Temple, when the Priestly Code received
paramount attention, and when the national life was
none of the happiest, even the most solemn feasts of
Israel were occasions of joyful merrymaking, and
some of them remarkably so. It is shallow and unnatural to speak, in this connection, of " the antithesis between spiritual earnestness and secular joyousness" (p. 76). For a people, as Delitzsch says,
"is and remains a natural, not a spiritual quantity,
and therefore celebrates even religious festivals with
a natural outburst of feeling, simple mirth, jubilant
exultation. It lies in the nature of a people as
such." [2] We have only to think of the infectious influence of a great throng at any public celebration,
of the thorough and hearty manner in which all
Orientals enter into any occasion of public rejoicing,
and finally, of the aid to enjoyment furnished by the
kindly climate, to see that Wellhausen's position is
altogether opposed to human experience. And over
against this sapient talk of the individual losing himself in the great crowd, and the depressing influence
of "exercises of religion," I would simply set those
psalms that speak of the festive throng, and express
the psalmist's delight in the public celebrations of
religion. If these psalms be early, or if they be
late, they tell equally against the theory; for they ex-

---

[1] "Dancing and the Criticism of the Pentateuch in relation to one
another," now published along with other papers in 'Iris, Studies in
Colour and Talks about Flowers,' 1889.

[2] Iris, p. 196.

hibit a delight not only in nature, but in the God of nature, and above all, in the service of a God who had, in the nation's history, done great things for them, whereof they were glad.

(*c*) Once more, Wellhausen fails to prove that mere nature feasts passed over in the time he mentions into the religious festivals of the Deuteronomic or Priestly Codes. That the three great cycle feasts, Passover, Pentecost, and Succoth, fell at or were fixed at turning-points in the natural year, and that the celebration of them had pointed reference to the agricultural seasons, is very far from being the same as to say that they grew out of and for centuries remained merely agricultural festivals. One might as well argue that all the festivals of the "Christian year" have their sole reference to the natural seasons. What Wellhausen says of the soil being the basis of religion, has this much of truth in it, that the teachers of religion always, and rightly, sought to impress upon the people the material blessings which God bestowed. The task, however, before him is to explain how the historical references in these feasts came in, as they did come in somehow, sooner or later. Having described, as an instance of what he is pleased to call "the manner of the older worship as we are made acquainted with it in Hos. ii., ix., and elsewhere,"[1] the celebration of the vintage festival by the Canaanite population of Shechem (not very high authorities on such matters, we should say); and having referred to the yearly festival in the vineyards at Shiloh, as men-

[1] Hist. of Israel, p. 107.

tioned in the book of Judges,[1]—he looks about for
proof that these or suchlike are the three cycle
feasts prescribed in the book of the Covenant or
Jehovistic legislation.   And what does he find?
"Amos and Hosea, presupposing as they do a splen-
did cultus and great sanctuaries, doubtless also knew
of a variety of festivals, but they have no occasion to
mention any one by name " (p. 95).   This is extraordinary meekness in one who is in the constant
habit of declaring, when a prophet does not mention a thing, that he knew nothing at all about it because it had no existence.   But stay!   "More definite notices occur in Isaiah.   The threatening that
within a year's time the Assyrians will be in the land
is thus (xxix. 1) given : 'Add ye year to year, let
the feasts come round; yet I will distress Jerusalem,'
and at the close of the same discourse the prophet
expresses himself as follows (xxxii. 9 *seq.*): 'Rise up,
ye women that are at ease; hear my voice, ye careless daughters; give ear unto my speech.   Days
upon a year shall ye be troubled, ye careless women;
for the vintage shall fail, the ingathering shall not
come.   Ye shall smite upon the breasts, for the
pleasant fields, for the fruitful vine.'"   Putting
these two passages together, he pictures Isaiah,
after the universal custom of the prophets, coming
forward at a great popular autumn festival, in which
the women also took an active part.   But this
autumn festival, he argues, takes place at the change
of the year, as may be inferred from the phrase "let
the feasts come round," and "closes a cycle of festi-

[1] Hist. of Israel, p. 94; Judges ix. 27, xxi. 19 f.

vals here for the first time indicated" (p. 95). It gives me pleasure to say that I quite agree with the sentence that follows: "The preceding survey, it must be admitted, scarcely seems fully to establish the alleged agreement between the Jehovistic law and the older praxis." "Names," he goes on to remark, "are nowhere to be found, and in point of fact it is only the autumn festival that is well attested, and this, it would appear, as the only festival, as *the* feast. And doubtless it was also the oldest and most important of the harvest festivals, as it never ceased to be the concluding solemnity of the year." All that needs to be said on this part of the argument is this: Isaiah's reference to feasts "coming round" may quite as suitably apply to feasts which have a religious and historical meaning as to purely agricultural celebrations, and his references in the close of his address, if they are not indeed quite general, may equally apply to the feasts as they are prescribed in the law. If on these slight notices the modern critics are satisfied to base the proof of a set cycle of agricultural feasts, we ought to hear less of the argument from silence as conclusive of the non-existence of the Mosaic feasts: but of this again.[1] Attention should be given to the difficulty experienced by Wellhausen in accounting for the historical reference which undoubtedly is attached to the feasts in the Codes, even in the earliest.[2]

"According as stress is laid upon the common character of the festival and uniformity in its observance, in precisely the

---

[1] See below, p. 401.　　　　[2] See Exod. xxiii. 15,

same degree does it become separated from the roots from which it sprang, and grow more and more abstract. That it is then very ready to assume a historical meaning may partly also be attributed to the circumstance that history is not, like harvest, a personal experience of individual households, but rather an experience of the nation as a whole. One does not fail to observe, of course, that the festivals—which always to a certain degree have a centralising tendency—have *in themselves* a disposition to become removed from the particular motives of their institution, but in no part of the legislation has this gone so far as in the Priestly Code " (p. 103).

"For after they have lost their original contents and degenerated into mere prescribed religious forms, there is nothing to prevent the refilling of the empty bottles in any way accordant with the tastes of the period " (p. 102).

And so in a word—

"One can characterise the entire Priestly Code as the wilderness legislation, inasmuch as it abstracts from the natural conditions and motives of the actual life of the people in the land of Canaan, and rears the hierocracy on the *tabula rasa* of the wilderness, the negation of nature, by means of the bald statutes of arbitrary absolutism " (p. 104).

A great deal of this mode of representing the Priestly Code arises from ignoring or misstating the character of that Code, which is brief, terse, technical, a manual for ceremonial to the priests, rather than a book of exhortation and guidance to the people like Deuteronomy. For the rest, Wellhausen fails entirely to show any occasion for this *late* turning of the reference from agriculture to national history. These ceremonies, we are to suppose, went on from year to year with their accompaniments of presentation of fruits and so forth. That is to say, they were never "separated from the roots from which they sprang." The mere fact of centralisation might add to the richness of the ceremonies, as is always the case; but this, one would suppose, would prevent them from becoming "more and more abstract." The people were as much an agricultural people after Josiah's time as before; probably they were much less of a mercantile people than they had been at an earlier period of the monarchy. If the great events of the exodus, the conquest of Canaan, and in general the experiences which had made them a nation, did not impress the national consciousness when it was plastic and fresh, are we to suppose that, for the first time when foreign nations were about to sweep them away, they began to read into their worship and cere-monial a meaning which had not occurred to them for centuries? If at a time when Hosea and Amos were reminding them of the days of the youth of the nation, and thus appealing to the strongest motives that could influence them—if at such a time there were many feasts and imposing rituals, are we to suppose that not once in all these was there a com-memoration of the founding of the nation, and of the achievement of the nation's success? No doubt the feasts, at such times as those of Hosea and Amos, would be overlaid with superstitious observances. But that is not the point. Because the modern Greeks at Jerusalem make Easter a time of riot, are we to conclude that Easter does not com-memorate the resurrection? What country has not, at one time or another, thus buried its holiest associations under carnal and sensuous forms? All

this does not suffice to show that the better meaning
does not underlie the institution; much less that a
better meaning is merely an afterthought, read into
an empty form, just because it is empty. Forms
are never empty in the strict sense. They are full
of something. The corrupt must be purged out
before the clean can be poured in; and we can find
no time in Israel's history at which a *tabula rasa*
was formed, and history made out of nothing.
Even the critical school has to admit, as we shall
see, that the Priestly Code was a gathering up of
the practice which had prevailed before the exile;
and without coming so far down, we see enough
already in the Deuteronomic Code to convince us
that the historical reference was full and clear when
that Code was drawn up. Nay, even in the
Jehovistic book of the Covenant, the Passover is
made distinctly to refer to the coming out of Egypt.

Wellhausen's difficulties over the Passover may
indeed be pointed to as evidence of the weakness of
his theory at its foundation. The following is his
account of the matter: As the Israelites were a
pastoral people before they became agriculturists,
their oldest feasts must have had a pastoral basis
(p. 92 f.) The Passover is a remnant of these, and
is, from the nature of the case, the oldest of all the
feasts, its primary form being the offering of the
firstlings; and so, with perfect accuracy, it is postulated as the occasion of the exodus (p. 87). The
exodus was not the occasion of the festival, but the
festival the occasion, if only a pretended one, of the
exodus (p. 88). "Let my people go, that they may

keep a feast unto me in the wilderness, with sacrifices and cattle and sheep;"—this from the first is
the demand made upon Pharaoh. And because
Pharaoh refuses to allow the Hebrews to offer to
their God the firstlings of cattle that are His
due, Jehovah seizes from him the first-born of
men. "But it is curious," says Wellhausen (p. 93),
"to notice how little prominence is afterwards given
to this festival, which, from the nature of the case,
is the oldest of all. It cannot have been known at
all to the book of the Covenant, for there (Exod.
xxii. 29, 30) the command is to leave the firstling
seven days with its dam, and on the eighth day to
give it to Jehovah." There are, however, two
names given to this feast, *Mazzoth* (or unleavened
bread), and *Pesach* (passover). The latter indicates
the original character of the feast, as a sacrifice of
the first-born; but the other name throws light upon
the manner in which this came into the cycle of the
agricultural feasts. *Mazzoth*, or unleavened bread,
denotes the hastily made cake of the first corn,
which was eaten at the time the sickle was first put
in to commence the harvest, when a sheaf was presented to the Lord. This happened at the season of
the year when tradition fixed the exodus, the spring;
and in the account of the exodus it is mentioned
(Exod. xii. 34) that in their haste to leave Egypt
the Israelites "took their dough before it was
leavened;" and these two circumstances assisted in
the transition of the conception to a commemorative
feast. "Probably," says Wellhausen, "through
the predominance gained by agriculture, and the

feasts founded on it, the Passover [in its original
sense] fell into disuse in many parts of Israel, and
kept its ground only in districts where the pastoral
and wilderness life still retained its importance"
(p. 93). "The elaboration of the historical motive
of the Passover," however, we are told, "is not
earlier than Deuteronomy, although perhaps a certain inclination to that way of explaining it appears
before then, just as in the case of the *Mazzoth*
(Exod. xii. 34). What has led to it is evidently
the coincidence of the spring festival with the
exodus, already accepted by the older tradition, the
relation of cause and effect having become inverted
in course of time " (p. 88).

A very ingenious piece of patch-work! But the
facts are these: The book of the Covenant (Exod.
xxiii. 15, 16), and the related Law of the Two Tables
(Exod. xxxiv. 18 f.), which are said by critics to be
older by at least two centuries than the Code of
Deuteronomy, call the feast Mazzoth or unleavened
bread, and in both cases give the reason for keeping
the feast that in the month Abid the people came
out of Egypt. The Code of Deuteronomy, according
to Wellhausen's own authority (p. 87), is the first
that mentions *Pesach*, but it has the name Mazzoth
as well; and the elaboration of the historical motive,
he has just told us, is not earlier than Deuteronomy.
" The only view," he says, " sanctioned by the nature
of the case is, that the Israelite custom of offering
the firstlings gave rise to the narrative of the slay-
ing of the first-born of Egypt: unless the custom be
presupposed, the story is inexplicable, and the pe-

culiar selection of its victims by the plague is left without a motive " (p. 88). As to this conclusion, if critics are to determine historical questions by the nature of the case as they judge it, and to assume a liberty of putting effects for causes when it suits them, we may get startling "scientific results," but we make no solid progress. What requires explanation is the fact that Mazzoth is mentioned as a feast commemorative of the exodus, in what is pronounced the earliest legislation, and no reference made therein to the offering of the firstlings; and that only two centuries later the name which is supposed to point to the original character of the feast is for the first time employed, and yet the description of the feast agrees (only being fuller) with the older. The truth is, as any fair-minded person may see, this laborious attempt to foist in the historical reference at a late date breaks down just because the historical reference was present from the first. The fundamental fallacy of this whole argument is the assumption that "in the land and through the land it is that Israel first becomes the people of Jehovah." For this assertion there is not a scrap of evidence, whereas the concurrent testimony of all Israelite antiquity is, that it was because He had chosen his people, and after he had signalised His choice, that He brought them into a goodly land. And the conclusion of the matter is, that as there was a formal system of law at a much earlier time than the critical theory postulates, so also there was an earlier reference in their worship and ceremonial to the events in the nation's religious history which marked them out as Jahaveh's people.

CHAPTER XV.

THE THREE CODES.

The legislative elements in the Pentateuch a subject of difficulty —The traditional theory makes it unnecessarily difficult, while the critical theory raises greater difficulties—The three positions of the modern theory as to the Codes: I. there are three Codes; II. far apart in time; and III. inconsistent with one another—As to I. there is nothing inconsistent with Biblical theory or nature of the case in variation or progression of Codes—Law is modified even after it is codified—II. But the critical position is that the Codes belong to times far apart—How this conclusion is reached—The evidence of dates is inferential—Argument examined—The book of the Covenant—No satisfactory account given of introduction of this Code at the alleged time, and why codification, once begun, should have stopped for two centuries—What happened in the intervals of the Codes?—Wellhausen's position, legem non habentes, &c. —The two points involved in this position: (1) argument from silence and non-observance; (2) praxis and programme—III. Alleged inconsistency of the Codes, particularly as to the centralisation of worship—The argument examined.

THE legislative parts of the books of the Pentateuch, in their form and setting no less than in their contents, present many difficulties. The laws are found, not collected together and systematised, but scattered over several books. Not only is there a repetition in one collection of what may be found in another, but the same laws may be repeated with little or no alteration in the same collection.[1] And then there are discrepancies in the regulations found in different places on the same subject; and laws relating to subjects apparently the most diverse are brought into strange juxtaposition, as also are laws bearing upon what seem very different conditions of life and states of society. We should have expected a writer, if he were the author of all the legislation, to work more systematically: whether he was early and looked forward to the future, or late and looked back upon the past, we should have expected a better arrangement of details, a more completed whole. On what is called the traditional theory, that Moses not only gave the law, but wrote substantially the books in which it is contained, the literary difficulties are very great indeed, and the expedients that have been resorted to in order to remove them are very often artificial and hazardous. The modern critical theory, on the other hand, starting with a good motive, gets involved in what I consider a vicious method, and ends by raising greater difficulties than those which it attempts to remove. Advocates of the traditional theory burden themselves with an unnecessary difficulty by assuming that the books of the Pentateuch were written by Moses; for the books do not say so of themselves, and even the older Jewish tradition that Ezra "restored" the law,

[1] Compare Num. xv. 1-16 with Levit. i.-vii.; Num. v. 5-10 with Levit. v. 5 ff., vi. 5 ff.; Num. xv. 22-23 with Levit. iv. 13 ff.

pointed to redaction as a probable solution of many of the difficulties. Too much praise cannot be given to those who have laboured in the field of Pentateuch criticism, for the minute examination they have made of details, in the endeavour to sift and distinguish the sources; and as a literary feat, the labour may be pronounced on the whole successful, although it will hardly be asserted that the last word on the subject has yet been spoken.[1] At the same time, it seems to me that the difficulties of the critical theory increase at every step when the attempt is made to determine the origin of the Codes, and their relation to one another and to the history. The three leading positions of the modern critical theory are: I. That there are three distinct Codes of Law. II. That these belong to three different periods far separate. III. That on essential points the Codes differ. How these positions are established, and what consequences are drawn from them, will be seen as we proceed.

I. By a process of critical analysis, into which we do not here enter at length, the legislation contained in the Pentateuch is divided into various Codes, distinguished by certain literary and material characteristics. (1.) The Code contained in Deuteronomy stands by itself, marked by a certain hortatory tone, and by the absence of the minute ritual prescriptions and distinctions found particularly in the book of Leviticus. (2.) There is also distinguished a book of the Covenant attached to the Jehovistic historical portion of the Pentateuch, and embraced

[1] See Note XXVI.

in Exod. xx.-xxiii. ; closely related to which, and usually classed along with it, is chap. xxxiv. of the same book, sometimes called the Law of the Two Tables. (3.) Then, in the remaining parts of Exodus, in the whole of Leviticus, and in some chapters of Numbers, are found a number of laws, moral, civil, and ceremonial, which are all classed together as the Levitical Code or Priestly Code, so named from the prevalence of the ritual element in its contents. A portion of this Code, contained in Levit. xvii.-xxvi., is sometimes spoken of as a code or collection by itself, the "law of holiness," and supposed to have a special history of its own. Moreover, there is a collection of regulations, mostly ritual, found in Ezekiel (from chap. xl. onwards) which it is customary to take into account in the critical history of the Codes. So far as the legislation of the Pentateuch, however, is concerned, we have to deal with the three collections—the Jehovistic book of the Covenant (with related chapter), the Deuteronomic Code, and the Priestly Code; and it is maintained that they are to be historically arranged in the order in which they have just been mentioned.

So far there is nothing in the modern theory essentially incompatible with the Biblical account of the matter, except the order of the Codes. The Biblical order is: Book of the Covenant, Levitical Code, Deuteronomic Code; but they are ascribed to different times, although these periods all fall within the lifetime of Moses. There is nothing unreasonable in itself in the supposition that laws or codes of laws were promulgated at different times; and different sets of laws, so given, for special purposes or on special occasions, might run severally their respective literary courses. Nor is it difficult to conceive how such several collections might overlap one another, and after a time have certain features of inconsistency. The law-books themselves give us to understand that, as the situation of the people changed, the law had a varying reference, and even that a law on a certain subject might be abrogated or modified to suit altered circumstances. So that, even in the Biblical theory, not to speak of what is known of the course of law generally, it is possible for law to undergo modification even after it is codified. We find, for example, within the compass of one book, a modification in the age at which the Levites were to serve at the sanctuary.[1] Music of an elaborate kind, we know, was introduced into the Temple service, though it is not prescribed, as we should expect to find it, in the Levitical Code. Again, the law of inheritance, contained in Num. xxvii., is modified within the Levitical Code itself by Num. xxxvi.; and it is notorious that by New Testament times and in modern Jewish usage there are modifications in the manner of celebrating the Passover, particularly in the use of wine and certain hymns that constitute very considerable variations from the ceremonial prescribed in the law. Nay, Ezra, to whom, on the modern theory, the introduction of the Priestly Code is ascribed, makes a modification on the amount of the tax payable for the

[1] Num. iv. 3, viii. 24; comp. also 1 Chron. xxiii. 3, 27; 2 Chron. xxxi. 17.

expenses of the Temple,[1] fixing it at a third of a shekel, whereas the code which he is said to have drawn up fixes it at half a shekel.[2]

It seems, therefore, reasonable to suppose that, just as the Passover is an institution of ancient Israel, although it has gathered about it usages of a comparatively recent time, so many of the laws contained in the Pentateuch may, before reaching the form in which they now stand, have been modified through changing circumstances in the national life, and yet be in their origin and character Mosaic. Even if we supposed that all the laws of the Pentateuch were originally written down by Moses— though the Biblical writers never say that they were—there is the probability—nay, the certainty— that these were copied from time to time in whole or in portions. And seeing that practice, in regard to some things at least, varied, and there was no hesitation about introducing certain alterations in the observances, the transcriber in a later age, in writing out a code for practical use, might, so to speak, translate the details of prevailing ordinances into the language of his own time, and describe the thing in the form in which he knew it. If such a double process went on, it would go far to account for the strange mixture of new and old that we find in these laws, some relating to and only practicable in the desert life or a more primitive state of society, and others denoting a time when the national life was in a more consolidated position. In short, we should have before us a kind

---

[1] Neh. x. 32 ff. [2] Exod. xxx. 13.

of history of the observances, on the understanding,
however, that the rites had been observed. The
aspect of the Levitical Code, in particular, is hardly
intelligible on any other supposition. To say that
it was all drawn up at one time by persons setting
themselves to the systematic work of framing a code
without written materials before them, is to ascribe
to the writers either great want of skill on the one
theory, or a design to deceive on the other. In
view of the only statements which the Biblical
writers themselves make on the subject, there is
nothing to preclude the supposition of various
editings of the laws at different times, while yet the
system as a whole, and even the three separate
Codes, had a positive basis in Mosaic legislation.

II. This, however, does not satisfy the modern
critical writers. They think they can prove, by a
comparison of the Codes, and by references to history, that the Codes belong to periods very far apart.
This, in fact, has been a great part of the laborious
task of Pentateuch criticism; and while, on the
one hand, it has been claimed that by pure literary
criticism the three Codes have been distinguished
from one another, it has been finally confessed, on
the other hand, that the order of the Codes and
their respective dates cannot be determined solely
from the Codes themselves, but must be ascertained
from an examination of the historical and prophetical
books which follow them in the Canon. The line of
argument has been as follows: If from a consideration of the books relating to a time subsequent
to Moses, we find a state of matters corresponding

with the requirements of one of these Codes, it is concluded that the Code in question was known and recognised and in operation; if, on the contrary, the state of matters shows that what were the requirements of any one Code were not put in force, and were ignored, not only by the people, but by the religious leaders and guides of the people, we conclude that such a Code, not receiving official recognition, was in fact non-existent. According to this principle, then, it is argued that the Deuteronomic Code was not known, and therefore was not existent till the time of Josiah; because up to that time not only the nation at large, but even the religious teachers of the nation, openly and without compunction practised the worship of Jahaveh at the high places, in direct contradiction to the command reiterated in Deuteronomy, that there was to be a central sanctuary, at which alone the former rites of worship were permissible. In the same way, it is argued that the distinction of priests and Levites so clearly marked in the Levitical Code did not in fact come into existence till after the Deuteronomic Code; that many of the laws contained in the Levitical Code were not know, and did not exist till the time of Ezra; and therefore that the Levitical Code as a whole belongs to the time of Ezra, or even a subsequent date. The order of the Codes, therefore, on this view, is—Book of the Covenant, Deuteronomic Code, Levitical Code, and they are separated by wide distances; for whereas the Book of the Covenant belongs to the earliest period of written composition—the century B.C. 850-750—the next in

order, the Deuteronomic, comes at least two centuries later—viz., in 621 B.C.; and the Levitical
Code, if placed, at the earliest, in the time of Ezra,
falls two centuries later still—viz., about 444 B.C.

It does not require to be said that there is no
direct historical evidence of the introduction of the
various Codes at the dates assigned. It is by a process of inference from the history, and by a comparison of the Codes, that the conclusions are reached
that under certain definite historical circumstances
each successive Code was introduced, and that certain appreciable influences were at work to bring
about their acceptance. Let us therefore look a
little more closely at what the position implies, and
how it is related to certain admitted facts.

It is obvious that the general position here is part
of the whole scheme of reconstructed history, according to which the law came gradually into existence
and authoritative recognition. In connection with
this part of the argument, the positions considered
in the preceding chapters should be borne in mind,
as to the alleged *basis* of the law in custom and in
spontaneous nature feasts, because we ought now to
find some precise information as to the circumstances
that led to the stamping of custom with authority,
and the transition from a mere nature reference to
religious significance. We come, in fact, face to
face with the questions, when and under what circumstances the respective laws became *codified*.

Critical writers prefer to commence their investigations with Deuteronomy; we prefer, for reasons
that will appear, to take the Codes in the alleged

order of their promulgation. Now it is not a little remarkable that modern critics, while they tell us very particularly the historical circumstances under which the Deuteronomic and Priestly Codes were produced, can tell us very little about the earliest of all the Codes, the Jehovistic. Yet this is the very one which we should think must have had a controlling influence on subsequent legislation and codification. Wellhausen, it will be remembered,[1] in fixing the period at which Hebrew literature first flourished, makes this collection of laws contemporaneous with the earliest historiography, and somewhat earlier than the legends about the patriarchs and primitive times. He says[2] that both the Jehovistic law and the Jehovistic narrative "obviously belong to the pre-prophetic period"; for it is inconceivable that the prophets Hosea or Amos, or any like-minded person, could glorify (in connection with the history of the patriarchs) the local sanctuaries in the way that these narratives do. Therefore at some period earlier than the first writing prophets—earlier than or about as early as the patriarchal histories—"certain collections of laws and decisions of the priests, of which we have an example in Exodus xxi., xxii., were committed to writing." We are told in another passage that the Jehovistic history-book, whose character is best marked by the story of the patriarchs, has legislative elements taken "into it only at one point, where they fit into the historical connection—namely, when the giving of the law at

---

[1] The passage is quoted above in chap. iii. p. 60 f.
[2] Hist. of Israel, p. 32.

Sinai is spoken of, Exod. xx.-xxiii., xxxiv." (p. 7), although soon after we are also told that "the Jehovist does not even pretend to being a Mosaic law of any kind; it aims at being a simple book of history" (p. 9.) All this throws very little light upon this first collection of written laws, which, one would have thought, was epoch-making. Indeed Wellhausen goes on repeating that the Torah of Jehovah still continued to be the special charge of the priests, though "it was not even now a code or law in our sense of the word; Jehovah had not yet made His Testament; He was still living and active in Israel; . . . the Torah had still occupation enough, the progressive life of the nation ever affording matter for new questions" (p. 468). And as to the outward observances of religion, we are told "the cultus, as to place, time, matter, and form, belonged almost entirely to the inheritance which Israel had received from Canaan; to distinguish what belonged to the worship of Jehovah from that which belonged to Baal was no easy matter" (p. 469).

Now, suppose we grant that the book of the Covenant was codified as late as is here asserted, it bears on the face of it, at all events, a testimony to Mosaic authorship, and authoritative sanction, and has a strictly religious basis. It is misleading in Wellhausen to say that "the Jehovist does not even pretend to being a Mosaic law of any kind." It aims at being a true history, and it brings in this Code under definite historical conditions as given by Moses. What more do the writers of the other law-books? Moreover, to whatever extent the worship may have followed Canaanite practice, a sharp line is drawn here between Mosaic requirements and the worship of the nations (Exod. xxii. 20, xxiii. 23 ff.) Let it be supposed that this Code is merely the embodiment of praxis or the crystallisation of custom—and it is certainly more—the praxis or custom was at all events by that time of so high antiquity and invested with such authority that the Code was made Mosaic; and we ask the critics in vain for an explanation of this ascription of the very earliest laws to a time so long antecedent, and to circumstances so positively historical.

But what we want very particularly to know is the occasion that at this precise time called for a codification of law even of this modest compass. What set the process of codification agoing at least two centuries before it occurred to any one to prepare an authoritative book of law? For this is the way in which Deuteronomy is spoken of: "The idea of making a definite formulated written Torah the law of the land is the important point; it [viz., the Deuteronomic Code] was a first attempt, and succeeded at the outset beyond expectation."[1] This book of the Covenant, however, shows that such an *idea* is much older, though the fact is simply slurred over.

Further, if this Code was the statement of the legal customs of that comparatively late time, it cannot have been the statement of the whole of them. By the time assumed the national life had taken definite form; the Temple of Solomon had long been in existence, priests as well as prophets were a nu-

[1] Wellhausen, Hist. of Israel, p. 402.

merous and influential class. The mere appearance
of this Code at what is called the earliest period
of literary composition presupposes, as we have argued,[1] an antecedent education, and a literary activity in priestly circles. Thousands of cases of casuistry, jurisprudence, and ceremony had arisen and
been settled in some way before the time this Code is
alleged to have existed. At length (we are told) it
had occurred to some person or persons to draw up
this Code, brief though it be, in all the sententious-
ness of this class of composition. Now it does seem
very remarkable that, a beginning having been made,
at the very earliest period of written composition,
the thing was entirely discontinued for at least two
centuries, and *that* during a period when literary
composition of other kinds attained its bloom; at a
time too when the civil, religious, and commercial
situations of the people were such as would demand
authoritative regulation and control. A glance at
the prescriptions contained in the book of the
Covenant will show that it contains, though in a
brief and germinal manner, legislation in all the
directions that are followed out more fully in the
larger Codes, and is enough to suggest the hundreds
of cases and relations similar to those then provided
for that must have arisen in the daily life of the
people, and demanded standing rules for their settlement. If it be said that oral teaching would determine all these, we ask, Why were not such other
matters as, *e.g.*, of fire arising in a corn-field, or of
an ox goring a man, left to the same authority? The

[1] See above, chap. iv. p. 105.

marvellous thing is that, codification having begun, even at the time to which this Code is assigned, it did not go on. Is there any class of literature more voluminous, more liable to grow from its own inherent impulse, than the legal? And when history, prophecy, poetry, flourished, when every kind of literature, in fact, which Israel produced had reached its best before the time of Josiah, that the legal and ceremonial should have once taken a start and then stood still is surely something which it requires the faith of a modern critic to believe. It is much more probable that when Hosea speaks of the writing of ten thousand precepts,[1] he was familiar with and alluded to a literary activity in this field of composition of a much more copious extent than the brief book of the Covenant.

Difficulties like these, arising out of the theory so far as it refers to the book of the Covenant, suggest other difficulties in connection with the succeeding Codes and with the process of codification in general. There is, for example, the difficulty of explaining the source of the laws embodied in the succeeding Codes. The book of Deuteronomy contains laws that relate to circumstances of the desert life, and so does the Levitical Code. Where were these laws preserved up to this time, if they had an existence at all? If they did not exist, whence came they into codes which were for quite different circumstances? Again, the Code of Deuteronomy, which is said to have been introduced for the specific purpose of centralising the worship at the Temple of Jerusalem, is

[1] See above, chap. xiii. p. 342.

singularly poor in regulations for ritual, the very thing we should have expected to be attended to, when a multitude of local sanctuaries, with presumably varying, not to say corrupted, worship, were abolished. On the other hand, the Levitical Code, drawn up, as is alleged, at a time when the Temple was in ruins and ritual worship impossible, deals above all, and in minutest detail, with ceremonial matters. One naturally asks, What was the source whence came the ritual and ceremonial laws which bulk so largely in the final Code of Leviticus? And then, what occurred in the long intervals between the successive Codes? Were these Codes sudden appearances, something quite new for their respective times, or did they come about gradually and receive acceptance as a matter of course?

It must be confessed that it is not very easy to follow the reasoning of Wellhausen in his treatment of these and suchlike questions, for he seems to be not quite consistent with himself in the positions he takes up at different parts of his argument. For example, he says at one time that " proofs of the existence of the Priestly Code [previous to the exile] are not to be found—not a trace of them " (p. 365); that the Code was not only not operative, but "that it did not even admit of being carried into effect in the conditions that prevailed previous to the exile " (p. 12). On the other hand, he says that the " real point at issue " is "not to prove that the Mosaic law was not in force in the period before the exile;" that he and his school " do not go so far as to believe that the Israelite cultus entered the world of a sudden—as little by Ezekiel or by Ezra as by Moses; " and that it is a mistaken assumption that on the modern hypothesis "the whole cultus was invented all at once by the Priestly Code, and only introduced after the exile " (p. 366). In brief, he sums up his position in the words which he prefixes as a motto to the first part of his book, "These having not the law, do by nature the works of the law." If this merely meant, as it might at first sight seem to mean, that the respective Codes were all actually observed in some form previous to the times at which they are said to have been introduced, and that only the *writing* of them in the forms in which they appear was a matter of later date, there would not be much objection to the position; and I do not know that it would be irreconcilable with the Biblical theory; but we shall see that the hypothesis involves a much more serious assumption. It is plain that for the establishment of Wellhausen's thesis there must be historical proof of two things: (1) that the law, as expressed in the Codes, was not in the possession of Israel up to the time the Codes were introduced, according to the one half of his motto—" these having not the law; " and (2) that the things contained in the law, the works of the law, were practised by nature—*i.e.*, without pre-scription—before these dates. Attention must be drawn to the different reference of the words as used by St. Paul and by Wellhausen. The apostle is speaking not of a ceremonial or ritual law, but of moral principles " written on the heart," the opera-tion of which can be traced in the Gentile world.

What Wellhausen has to prove is, that a law such as that contained in the Priestly Code was taught by nature and practised as a custom by Israel before its details were prescribed by any authority,—a very different matter.

(1.) For the establishment of the first position reliance must be placed for the most part on the argument from silence, as it is called—*i.e.*, if the thing we are in search of is not mentioned, particularly if it is not mentioned where we should look for it, it is assumed that the thing did not exist. Wellhausen objects to the process followed by him being called by his name, and says, " What the opponents of Graf's hypothesis call its argument *ex silentio*, is nothing more or less than the universally valid method of historical investigation " (p. 365). One would think it depended not a little upon the manner and the extent to which the process is carried out; and it would be easy to illustrate the havoc that might be made in general history by a reliance upon this argument.[1] We have already in a former chapter [2] observed the significant absence of all reference to education; and in regard to many other

[1] Whately, for example, in his ' Historic Doubts, ' draws attention to the fact that the principal Parisian journal in 1814, on the very day on which the Allied armies entered Paris as conquerors, makes no mention of any such event. So, too, the battle of Poictiers in 732, which effectually checked the spread of Mohammedanism across Europe, is not once referred to in the monastic annals of the period. Again, Sir Thomas Browne lived through the civil wars and the Commonwealth; yet, says a biographer, " no syllable in any of his writings, notwithstanding their profound and penetrative meditations upon vicissitudes in human lives and empires, betrays the least partisanship in the tragedy enacted on the world's great stage around him." And, once more, Sale notes that circumcision is held by the Mohammedans to be an ancient divine institution, the rite having been in use many years before Mohammed; and yet it is not so much as once mentioned in the Koran.

[2] Chap. iv. p. 75.

things, we are left in like ignorance by the Scriptural writers. Graphic as their descriptions are when they exist, there are hundreds of details of daily life and ordinary custom in regard to which we would fain have information. The prophet Isaiah, in one well-known passage,[1] gives a complete inventory of the wardrobe of a fashionable lady of Jerusalem; but a great number of the words he employs are found only in that passage, and are such that we can only guess at the precise things they are meant to signify. And to speak more particularly of customs and observances, who shall describe to us, from information drawn from the Biblical books, the mode in which the Sabbath was observed in the time of the prophets? We know from their references to it[2] that the Sabbath was specially sacred; and the book of the Covenant, at the latest, vouches for the existence of the Decalogue, which enjoins the sanctity of the Sabbath: yet we remain in almost total ignorance of the manner in which its sanctity was preserved. And the same thing holds of other feasts, whether we regard them as matters of custom or of prescription. Things of daily occurrence and of standing observance, just because they are such, are most naturally passed by without notice. It is perfectly evident that the Old Testament writers contemplated as their readers those who were familiar with the most familiar things in their national life and history. As for Hebrew prophets not referring to legislative books, it is

[1] Isa. iii. 16-24.
[2] Amos viii. 5; Hosea ii. 11; Isa. i. 13: cf. 2 Kings iv. 23, xi. 5, 7, 9, xvi. 18.

much more remarkable that they do not refer to prophetical books, and scarcely make a quotation from
one another.   I do not know that we have positive
historical evidence (of a contemporary kind) that
would establish the existence of the great bulk of the
existing prophetic literature before the captivity;
and quite recently a French critic [1] has put forth the
view that the greater part of the literature of the
Hebrews is a free creation of a school of theologians after the restoration.

A mode of reasoning like this can be tested by
one striking instance, and such an instance is furnished in the great day of atonement (Levit. xvi.)
A ceremonial so imposing, one would think, would
not pass without notice, and the modern school
points with confidence to the fact that though the
institution bulks so largely in the Levitical Code, it
is not once referred to in the pre-exilic history, and
therefore it must have been devised first of all by
Ezra or his successors.   But the instance proves too
much, for, as a matter of fact, there is no positive
historical account of the observance till about the
beginning of the Christian era, at the earliest the
time of John Hyrcanus or even Herod the Great, 37
B.C., a date at which it was impossible that the
prescription of the ceremony could have been in-
serted in the Law Code, which, according to Wellhausen, was introduced in B.C. 444. [2]

<hr/>

[1] Maurice Vernes, Les Résultats de l'Exégèse Biblique, Paris, 1890.

[2] Delitzsch, Pentateuch-Kritische Studien in Luthardt's Ztsch. f.
Kirkl. Wissenschaft und Kirkl. Leben, 1880, p. 173 f.; Dillmann, Comm.
on Lev., p. 525; Bredenkamp, Gesetz u. Propheten, p. 116. The fact that
Ezekiel, in his [vision of] ritual, does not mention the day of atonement, is taken by the critics to prove that he was not aware of the

But, indeed, we do not need to come so far down in history for evidence that the non-observance or the absence of mention of a law is not a proof of its non-existence. On the position of the modern critical writers, the Jehovistic book of the Covenant was in existence two centuries before Deuteronomy. And yet, not to speak of the moral precepts with which the Code is charged, and which were so sadly violated in the life of the people, can distinct proof be produced that the Sabbatic year prescribed in Exod. xxiii. 10, 11, or even the weekly Sabbath itself, was observed in the time during which this Code is said to have been the sole law-book? Why, the Deuteronomic law itself was systematically violated after the time of Josiah.[1] Down even in the times after the exile, among a community which had learned by misfortune the evil of breaking the law, and which had returned through hardship to set up a new state at Jerusalem, Ezra and Nehemiah had to contend for the observance of the most fundamental principles that lay not only at the basis of the Deuteronomic Code, but at the foundation of Israel's national existence.[2]

So far, then, as the first part of Wellhausen's thesis is concerned, it cannot be sustained. The

legislation of the Priestly Code in which it is prescribed. It is urged, however, in reply, that Ezekiel's idea of a double atonement for the sanctuary (Ezek. xlv. 18-20) may be an intensification of the atonement required in the Priestly Code. And Dillmann remarks, "Why Ezekiel should first have produced the idea of such an atonement is not at all apparent, still less how people of a later time ventured to hit upon quite different characteristics, and to give out these as Mosaic.

[1] Compare Deut. xv. 12 f. with Jer. xxxiv. 13 f.

[2] Compare Ezra ix. 1, 2, Neh. x. 30, xiii. 23, with Exod. xxxiv. 16, Deut. vii. 3. Compare also Neh. x. 31 with Deut. xv. 2; and Neh. x. 37, 39, with Deut. xii. 17.

argument from silence does not prove it, since we know that many things of much greater significance to the prophets than ritual are not mentioned by them. The argument from non-observance does not prove it, since the Deuteronomic and Levitical Codes themselves were broken systematically after the admitted dates of their introduction. And the existence of the book of the Covenant, or even of such a part of it as would satisfy Wellhausen's own account of its origin, flatly disproves the assertion that up to the time of Deuteronomy the Israelites were in the position of people "having no law."

(2.) The other part of Wellhausen's motto that has to be established is, that Israel, without the law, did the works of the law; in other words, that the Codes were not suddenly introduced. On this subject, the use of the two terms, "praxis" and "programme," plays a prominent part in the discussions; and we can understand a code coming into existence by either process. The practice or usage of the time is systematised more or less, and put down in the form of prescription; this is the codification of praxis. Or, on the other hand, a person or persons, considering the existing state of matters unsatisfactory or insufficient, may devise a better scheme, and set it forth in orderly form as a legislative programme. It is remarkable how, on either hypothesis, the critical writers find it difficult to get rid of the postulate of Mosaic legislation, to which they have so much objection. For they tell us that the Deuteronomic Code was a programme drawn up by prophets and priests combined for the centralisation of worship, without which they saw there could be no purity of worship. It could not, on the hypothesis, have been a codification of the praxis, for the whole drift of the theory is, that up to the introduction of this Code, worship at any place was the practice. Yet the men who brought about the introduction of this Code were the Mosaic party—the party who strove to preserve what they regarded as the true religion of Israel,—and they appealed to Mosaic authority in ascribing the Code to him. Wellhausen gives us to understand that the movement for centralisation was connected with the growth of monotheistic conceptions. In all this there is a testimony to the fact that Mosaism, in its essence, was monotheistic, and that the Deuteronomic Code rested on Mosaism at its best, to such an extent that the authority of Moses had to be invoked to secure its acceptance. Again, Ezekiel is said to have put forth a legislative programme; this, however, he did not ascribe to Moses, and his Code was not adopted. Was there any connection between the two things? In all this talk about programme, it seems to me the critical writers are in an uncomfortable dilemma. Either the programme is something new, and then their position that the law did not suddenly come into force becomes untenable; or else it is a departure in the spirit of the Mosaic legislation, which amounts to the Biblical view that what took place was a reformation of the worship, not an innovation.

The same perplexing situation arises when resort is had to praxis as an explanation of the origin of the Codes. This is particularly the case with the

Priestly Code.   We are told [1] that when the Temple
was in ruins, and there was no longer a possibility
of the worship being carried on, a body of men in
the captivity set themselves to a careful study of the
praxis as it had been carried on, and drew up what
their memory had fondly preserved of the cultus, and
that this assumed finally the form of the Priestly
Code.   The question at once occurs, What praxis?
Was the worship of the temple, as Ezekiel and
others remembered it, of the pure Mosaic type prescribed in the Code which men of his spirit elabor-
ated?   What then becomes of Wellhausen's assertion
that the observance of the Priestly Code was impossible in the conditions prevailing before the exile?
What becomes also of all the burden of denunciation,
of which the prophetic and historical books are full,
of the corruptions that prevailed?   But if the praxis
was corrupt, what guided Ezekiel and Ezra to produce a Code which was in "the spirit of the Mosaic
legislation"?   Again we fall back upon the Mosaic
legislation, which, unless we are to give the lie to
all history, was something better than the corrupt
practice.

Further, if the critics will have it that the Priestly
Code is a codification of the praxis, we may employ
their own argument, and ask them for historical
proof of the praxis of anything that can be supposed
to have formed the materials of the new Code.
Wellhausen professes indeed to give what he calls
"a sort of history of the ordinances of worship;"
but he is constrained to add, "Rude and colourless

[1] Wellhausen, Hist. of Israel, pp. 59 f., 404 f.

that history must be confessed to be—a fault due to the materials, which hardly allow us to do more than mark the contrast between pre-exilic and post-exilic, and, in a secondary measure, that between Deuteronomic and pre-Deuteronomic."[1] Let us, for example, take the three great feasts of the Passover, Shebuoth or Weeks, and Tabernacles. These, as agricultural feasts, are admitted by the critics to date back to the time of the settlement in Canaan, though the distinctive religious or national character attributed to them by Biblical writers is disputed. Things of such regular recurrence could not be kept hid, and surely here the critical canon of observance may be applied. Yet we have already seen[2] the difficulty Wellhausen has in proving their existence; for in regard to the celebration of the feasts in question before the exile, we have only very few notices, and these mostly very slight. The observance of all the three is only mentioned twice, once in the most general terms in the book of Kings (1 Kings ix. 25), and again in the parallel passage in Chronicles (a book on which the critics are wont to place no confidence), where they are mentioned by their usual names (2 Chron. viii. 13). The celebration of the Passover is mentioned at most twice— viz., in a very general way, if it *is* this feast that is referred to, in Isa. xxx. 29, and again at the reformation in Josiah's reign (2 Kings xxiii. 21 ff.) Of the Feast of Tabernacles (Succoth) we have four notices—viz., two very doubtful ones in Judges xxi. 19 and 1 Sam. i. 20, 21, and another two very general

[1] Hist. of Israel, p. 13.   [2] See before, chap. xiv. p. 374.

references in 1 Kings viii. 2, xii. 32.   The observance of the Feast of Weeks is only once mentioned,
and that is in 2 Chron. viii. 13, where it is mentioned
with the other two.   The critics are in the habit of
making light of the statement of the chronicler and
the author of the book of Kings,[1] that such celebrations as took place in the times of Hezekiah and
Josiah had not been seen since the times of the
Judges, or in all the reigns of the Kings.   This, they
says, amounts simply to the fact that the Passover,
as enjoined in the law, had not been observed at all
till the late period to which the narrative refers.[2]
But in view of the paucity of references, and the
vagueness of the references which have been pointed
out, we may ask, What then was observed at all?
What proof have we that even the nature feasts
were kept up, on which this new religious observance
might be grafted?   In the same way we could argue
against the whole "praxis" of which so much is
said.   We have no more evidence of the existence
of a praxis which could be subsequently codified than
we have of the ordinances which are prescribed in
the Codes; and the passages that may be supposed
to refer to a cycle of nature feasts may as well be
taken to refer to the legally sanctioned observances.

III. Modern critics, however, pronounce the
Codes to be so incompatible on vital points as to
give indication that they cannot have been all the

---

[1] 2 Chron. xxx. 5, xxxv. 18, with 2 Kings xxiii. 22.   Cf. Neh. viii. 17.

[2] One would have expected of the chronicler, if he was such a stickler
for ceremonial, and so unscrupulous in his statements of their earlier
observance as the critics make him out to be, that he would have rather
pointedly told us how faithfully the Passover had been observed all
along, than give this intimation that it had been persistently neglected.

production of one man, or the product of one age. On one subject, in particular, it is held they give clear evidence of a progress from the simple to the complex, of a development which required centuries to accomplish, and that subject is the legislation relating to the place of worship. It is maintained that the book of the Covenant permits sacrifice anywhere, or what amounts to that; that the Deuteronomic Code prescribes one central sanctuary; and that the Levitical Code makes no formal prescription on the subject, taking for granted that a central sanctuary exists, and that worship is there observed. These three stages of legislation, it is maintained, correspond to three periods in Israel's history. Up to the time of Josiah the worship of the Bamoth or high places, up and down the land, at the holy places consecrated by hallowed associations, was the rule and custom. Then came the struggle which culminated in the victory in Josiah's time, when the high places were abolished, and the legitimate worship confined to the Temple. And finally, after the Temple was no more, and the people in exile had time to reflect on the privileges they had lost, the work of gathering up the ritual praxis that had been observed at Jerusalem was undertaken; and when the restored community returned to their native land, they came with a book in their hand regulating the service of the new sanctuary, the book being the Levitical Code.

It will be observed that the great difference on this view lies between the book of the Covenant and the Deuteronomic Code; and as the primary object of our inquiry is the earlier condition of things, the pre-prophetic and early prophetic religion, this part of the subject demands more attention. The difference between the two Codes in question is not one that resolves itself easily into a case of development, for the introduction of the Deuteronomic Code is represented as having been effected in fact by a religious revolution. A true case of development would be that centralisation of worship was the idea and the ideal from the first, but that it gained realisation by slow degrees. If this can be made out by a comparison of the Codes, and can be shown to be borne out by the history, the objection of modern critics to the discrepancy of the Codes will have comparatively little weight; and a development of the proper kind, from germ to full manifestation, will be established. It will then not necessarily follow that the Codes are far distant in time; or if, in their final form, they belong to periods far apart, yet they will be seen in the essential point to agree, and the stronger emphasis laid by the Deuteronomic Code than by the book of the Covenant on this requirement, will be explicable on the greater fulness of the longer Code, on the special object which it aimed at, or even on the supposition of a later editing or revision of it. I think good reasons can be given for taking this position:—

(1.) No formal sanction is given by prophetic men before Josiah's time to a multiplicity of sanctuaries in the sense in which the modern writers speak. When Amos and Hosea speak of the worship performed at such places as Bethel and Gilgal, there is nothing in their words to lead us to suppose that these places were regarded by them as set apart by any divine authority as places of worship. They were certainly invested with old sacred associations (every country has such places); they were certainly, in the time of these prophets, resorted to for religious purposes by the people generally, but the prophets mention them for the purpose of rebuking the idolatrous or corrupt religious observances of which they were the seat, and never are such expressions applied to them as to Jerusalem and Zion. It is quite possible that, in the northern kingdom after the schism, such places as these, hallowed by patriarchal associations, were the only places, or the special places, at which those who wished to sacrifice to Jahaveh, debarred from attendance at Jerusalem, performed their worship. But as the prophets recognised only the Davidic house as the legitimate depository of the monarchy, so they regarded Jerusalem as the seat of Jahaveh, and the place of His special manifestation. The very first words which Amos utters to the people of the northern kingdom are: "Jahaveh shall roar from Zion, and utter His voice from Jerusalem;"[1] words which could only mean that from Zion and Jerusalem God's authority was in a special way manifested; that there, by preeminence, His presence was to be sought and His law to be found, just as the oracle said, "Out of Zion shall go forth the law " (Isa. ii. 2; Micah iv. 2). Whatever may be said of sanctuaries in the northern kingdom, there is no sanction given to such places as

[1] See Note XXVII.

of co-ordinate authority with Jerusalem. Much less is there any trace of the recognition of any number of places in the southern kingdom, as some would have us suppose, which were regarded as equally sacred with Jerusalem.

(2.) Nor does the history prove that a multiplicity of sanctuaries, in the modern sense, was a recognised thing in the nation. When it is said that in the stories of the patriarchs the writers represent the fathers of the nation as freely erecting an altar wherever they encamped, and that therefore the writer of these stories saw nothing wrong in this proceeding, there is surely a confusion of thought, or a false inference, when it is concluded that in the writers' day a multiplicity of sanctuaries was recognised. For how, indeed, could the patriarchs have sacrificed at all, except in the manner indicated? There was to them no law of central sanctuary, and the writer of these accounts simply represents the patriarchs as doing the only thing that it was possible for them to do. If the writer knew of the law of a central sanctuary, he could not have blamed the patriarchs for ignoring it, simply because it did not exist in their day. Of course the contention is that the writer knew nothing at all about the worship of Abraham and the other patriarchs, but simply *projected* into the past the ideas and practices of his own time, and made them do sacrifice at the various places which in the writer's day were resorted to as sanctuaries. But all this is mere assumption. The cases referred to of Samuel and the Judges, who are described as offering sacrifices at various places, are not more conclusive on the point in hand. The places at which such sacrifices are offered are not regarded by the writers as places sacred in themselves; nay, they are mentioned generally only on the special occasions on which sacrifice was performed at them, and again disappear from the history. There is always some special reason for the performance of the sacrifice; there is not one of them that is spoken of as habitually the seat of worship, except Shiloh, which was consecrated by the presence of the ark, and which was, so long as it stood, the central sanctuary of Israel. That it was so regarded as the predecessor of Jerusalem itself is proved by the reference to it so late as the time of Jeremiah (vii. 12), a reference which shows that the nation had regarded it as, for its time, similar to the sanctuary at Jerusalem in the days of its glory.

(3.) Moreover, the ideal even in the book of the Covenant is that of a central sanctuary. Much has been made here of the words, " In every place where I record my name, I will come unto thee, and I will bless thee " (Exod. xx. 24), which have been taken to mean a permission to worship indifferently at any place. Wellhausen indeed makes a show of meeting the limitation expressed in the words "where I record my name "; but all he can say [1] in explanation of them is, "that the spots where intercourse between earth and heaven took place were not willingly regarded as arbitararily chosen, but, on the contrary, were considered as having been somehow or other selected by the Deity Himself for His service,"

[1] Hist. of Israel, p. 30.

which is simply saying nothing. The promise here given must be taken to mean something of a positive kind, and coming after the direction how to make the altar, must be supposed to have some reference to worship. If, after the manner of modern critics, we were to ask the *polemic* the words imply, it might almost seem, on their mode of reasoning, that the writer of these words was protesting against such a centralising of worship as took place in Josiah's days![1] At all events, it seems strange that such a permission to worship anywhere should be given in this formal way at a time when, it is alleged, no one dreamed of doing anything else, for the book of the Covenant dates (on the hypothesis) from the earliest writing period, when the law of a central sanctuary was unknown.[2] If the words were meant merely to sanction places which had been elevated into sacredness by association with patriarchal theophanies and the like, they might be urged as an argument for the worship at a certain number of places; but this is less than what the words express, and less than the example of the patriarchs would warrant, for they seem to have erected an altar as a matter of course wherever they went.[3] And if the words are really intended to mean that Jahaveh may be wor-

---

[1] I see that Wellhausen notes that " Exod. xx. 24-26 looks almost like a protest against the arrangements of the Temple of Solomon, especially v. 26. "—Hist. of Israel, p. 96, footnote.

[2] So that we have here something very like " a positive statement of the non-existence of what had not yet come into being," which Wellhausen thinks it so unreasonable to ask.—Hist. of Israel, p. 365.

[3] Wellhausen, however, says that they did not worship at indifferent and casual localities, but at famous and immemorially holy places of worship; which is just assuming his hypothesis.—Hist. of Israel, p. 30. This is also the view Stade takes, connecting these sites with the worship of ancestors.

shipped anywhere, in the sense that "a multiplicity of altars was assumed as a matter of course,"[1] it may be objected that this is hardly consistent with the materialistic conception of the national God which is ascribed to Israel. One would have expected that, at a period when Jahaveh was no more than a national God, as the theory maintains, the tendency would be to a narrow centralising of worship, or at least to a worship in regularly authorised places; and that, when once "ethic monotheism" was reached, a free and more unrestricted worship would be permissible. But this is another of the many perplexities of the modern theory, that the development was quite the other way.

As it stands, the book of the Covenant is represented as antecedent to the appointment of the tabernacle in the wilderness, and may therefore be taken as meant to state the fundamental idea of worship that was inculcated upon Israel. As the Covenant precedes the law and is not annulled by it (Gal. iii. 17), this more spiritual conception of God, as ever near to the worshipper who seeks Him in the right way, represents the idea that we find everywhere held by prophetic men. It was a protest, or polemic, if we may so say, against the localising tendencies of other religions, an assurance that the God of Israel could and would come near to bless His people in every place where He recorded His name. It thus formed the guiding principle of prophetic men, to whom, as it would seem, the ordinances of ritual worship were "a figure for the time

[1] Wellhausen, Hist. of Israel, p. 29.

present," and who never allowed themselves to fall
into the belief that their God was confined to temples made with hands.   Had there not been such an
assertion of this fundamental principle in the very
earliest legislation—the omnipresence of Jahaveh—
we should no doubt have been told by modern critics
that this is another proof that at this early stage of
religious belief He was conceived of as limited to
some high mountain, or accessible only in some
special sanctuary.   The duty of united worship in a
central place is not incompatible with God's power
to bless anywhere.   The book of Deuteronomy itself,
which is said to restrict worship to the Temple of
Jerusalem, contains an injunction to set up an altar
and offer sacrifices between Ebal and Gerizim (Deut.
xi. 29; xxvii. 4, 13).   Still the limitation stands,
"in every place where I record my name," which
cannot simply mean "in all places indifferently."
There was to be some indication of Jahaveh's name
given by Himself; and after all, the old explanation
that saw a reference to the movements of the tribes
through the wilderness, under the direction of God,
who appointed their halting-places, and to a time
before the tribes were a settled people with fixed
dwelling-place, though it does not seem to exhaust
the reference, is not inappropriate.   At most the
words may imply the acceptable worship of Jahaveh
at a number of successive places, but they do not
necessarily, nor perhaps possibly, imply the recognition of simultaneous sanctuaries in different
places.   With this idea the whole tone of the passage is at variance.   The people to whom the words

are addressed are *one* people; it is not to *individuals* that the permission or promise is given.[1] Wherever Israel as a whole is, and wherever Jahaveh, their *one* God, records His name, there acceptable worship may be offered. The very idea of the unity of the national God, and the correlative idea of the unity of His people, imply a unity of worship and of sanctuary. The corporate reference is confirmed by the fact that this same book of the Covenant ordains that three times in the year all the males should appear before Jahaveh. It is inconsistent with the fundamental ideas of the unity of the tribes at that early time to suppose that such a command could mean that three times in the year all the males were to make a pilgrimage to some shrine or other, some tomb or holy place of a tribal ancestor, and thus fulfil the command here given. The mere possession of a sacred ark, with a tent for its habitation, and these as the common possession of all the tribes, was in itself a centralising of worship. Though the existence of a tabernacle such as is described in the Pentateuch is denied by the modern historians, it is not denied that an ark, and a tent for its covering, were in the possession of Israel, and held in general regard in connection with the

---

[1] The ten commandments, says a very docile pupil of Wellhausen, "are not addressed to individuals, but to a nation. The 'thou' to whom they speak is the people of Israel, and they are prefaced by a sentence in which Jehovah states how it is His right to give laws to Israel" (Allan Menzies, National Religion, p. 42). Wellhausen would have us believe that the notion of the "congregation" as a sacred body was "foreign to Hebrew antiquity, but runs through the Priestly Code from beginning to end" (Hist. of Israel, p. 78). I think we have it here clearly marked in the "thou" of the book of the Covenant in formal connection with worship (comp. above, p. 303 f.) But indeed it was present in essence in the first self-consciousness of Israel as Jahaveh's people.

Jahaveh religion. Nor can it be denied that Shiloh was a sanctuary of a quite special importance in the times of the Judges and Samuel, and no one who believes that the Hebrew writers knew anything at all of their history will accept the assumption that the Temple was merely the court sanctuary of the kingdom of Judah, or even only one of many co-ordinate holy places in that kingdom. Wellhausen says [1] that the principle "one God, one sanctuary" is the idea of the Priestly Code. It is, in point of fact, the idea of the book of the Covenant also, though neither in the one nor in the other is it held to mean that the one God was only present, and could only manifest His power at one particular spot. "*An* altar shalt thou make to me," the command runs, not "altars." The altar of God is always only one. It ceases to be an altar the moment His people and His manifestation to them are at another place. It is not the sanctity of the place that constitutes the sanctity of the altar, but the presence of Him who makes His name manifest. It is remarkable that we do not find in all the Old Testament such a divine utterance as "my altars"; and only twice does the expression "Thy altars," addressed to God, occur. It is found in Elijah's complaint, which refers to northern Israel, at a time when the legitimate worship of Jerusalem was excluded; and in Psalm lxxxiv., where it again occurs, no inference can be drawn from it. On the other hand, Hosea says distinctly, "Ephraim hath multiplied altars to sin" (Hosea viii. 11).

[1] Hist. of Israel, p. 34.

I think, therefore, it is not proved that the book of the Covenant allows worship at any indefinite number of places as co-ordinate sanctuaries; nor does the history show that this was recognised by the religious leaders of the nation. Previous to the building of the Temple at Jerusalem, and especially when the ark was removed from Shiloh, we find what may be called a freer or less regulated practice; and this was the result of the exigencies of the period. But from the erection of the Temple, not only is there no proof that any other sanctuary was allowed, but there are positive indications that that was regarded as the one authoritative place of worship in the sense in which we here speak. The practice in the northern kingdom proves nothing, for all the assertions of modern writers to the effect that the history mainly evolved itself there, and that the kingdom of Judah counts for little, are opposed to the spirit and distinct utterances of the earliest prophets. Not less are they inconsistent with the earliest legislation. The book of the Covenant, at whatever time written, and whether composed in the northern or the southern kingdom, makes no distinction between the two, and lays down one law for all Israel. The schism of the ten tribes was a breaking away from national unity and from the national God; and no proof can be adduced that prophetic men looked with anything but disfavour on the idolatrous worship that was practised in the southern kingdom, whether at Jerusalem or at local sanctuaries.

CHAPTER XVI.

THE LAW-BOOKS.

Distinction of Books and Codes—Wellhausen's personal experience—The hypothesis of Graf; not the result of criticism—The great objection to it its assumption of the fictitious character of the history, thus leaving no solid materials for a credible history—I. The book of Deuteronomy is neither (1) *pseudonymous nor* (2) *fictitious—II. The books containing the Levitical Code—*(1) *The position that Ezekiel paved the way for this Code—*(2) *The pious remnant and the reformation ideas—*(3) *Fictitious history in an aggravated form—*(4) *The literary form of this Code—Multiplicity of sources a proof of long-continued literary activity—But the main course of the history rests on its own independent proofs.*

In the preceding chapters we have seen reasons for concluding that the modern theory does not sufficiently account for the persistent ascription of law and religious ordinance to Moses; that it fails to exhibit the transition from natural to religious observance, and from oral to authoritative written law; that its argument from silence tells as much against its own assumption as against the Biblical view; and that its sharp distinction of the Codes in essential matters is not well founded. With the literary fates of the various law-codes we are not much concerned, because this is a subject on which the Biblical theory, which it is our main purpose to test, leaves great latitude for different views; and the same may be said of the question of the composition of books. We must, however, look somewhat particularly into the relation of the law-books to the Codes and to the general history; for in regard to this matter the Biblical theory and the modern are radically at variance in important points.

Wellhausen in one passage [1] gives us an interesting piece of his own personal experience. He tells us that in his early student days he "was attracted by the stories of Saul and David, Ahab and Elijah;" that the discourses of Amos and Isaiah laid strong hold on him, and that he read himself well into the prophetic and historical books of the Old Testament; but that all the time he "was troubled with a bad conscience, as if he were beginning with the roof instead of the foundation." At last he took courage, and made his way through the books of Exodus, Leviticus, and Numbers; but looked in vain for the light which he expected these would shed on the historical and prophetical books. "At last," he says, "in the course of a casual visit in Göttingen in the summer of 1867, I learned through Ritschl that Karl Heinrich Graf placed the law later than the prophets, and, almost without knowing his reasons for the hypothesis, I was prepared to accept it; I readily acknowledged to myself the possibility of understanding Hebrew antiquity without the book of the Torah."

[1] Hist. of Israel, pp. 3, 4.

So far as his experience in the reading of Scripture goes, there is nothing very peculiar in it. I suppose that few of those who have formed for themselves any defined view of Bible history, have acquired this by reading through the law-books before approaching those that are historical. He tells us nothing of his experience in regard to the book of Genesis, whose stories of the patriarchs, one would have thought, would have as powerfully attracted the young student as the history of Saul and David; and it is difficult to fancy what idea he could have obtained of even the historical and prophetical books, without accepting the underlying assumption of these books that the history went back to the patriarchal period. The whole history hangs in the air, if we begin with Saul and David—implying, as it does, a great deal for which we must turn to the writings which Wellhausen must include in his expression, "the book of the Torah." But in using this expression, and in his reference to the theory of Graf which he says he found himself ready to accept, he leads the unwary reader to confuse two things which ought to be kept distinct, and to jump to a conclusion which is not warranted by the experience which he relates.

Our examination of the early prophetical writings, and of the histories which are said to be of about the same date, always threw us back upon an antecedent history, and gave at least a strong presumption of the truth of the narrative contained in the books of the Pentateuch. Yet for the fundamental facts and main course of the history we did not require to refer to the Pentateuchal laws, although we found a coherence and consistency between the accounts contained in the two sets of books. The history, in fact, does not turn upon laws and the observance of ceremonies, and so far it is true, as Wellhausen says he experienced it, that the history is intelligible without the Torah. But in saying " the book of the Torah," if by that he means the whole Pentateuch, and not merely the legal part of it, it is not the case that the history is thus intelligible.

The law-books of the Pentateuch, as is well known, exhibit two component elements,—narrative and legislation; and it has been found impossible by literary analysis to separate them. Whether the two parts originally came from different hands or not, in part or in whole, they are so inextricably blended or woven together that it has to be confessed they must go together. That is to say, the narratives imply that the laws were given under historical circumstances, and the laws imply the circumstances under which they were given. If, then, we are satisfied with the testimony given by later writers to the history; if, in other words, we take the references to earlier times contained in the writings of the eighth and ninth centuries as confirming, in the main, the narrative of the Pentateuch, we might conclude that the laws, which are by confession bound so closely in the bundle of narrative as to be inseparable from it, are also the laws and statutes to which the prophets appeal. The laws would go with the narrative, in which they are enclosed. And this is what the Old Testament writers take for granted. The reverse process, however, since the time of Graf, has been followed by those who advocate his theory. They say the narratives must follow the laws. How this conclusion was reached, and what it involves, must now be considered.

Graf at first attempted to make a separation between the legislation and the accompanying history contained in the Pentateuch; and having proved to his own satisfaction that the narratives attached to the Levitical Code were implied in the book of Deuteronomy, and known to the writer of the latter, he said that the narratives were early, while the legislation was late. Being, however, afterwards convinced that the two elements were inseparable, he was clearly in a dilemma, from which be adopted a remarkable mode of escape. He simply said that as the laws had been proved to be of late origin, the narratives must also be of late composition—throwing over entirely the proofs which he had before considered sufficient to show that the narratives of the Levitical books were older than Deuteronomy, and introducing a fashion of regarding the contents of these books which is at once novel and startling. For if the laws of the Levitical Code are late in the literal sense that they became laws at a period as late as Ezra, the narratives which accompany them and describe in detail in regard to many of them the manner in which they were promulgated by Moses, cannot be true history at all: the events related as the historical setting of the laws must be nothing else than fictitious. The only thing that can be said in their favour is, that they were invented for the good purpose of confirming and sanctioning the laws, by ascribing them to Moses, to whom the national tradition looked back as the great originator of law in Israel.

The first thing that strikes one here is that the theory is not the result of a sustained and uniform line of criticism. It was a *volte-face.* Graf had satisfied himself that the narrative parts of the Pentateuch were early, and were referred to or implied in pre-exilian writings. If he was equally satisfied that the laws were exilic, or post-exilic, and yet were inseparable from the narrative, the proper conclusion was that his critical processes were incorrect somewhere, and he ought to have searched for the error. One would think that the national testimony to a series of historical facts would be more clear than the recollection of a body of laws, and that laws were more liable to change by usage than the national testimony to vary in regard to fundamental facts of history. At all events, to say bluntly that the narratives must go with the laws is no more a process of criticism than to say that the laws must go with the history. It is therefore inaccurate to describe the position of Graf as a conclusion of criticism. It was simply a hypothesis to evade a difficulty in which criticism had landed him.

And then, when it is considered what is implied in the position that the narratives must go with the laws, it cannot but be admitted that the hypothesis is so far-reaching and revolutionary that it should be accepted only when every other explanation of the phenomena fails. For it amounts to a thorough discrediting of the historical value of the narratives of these books with which the laws are so closely interwoven; and to an ascription of fiction, if not fraud, to the writers, which will render it extremely difficult for sober criticism to rely upon any testimony which is borne by the Hebrew writers to the facts of their national history. So that here again, when pushed home to its central position, we find that the modern view, claiming to be strictly critical, in reality throws discredit on the documents which it starts to criticise,[1] and which are the only sources available for obtaining information regarding the history which is to be described.

But there is no necessity, except that imposed by an unyielding hypothesis, for this last resource. If laws were not given by Moses, then certainly any narratives that describe them as so given must be false. But if Moses did deliver a body of laws to his people, then even if the laws, as they stand, indicate divergency, even if they underwent modification, even if the codes or the books, or both, are of much later composition, in their existing forms, than the time of Moses, we may still respect the *bona fides* of the writers of the books, and maintain them as substantially true history.

I. To begin with the book of Deuteronomy. Some who believe that this book is of late date, written at the time of Josiah in order to bring about a reformation, and yet seek to maintain the *bona fides* of the

---

[1] Compare above, chap. vi. p. 149 f.

writer, are in the habit of saying that the book is an example of pseudonymous composition. Briggs, for example,[1] has argued at length and ingeniously to show that there is nothing unreasonable in the supposition of pseudonymous literature in the Bible, and by reference to the book of Ecclesiastes has tried to save this book of Deuteronomy from the category of forgery or fiction. But in point of fact, the book is not pseudonymous in the same way that Ecclesiastes is. The latter book, except the heading at the beginning and the epilogue (chap. xii. 9 ff.) at the end, is all written in one person. "I, the preacher," did so and so throughout; and his personality, "son of David," and magnificence, are so accentuated as to lead to the conclusion that Solomon is meant. But the writer by saying, "was king over Israel in Jerusalem," lets us at the outset into his secret, which is simply this, that he is writing in the name of Solomon, to represent what might have been Solomon's reflections upon life. There is not only no intent to deceive, but there is scarcely the possibility of deception. The circumstances of a historical kind that are introduced are so few and so general that we are not misled or misinformed as to matters of fact; all the rest is meditation, moralising, and the scheme of the book is so far transparent. But it is quite different with the book of Deu-

[1] Biblical Study (1887), p. 223 ff. He appeals also, among others, to Robertson Smith, "who uses the term legal fiction as a variety of literary fiction" (see Old Testament in the Jewish Church, p. 385). What is there described, however, as "found more convenient to present the new law in a form which enables it to be treated as an integral part of the old legislation," though probably applicable to the present form in which the collections of laws appear, does not seem to cover the case of the *book* of Deuteronomy with which we are concerned. Compare Cheyne, Jeremiah, His Life and Times, p. 77.

teronomy. As a book, it does not profess to be written by Moses; it is, in fact, one of the many anonymous books of the Old Testament. The writer, whoever he was, and at whatever time he lived, tells us certain things that Moses did, and especially produces long addresses which Moses is said to have uttered. These long speeches, however, are all set in a historical framework; and if the framework is not historical, the book is more than pseudonymous —it is pseudo-historical. The speeches by themselves might be taken to fall into the category of the book of Ecclesiastes, where the preacher is made to give the thoughts that passed through his mind. But if the writer, who has set these speeches down at definite times and under definite circumstances, is not correct as to the time and circumstances, or if the events he weaves into the speeches never occurred, he is manufacturing these, not studying to reproduce them by historical imagination. The book declares that at a certain time, and under certain circumstances, Moses gathered the people and addressed to them long speeches recalling certain facts. If Moses never did such a thing, and if such facts never occurred, the book must be simply described as unhistorical or fictitious.

And yet I do not think it is to be so regarded. Whoever was the author, and whatever time may be assigned for its composition, this is what the book presents to us. It declares that Moses at the close of the wilderness journey, when the people were ready to cross the Jordan, made formal addresses to them, in which he recounted the events of their past history, recapitulated the laws which he had laid down for their guidance, and warned them against the temptations to which they would be particularly exposed in Canaan; threatening them, in case of disobedience, with God's judgments, and promising them, in case of obedience, His blessing. Now, if Moses sustained anything at all like the office which is invariably ascribed to him in the books of the Old Testament; if he was the leader of the people to the borders of Canaan, the founder of their national constitution, the lawgiver in any positive and definite sense,—it was the most natural thing in the world that he should, at the close of his life, have given such parting counsels and addresses to the people whose history was so closely bound up with his own life's work. That is to say, the situation which the book of Deuteronomy presents to us is a situation not in itself improbable, but on every ground exceedingly probable; and the statement by the writer of the book that this situation presented itself is such that it would be accepted as matter of fact in any secular historian. Further, if a writer, whether early or late, set himself to tell all this, he could only do so in the form in which the book of Deuteronomy comes before us.

Let us not be misled by the direct form in which these speeches are expressed. Wellhausen, in one place,[1] speaks contemptuously of our being treated to long addresses instead of historical details. It is somewhat remarkable that he, and many likeminded, have not taken note of the peculiarity of

---

[1] History of Israel, p. 340.

the Hebrew language, that it has not developed what we call the indirect speech—a peculiarity which necessitates the regular introduction of speeches or addresses. Take such a passage as the following: When the children of Israel, after their long wanderings in the desert, were on the point of crossing the Jordan to take possession of the land to which they had looked forward as their inheritance, Moses, who had been their constant guide and legislator for forty years, seeing that the close of his life was near, and solicitous for the welfare of the people whom he had hitherto guided, assembled them about him, and in various addresses recapitulated the striking events of their past history, dwelling particularly on details that exhibited most clearly the guiding hand of God and the fallibility and frailty of Israel, restated the fundamental principles on which the nation was constituted, and by warning and promise directed them to the dangers that lay in the future if they proved unfaithful, and to the blessings in store for them if they adhered to allegiance to their national God. Let any professor of Hebrew set himself to state in idiomatic Hebrew what all this implies in detail, and he will be bound to state it just as it is put down in this book. The absence of the indirect speech in Hebrew can be made quite clear to the English reader by a reference to any page of the historical books. If a writer wishes to say that one person made a verbal communication to another, he must say, "So-and-so spake to So-and-so, saying," and must give the *ipsissima verba*. And yet, strictly speaking, the writer is not to be taken as vouching for the actual words spoken. He is simply producing, in the only way that the laws of his language allow him to produce, the substance of the thing said; and from beginning to end of the Old Testament writings, the language remained at that stage, only the faintest attempts to pass beyond it being visible. It is part of that direct, graphic style of Old Testament Scripture, which is of wide extent, and is based on the intuitive, presentative mode of thought of the sacred writers, who must describe a scene by painting it and its actors, with their words and gestures, and reproduce a communication in the actual words supposed to have been uttered.[1]

It is easy to see now how a writer, soon after or long after Moses, recalling the events which we may suppose tradition preserved in the nation's mind, and using we know not what documents, produced a book like Deuteronomy. The situation was not one of active events, but of reflective pause and consideration, preparatory to the arduous work of the contest, and hence the literary form of the book is different from that of the other books of the Pentateuch. Not by any fiction, not by inventing a story for a purpose, but in perfect good faith, he represents the aged lawgiver, surrounded by the people whose welfare lay so much at his heart, giving them such counsel, warning, and encouragement as were suited to their circumstances. It was but natural that a writer, setting himself to such a task, should

---

[1] I may be allowed in this connection to refer to a paper on the "Graphic Element in the Old Testament" in the Expositor, second series, vol. vi. p. 241 ff.

mingle much of his own in the composition. **No** writer can divest himself of his own personality, or write entirely without reference to the time in which he lives. And a writer succeeding Moses, at a greater or less interval, could not but see the development of events which were only in germ in Moses' time, and could not help representing them more or less in their developed form. In this sense, and to this extent, it is true that any late writer writes under the influence of later ideas; and the objection taken by critical writers to such a course is an objection that would apply to all writing of history. But between this—which is done in absolute good faith—and the wholesale manufacturing of incidents and situations, there is all the difference between history and fiction. We cannot think of such a writer imagining his events so as to represent Moses recapitulating a series of occurrences that did not take place, or which the writer did not firmly believe did take place, or ascribing to him laws which he did not consider to have been in their form or substance propounded to the people whom Moses addressed.

Laws are indeed, as has been already said, subject to change with changing circumstances, and observances are liable to assume new phases to meet new emergencies. A law, given at first with a general reference, may come face to face with actual states of society which force it to take a more definite shape to meet the cases that have arisen. This is development of law, but it is not change of the substance of the law. Now if, as is surely most reasonable to assume, Moses did warn his people against the idolatries of the nations of Canaan, and enjoin them to maintain their own religious faith and observances, the force of such warnings and admonitions would be accentuated when the actual dangers emerged; the law would be seen in its farther reference, and assume a more specific and precise form in the minds of those who looked at it. If, then, a later writer, believing in all good faith that Moses gave such admonitions, had before his eyes the actual dangers which the lawgiver had in a general way foreseen, he could not help, in restating the laws, giving them a sharper and more incisive point; but he was not thereby either changing or inventing a law. This would be to develop law in the spirit of the Mosaic legislation, on the understanding, however, that there was a positive Mosaic legislation to be developed. And all this again, it seems to me, is compatible with the good faith of the writer and with the substantial historical accuracy of his narrative. It is, however, quite a different thing from the supposition that the writer, after he had seen certain dangers and abuses emerge, set himself to devise a law which was quite new, in order to meet these, and deliberately contrived a whole set of historical occurrences, in which it was feigned that the laws were given forth in Mosaic times.

It will be remembered that those who make the Code of Deuteronomy late, usually say that the writer drew up laws in *the spirit* of the Mosaic legislation; and even Wellhausen says that the book of

" Deuteronomy presupposes earlier attempts of this kind, and borrows its materials largely from them." [1] The Biblical account of the matter is, that Moses actually wrote down the laws contained in the book. There was, in other words, a Deuteronomic Code prior to the book of Deuteronomy; this is what the critics themselves say, and what the book itself says. The question is, Did the Code, in a written form and to an appreciable extent, come from Moses himself? On the one side we have these vague admissions as to the "spirit of the Mosaic legislation " (and how was a late writer to know what that spirit was unless by positive enactment?), and the equally vague admission of "former attempts," without positive specification of the time and extent of the attempts that were made. On the other hand, we have the positive statement that Moses, at his death, left a body of laws such as are included in the book of Deuteronomy. That we have the very words of the laws as he penned them, the custom of literary composition, and the ordinary fates of legislative codes, show us we are not forced to suppose. What became of the actual collection of laws, beyond the fact that it was delivered to the Levites, and deposited in the side of the ark, [2] we are not told. And moreover, at what time and by whose hands the whole of the book of Deuteronomy, as we now have it, was composed, is a matter which literary criticism alone cannot decide. It is only by inferences, not very clear in themselves, that the conclusion is reached that the book belongs to the age of

---

[1] **Hist. of Israel,** p. 402. See above, p. 399 f.   [2] Deut. xxxi. 26.

Josiah; but even if, as a book, it belongs to that age, or later, I think the considerations advanced will show how it may be still historical and trustworthy, exhibiting at once the working of a later development of old principles, and preserving also—not inventing for the occasion—elements which are ancient and Mosaic.[1]

II. Of the other law-books, we have to deal particularly with those that embody the Levitical Code. Here the narrative and the legal elements are very closely blended; but I think it is possible, even on the supposition that the Code underwent modification in course of time, to accept the books as trustworthy historical records. Let us, however, first of all, see how the critical writers account for the introduction of the Code and its related narratives.

It is said that Ezekiel

" in the last part of his work made the first attempt to record the ritual which had been customary in the Temple of Jerusalem. Other priests attached themselves to him (Levit. xvii.-xxvi.), and thus there grew up in the exile from among the members of this profession a kind of school of people who reduced to writing and to a system what they had formerly practised in the way of their calling. After the Temple was restored this theoretical zeal still continued to work, and the ritual when renewed was still further developed by the action and reaction on each other of theory and practice."[2] "So long as the sacrificial worship remained in actual use, it was zealously carried on, but people did not concern themselves with it theoretically, and had not the least occasion for reducing it to a Code. But once the Temple was in ruins, the cultus at

---

[1] See Note XXVIII.   [2] Well., Hist. of Israel, p. 404; comp. 496.

an end, its *personnel* out of employment, it is easy to understand how the sacred praxis should have become a matter of
theory and writing, so that it might not altogether perish, and
how an exiled priest should have begun to paint the picture of
it as he carried it in his memory, and to publish it as a programme for the future restoration of the theocracy. Nor is
there any difficulty if arrangements, which as long as they were
actually in force were simply regarded as natural, were seen
after their abolition in a transfiguring light, and from the study
devoted to them gained artificially a still higher value." [1]

All this may not be so " easy to understand " to
everybody as it seems to be to Wellhausen. Indeed
the things that he finds " no difficulty " in accepting
are very often the very things for which proof is
most desiderated. As to codification being the deposit
during the exile of an old, fully developed praxis,
we have already had something to say (p. 400 f.); and
Bredenkamp exclaims with justifiable astonishment,
" Clouds which are formed in the time of grandsires
are not in the habit of raining upon grandsons.
Could people not write in pre-exilic times? Must
they not be allowed to write? Why tear with violence the pen from the hand of the ancient Israelitish priests? " [2] We are told indeed by Wellhausen,
on his own authority, that the praxis of the priests at
the altar never formed part of the written law in
pre-exilic times. [3] But Dillmann, who has subjected
these books to a most thorough examination, not
only sees nothing against the idea, but finds positive proof for it, that the priests at the Temple of
Jerusalem were in the habit of writing down the

[1] Wellhausen, Hist. of Israel, p. 59 f.
[2] Gesetz und Propheten, p. 118.   [3] Hist. of Israel, p. 59.

laws and regulations for their ceremonial functions.[1]
Besides, Wellhausen has to assume for the nonce
that the praxis which was "zealously carried on"
anterior to the exile was just what underwent codification after it; although his general contention is
that in the pre-exilic period "no trace can be found
of acquaintance with the Priestly Code, but on the
other hand, very clear indications of ignorance of
its contents."[2] If, however, such "ignorance of
its *contents*" prevailed, how was an exiled priest or
a number of priests to carry the whole thing in
memory and reduce it to writing? Moreover, what
he ascribes to the time of the exile, seems ill to
agree with the statement of the matter which he
gives in another place. The Babylonian exile, he
says,

"violently tore the nation away from its native soil and kept it
apart for half a century,—a breach of historical continuity
than which it is almost impossible to conceive a greater. The
new generation had no natural but only an artificial relation to
the times of old; the firmly rooted growths of the old soil, regarded as thorns by the pious, were extirpated, and the freshly
ploughed fallows ready for a new sowing."[3]

He then goes on to say that it is

"far from being the case that the whole people at that time
underwent a general conversion in the sense of the prophets.
. . . Only the pious ones, who with trembling followed Jehovah's word, were left as a remnant; they alone had the strength
to maintain the Jewish individuality amid the medley of nationalities into which they had been thrown. From the exile there

---

[1] Die Bücher Exodus u. Leviticus, 2te Auflage, p. 386. He calls Wellhausen's position "an arbitrary assertion."

[2] Hist. of Israel, p. 59. Comp. above, p. 394.   [3] Ibid., p. 28.

returned, not the nation, but a religious sect—those, namely, who had given themselves up body and soul to the reformation ideas. It is no wonder that to these people, who besides, on their return, all settled in the immediate neighbourhood of Jerusalem, the thought never once occurred of restoring the local cults. It cost them no struggle to allow the destroyed Bamoth to continue lying in ruins; the principle had become part of their very being, that the one God had also but one place of worship, and thenceforward, for all time coming, this was regarded as a thing of course.

This aspect of the exile as a violent wrench from old associations is hardly consistent with the view that a priestly party from the very beginning of the captivity took up the minute study and arrangement of the sacrificial system which had just been broken up. Nor, although it is " no wonder " to Wellhausen, is it very clear that a people should so easily forget all that was bad in the past worship (and how much of it was bad!) and so readily begin life anew on an entirely new principle. Indeed this whole account of the influence of the exile on the codification of law does not by any means turn out to be so easy as Wellhausen would make us believe.

(1.) In the first place, we are told that "the transition from the pre-exilic to the post-exilic period is effected, not by Deuteronomy, but by Ezekiel the priest in prophet's mantle, who was one of the first to be carried into exile." [1] Ezekiel's so-called programme is so confidently appealed to as the precursor of the Levitical Code, that to assert anything to the contrary at the present day is to expose one's self to ridicule as incompetent to understand critical

[1] Hist. of Israel, p. 59,

processes.   Nay, so important are the chapters in
the book of Ezekiel which contain this programme,
that Wellhausen says they have been called, not in-
correctly, "the key of the Old Testament."[1]   The
chapters in question are xl. to xlviii.   They form a
connected piece, and tell us how the prophet was,
"in the visions of God," brought into the land of
Israel, and what he saw and was told there.   He
dwells at great length on the measurements and details of arrangement of the Temple, and communi-
cates directions for its dedication and for its service.
He also describes the waters issuing from under the
house and going to fertilise the desert; and he lays
out minutely the measurements of the sacred territory and the situation of the tribes in the land.
Now, surely, by all honest criticism, whatever mode
of interpretation is applied to one part of this vision
should be made to apply to the whole.   If one part is a
cool, deliberate programme, so should the others.   If
the other parts are clearly not to be taken in this
sense, neither should the ceremonial part.   Ezekiel
is just as precise and matter-of-fact in the divisions
which he makes of the Holy Land as in the ordinances he puts forth for the worship of the sanctuary.
Yet the critical school proceeds in the most elaborate fashion to examine this code or programme,
and tells us that it is the first attempt to arrange
what afterwards became the Levitical Code.   Why
do they not say also that his geographical sketch is
to be understood, say, as the starting-point for the
tribal divisions of the book of Joshua, or that his

[1] Hist. of Israel, p. 421.

sketch of the Temple is the groundwork of Solomon's? I must confess simply that I cannot understand the principle of a criticism that thus tears one piece out of connection and seeks to make it a serious historical programme, while not a word can be said in favour of treating the other parts in the same way. If two-thirds of the vision are clearly ideal, so must the other third, in whatever way we are to understand the ideal meaning which the prophet meant to convey. If it be urged that Ezekiel did not need to give details for ritual if a ritual law existed, and that he makes no reference to any law on the subject, it can be rejoined that he speaks in the same way of Temple and land. We cannot gather from his description that the Temple of Solomon was ever built or the land ever divided among the tribes before his day. "This," he says, "shall be the border, whereby ye shall divide the land for inheritance according to the twelve tribes of Israel: . . . concerning the which I lifted up mine hand to give it unto your fathers;"[1] and he gives all the measurements of some house seen in vision without referring to a house which he knew quite well as having stood for centuries. We need not therefore wonder at his bringing in a detailed ritual, as if this were the first time such a thing had been heard or thought of. He is not for the first time in history trying to fix a ritual for a people who had hitherto nothing but custom to guide them. His sketch is too brief altogether for such an attempt. No priesthood could have carried on the service of the sanctuary and

[1] Ezek. xlvii. 13, 14.

regulated the worship of the nation with such a vague and fragmentary manual. As to its being as a literary work the foundation of the later Levitical Code, it is not by any means certain that in language or matter the Levitical Code is dependent upon it. A careful examination has led competent judges to decide that the reverse is the case,[1] though I do not think it necessary to go into this.

But it may be urged, if there was a detailed authoritative law in existence, why did Ezekiel, even in vision, deviate from it? Well, on the critical hypothesis the Deuteronomic law at least existed as authoritative, and yet Ezekiel deviates from it. If it is still asked, How could he, prophet though he was, quietly set aside the recognised law? the question again arises, After he, a prophet speaking in God's name by direct revelation, sketched this law, how did priests in the exile pass by Ezekiel's draft, and frame a divergent code? In fact, there are insuperable difficulties on every side when this ritual of Ezekiel is taken as a cool, matter-of-fact programme of legislation, put forth as a first attempt at codification; and no argument can be based upon it for the modern theory.

(2.) And then, secondly, it is quite conceivable that the people in the exile should have turned their attention to matters of law. They would be compelled, in order to keep themselves separate from the surrounding heathen, to attend to those matters of personal, ceremonial, and social order which

---

[1] See, *e. g.*, Bredenkamp, Gesetz und Propheten, p. 116 ff.; Dillmann, Die Bücher Exodus u. Leviticus, p. 524 ff. See also Note XXIX.

were their national distinctions, and, so far, their very existence as a separate people in the exile is a proof of pre-existing law. But it is not so clear, by any means, that they should for the first time make a study of purely Levitical and sacrificial laws at a time when they had no cultus. Nor, in view of the zeal for the law shown at a later time by the Jews in Babylon, is it so clear that only a few underwent a "conversion in the sense of the prophets." Wellhausen has to suppose a school of people who gave themselves ardently to this study of ritual law. It was a large school, if the number of returning exiles is taken into account. All these must have been in Ezra's secret on this view,—all ardently devoted to the reformation ideas. Now, in point of fact, Ezra's own account is that he had a deficiency of Levites among his volunteers, and had to urge them to join him and to act as "ministers for the house of *our* God" (Ezra viii. 15 ff.) Moreover, Haggai shows us that the people were very far indeed from being devoted to the reformation ideas; the sacrificial system was slackly observed; and even in Ezra's and Nehemiah's time the picture of the people is anything but that of a community that "had given themselves up body and soul to the reformation ideas" of either morals or worship.[1]

(3.) But, further, difficult as it is to believe that the so-called school for the first time put down in writing what they treasured in their memories, this is not the whole of the hypothesis. Again, and in a much more objectionable form, comes in the sup-

[1] Ezra ix. 1 ff.; Neh. v. 1 ff., xiii. 4 ff., 15 ff., 23 ff.; Mal. i. 6 ff., ii. 8 ff.

position of fiction, whereby a false historical setting was invented for the laws of the Levitical Code, by carrying them back to Moses and the desert, simply in order to give the law higher sanction. Not only, for example, was there no tabernacle, such as is described in the Pentateuch, prepared in the wilderness, but even at the time when the story of its construction was fabricated, there was no such tabernacle to have given rise to the fable, nor had any such tabernacle ever existed to give a start to the story.[1] It was simply the legend-spinning invention of men of late time that cut down the dimensions of the Temple to half their size, and feigned that a tabernacle of that size existed in a portable form in the wilderness; and all this simply to make it appear that the Temple worship was of older institution than the time of the building of the Temple. So also a fictitious origin is given for what the Code represents as other early institutions. In every case in which a law is said to have been given in Mosaic times, the circumstances, if stated, must be similarly explained as invented or suggested in a late time. In this way, all sorts of divergences of the narrative of the Priestly Code from that of the Jehovist are accentuated, and it is made to appear— at the expense, it must be admitted, of wonderful ingenuity—that the former are of exilic time—*i.e.*, of the date of or subsequent to the introduction of the laws.[2]

The question is whether the palm of ingenuity is to be assigned to the writers of these books or to

[1] Wellhausen, p. 37 ff.   [2] See Note XXX.

the modern critics; whether a school composed of men like Ezekiel and Ezra were likely to have with boundless inventiveness concocted all this history, or our modern critics are ransacking the treasures of their wits to find an artificial explanation of a thing that is much more simple than they make it? For what could have been the object in inventing history wholesale in this way? To give sanction to the laws, it is said: but on whom was the sanction to bear? If on the men of the priestly school themselves, they were already, on the hypothesis, devoted to the reformation ideas; if on the people at large, the mere manufacture of a history that was new to them was not likely to rouse them from their lethargy and fire them with new zeal; and, so far as we can see, it did not. It is to be remembered—and the remark applies also to the production of Deuteronomy—that this was not a case of a person in secret devising an unheard-of scheme of history, and laying it away to be read by posterity. Nor was it, as I understand the theory, a case of gathering up for a present purpose the old and cherished traditions of a people. The thing was done, so to speak, in open day for a special purpose at the time, a considerable number of persons being engaged in it, and among a people who already had a definite tradition as to their history. Yet, though the people, at least in Jeremiah's days, were critical enough in matters of the national history (Jer. xxvi. 16 ff.), we never hear, either then or at the time of the restoration, of any suspicion being cast upon the account of the history which these law-books contain.

(4.) But the form in which the Levitical Code appears is not favourable to the modern theory of its origin. The laws are in many cases, it will be observed, provided with headings, which vary in a curious manner, as, *e.g.*, "The Lord spake unto Moses," "The Lord spake unto Moses and Aaron," and even "the Lord spake unto Aaron"; and the persons to whom the laws are directed are various, as "the children of Israel," "Aaron and his sons," "all the congregation of the children of Israel," and "Aaron and his sons and all the children of Israel." Such features as these, as well as the manner in which the laws are arranged, the same subject coming up more than once, and the same law being repeated in different places, give one the impression that the laws were collected together from different sources. It looks as if there had been smaller collections, regulating individual observances and perhaps intrusted to different persons for preservation and execution. At all events, the collection does not present the appearance of a systematic Code. This feature, I should think, is more opposed to the idea of composition by Ezra and a school, who would surely, when the whole system was for the first time to be set down in writing, have proceeded in a more systematic manner, than to the idea of Mosaic origin and gradual modification in course of time. I have already referred to the peculiarity of the Hebrew speech, whereby the direct words must be put into the mouth of the speaker, when we need only assume the substance of the thing delivered. The headings of those laws, on this common-sense mode of viewing the matter, mean no more than that the laws originally came from Mosaic times; the history is satisfied, and the *bona fides* of the writers is maintained. So that even if the final codification took place as late as Ezra, the Code, and still more the institutions, might with propriety and substantial accuracy be described as Mosaic.

The Biblical writers do not fix for us the time or times at which the laws as they lie before us were written down; and their statements, fairly interpreted, allow us to suppose that the books passed through many literary processes before they reached their final form. The multiplicity of the sources out of which the law-books are composed is a proof of long-continued literary history. The peculiar arrangement of the legal portions, nay, their very divergence from one another, prove that law was for long a living thing, and that the Codes are not resuscitated from the memories of priests or excogitated by scribes. If, as seems quite reasonable, the laws for various ceremonies were, in the hands of those who had charge of them, copied and handed on from generation to generation of priests, it is quite probable that in the course of time there might have happened alterations of the rubric with altered circumstances, and that the final transcript or redaction would thus have a more modern cast than the original. All this, however, does not disprove the antiquity of the legislation nor the early writing of the laws, and it is surely, though not so ingenious, yet a much more ingenuous explanation than to say that the laws were by a fiction ascribed to ancient

time in order to give them an authority to which
they were not entitled. By taking the statements
of the Biblical writers as they stand, and not burden-
ing them with conclusions for which they are not
responsible, we get a more consistent and natural
view of the whole history of the law—a view that
certainly in itself is more credible to one who is not
prejudiced against the Biblical writers, and set to
watch for their halting. For the rest, the order of
the Codes as Codes written, the relation of laws to
one another, and their modifications in detail with
advancing time—these are things that criticism may
exercise its ingenuity upon, and seek to exhibit in
their true lights and proportions. But they are
more of archæological than of practical interest in
reference to the great point which we wish to ascer-
tain, the origin and development of the religion;
and it is mainly because they have been too much
bound up with that question that they have acquired
so much importance. There can be no harm in
critical investigation of this kind, so long as the
main course of the history, which rests on its own
independent proofs, is taken as the guiding principle of the criticism. It is, to say the least, very
doubtful whether at this distance of two or three
thousand years we are in a position to determine,
with any measure of success, the dates of the respective sources of which the books of the Pentateuch
are made up. The extraordinary turns that modern
criticism has taken on the subject testify to the
difficulty of the problem, if they do not shake our
confidence in its ability to solve it. The curious

blending of elements in the composite structure of these books, while it impresses on us the magnitude of the task of criticism, suggests a gradual and repeated process of editing, transcribing and modification which is perfectly conceivable among a people well acquainted with literary processes. The essential point to be remembered—the point to which all our investigations have tended—is, that the law and the writing of it are much older than modern critics allow; and the phenomenon which the books as books present to us is much more reasonably accounted for on the Biblical principle than on the modern theory: they are a product, in a natural way, of history, both religious and literary —not compositions, framed according to a literary method altogether unparalleled in order to manufacture a history which never was.

CHAPTER XVII.

LAW AND PROPHECY.

The order of law and prophets reversed by modern theory, and this not merely as an order of written documents but of history—(1) Position examined that all the prophets denied the divine authority of sacrifice and ritual laws—Passages from Isaiah, Micah, Hosea, Jeremiah considered—(2) The position that the Deuteronomic Code was introduced through prophetic influence, and with it the impulse given to legalism—Inconsistent character in which the prophets are made to appear in modern theory—The whole position of the prophets as religious guides is to be taken into account—The Covenant, and what it implied—The historical situation in Josiah's time does not agree with modern theory—Nor does the situation at and after the exile—Fundamental harmony of law and prophecy—The history did not turn on a struggle of parties—Law and Gospel.

ACCORDING to the modern theory the Biblical order of law and prophets is reversed into the order of prophets and law. Did this merely amount to the assertion that some of the prophetical writings existed before the Pentateuch had assumed its present form, it might be a defensible position on grounds of literary criticism.[1] It is, however, maintained in the sense that prophetic activity comes

[1] Cf. Wellhausen, p. 409.

historically before the acceptance of authoritative law, and that, in fact, by a course of development, the prophets brought about the introduction of the law. The position which, on this theory, the prophets are made to assume from first to last, and the relation in which they are made to stand towards the whole movement of legislation, are so peculiar that the subject requires some special treatment.

(1.) We have already considered the contention that in all those passages in the earlier writing prophets in which law or laws are mentioned, the reference is only to oral and not to written law. The priests, we are told, like the prophets, gave forth their *toroth* or instructions orally to the people; and the substance of the priestly Torah was chiefly moral, but partly also ceremonial, relating to things clean and unclean. Whatever became of the concrete *toroth* on those subjects, we are assured that the practice of the priests at the altar was never matter of instruction to the laity, and was not written down in a codified shape.[1] It is not made very clear in all this wherein the Torah of the priests differed from that of the prophets; nor is it made clear to what extent, if any, the priests wrote down their moral and ceremonial Torah. What we have particularly to do with here, however, is the attitude of the prophets to the law. It cannot be denied that, in the expressions of a general kind which they employ, they show a high respect for the Torah of the priests. This, however, say the critical historians, was the moral part of the priestly instruc-

[1] Wellhausen, p. 59.

tion, and it is strenuously maintained that the prophets, down to the time of Jeremiah, denied the divine authority of sacrifice and ritual laws. The situation, as I understand the contention, was this: In pre-exilic antiquity, when the worship of the Ba- moth was the rule, the main thing in the service was not the rite, but the deity to whom the service was rendered. The historical books that date from pre- exilic time—the books of Judges, Samuel, and Kings —exhibit great varieties in the modes of sacrifice, some of which may correspond to the law of the Pentateuch, while others certainly deviate widely from it, proving that there was no fixed rule.[1] The prophetical books also, " in their polemic against confounding worship with religion," while they " re- veal the fact that in their day the cultus was carried on with the utmost zeal and splendour," show that this high estimation rested, not on the opinion that the cultus came from Moses, but simply on the be- lief that Jahaveh must be honoured by His depend- ants, just like other gods, by means of offerings and gifts.[2] " According to the universal opinion of the pre-exilic period, the cultus is indeed of very old and (to the people) very sacred usage, but not a Mosaic institution; the ritual is not the main thing in it, and is in no sense the subject with which the Torah deals."[3] So that, in a word, as far as regards the ceremonies of worship, " the distinction between legitimate and heretical is altogether wanting; "[4] the theory of an illegal praxis is impossible, and the

---

[1] Wellhausen, p. 55.
[2] Ibid., p. 56.
[3] Ibid., p. 59.
[4] Ibid., p. 55.

legitimacy of the actually existing is indisputable.[1]
The prophets, therefore, when they rebuke the people for their sacrifices and offerings, are not to be
understood as reproving them for the corruption of
a pure law of worship that existed, but as expressing disapproval of the whole sacrificial system, as
a thing of mere human device, and destitute of divine sanction.   Not only do they show, by thus
speaking, that there was no law such as the Levitical Code in their day; but even the prophets, before
the time of Josiah, have nothing to say against the
local sanctuaries (so long as they are devoted to the
worship of the national God), a proof that the Deuteronomic Code did not come into existence till that
period, and much more a proof that it had no divine
sanction.   The prophets, in a word, appear as the
exponents of a tendency the very opposite of the
legalising tendency which brought legal Codes into
existence.

Great stress, in this argument, is laid upon the
declaration of Isaiah.   His antipathy to the whole
ritual system finds expression, it is said, in the well-
known passage in the first chapter of his book: "To
what purpose is the multitude of your sacrifices unto
me? saith Jahaveh: I am weary with the burnt-offerings of rams, and the fat of fed beasts; and I delight not in the blood of bullocks, and of lambs, and
of he-goats.   When ye come to look upon my face,
who hath required this at your hands, to trample my
courts?"   This expression, Wellhausen asserts with
confidence, "the prophet could not possibly have

[1] Wellhausen, p. 60.

uttered if the sacrificial worship had, according to any tradition whatever, passed for being specifically Mosaic."[1] But what then becomes of the book of the Covenant, which was surely at this time accepted as an authoritative Code, and is expressly ascribed to Moses? It says, in the law of worship which the critics appeal to as existing up to Josiah's time, and therefore prevailing in Isaiah's days: "An altar of earth thou shalt make unto me, and shalt sacrifice thereon thy burnt-offerings, and thy peace-offerings, thy sheep, and thine oxen."[2] Or if it is maintained that Isaiah condemned even that early piece of legislation, surely the argument here employed proves too much. For it would make the prophet condemn also the Sabbath as a piece of will-worship, and even reject prayer as a thing displeasing to God, since, in the same connection, he says: "The new moons and Sabbaths, the calling of assemblies, I cannot away with; . . . and when ye spread forth your hands, I will hide mine eyes from you; yea, when ye make many prayers, I will not hear."[3]

If we allow to Isaiah the perception of a difference between sacrifice as an *opus operatum*, and sacrifice as the expression of a true and obedient heart—and surely the prince of the prophets was capable of drawing such a distinction—his words have a defi-

---

[1] Wellhausen, p. 58.   [2] Exod. xx. 24.

[3] Isa. i. 13, 15. König (Hauptprobleme, p. 90) endeavours to make a distinction between "I cannot away with" (v. 13) as applied to the Sabbath, and "who hath required?" (v. 12) as applied to offerings; and says that a "cautious exegesis" shows that the things enumerated in vv. 11-16 were looked upon as matters of worship, coming in different senses and degrees from God. "Cautious" is scarcely the term that I should apply to such exegesis; for I doubt very much whether such fine distinctions ever occurred to the minds of the prophets.

nite and precise meaning, eminently suited to the times and circumstances in which he lived. If we take them as a statement in this bald form, of the history of religious observances in Israel, they are emptied of their ethical as well as their rhetorical force, and land us in a position which is incomprehensible in the circumstances. For what, is it conceived or conceivable, was the worship of a true Israelite in Isaiah's days? Is there any outward worship left that a man like Isaiah himself could take part in? Is this prophet to be refined away into a kind of free-thinker who stood aloof from all outward observances of religion, who "never went to church," as the modern phrase goes, because the whole of the ordinary service of worship was a mere human device? Or if a prophet might thus attain to a position independent of the outward aids of devotion, what of the common people? What worship is to be allowed to them at all, if all that went on at the Temple is condemned, and if the condemnation means what the critics say? For, be it observed, Isaiah is not indifferent to these things, as things that might be good enough for the vulgar, but were too gross for him. Whatever the things are to which he is referring, he refers to them with displeasure; and if there is a possibility of legitimate worship at all, we must regard his words not as a condemnation of that, but of the spirit in which it was performed, or of the abuses with which it was surrounded. A mere historical, unimpassioned statement as to the origin of sacrificial worship is out of the question.

Again, it has been said that the words of Micah, the contemporary of Isaiah, prove the same thing: " He hath showed thee, O man, what is good; and what doth the Lord require of thee, but to do justly, and love mercy, and to walk humbly with thy God? " (Micah vi. 8). Says Wellhausen, " Although the blunt statement of the contrast between cultus and religion is peculiarly prophetic, Micah can still take his stand upon this: ' It hath been told thee, O man, what Jehovah requires.' It is no new matter, but a thing well known, that sacrifices are not what the Torah of the Lord contains," [1] which is not a fair interpretation of the prophet's words, for the command to do justly and love mercy does not exclude a command to offer sacrifice. But this is the very prophet who, in almost identical terms with Isaiah, anticipates the time when the mountain of the Lord's house shall be exalted, and all nations shall flow into it. So that the argument, if pushed to its conclusion, would prove that these two prophets denied the divine authority of all outward observances of religion; and yet would ascribe to them the absurdity of maintaining great sanctity for a Temple and an altar, whose service was otiose or altogether improper.

In the same way appeal is made to the well-known declaration of Hosea, " I desired mercy and not sacrifice " (Hosea vi. 6). One would have thought that the prophet's meaning was made quite clear by the words that follow, " and the knowledge of God more than burnt-offerings." I confess I am aston-

---

[1] Hist. of Israel, p. 58.

ished that a passage like this should be insisted upon
by professional students of Hebrew; but it would
almost seem that, in their anxiety to establish a hypothesis, some can not only ignore poetry and sentiment in the Hebrew writings, but even shut their
eyes to plain matters of grammar and rhetoric. The
slightest reference to the usage of the language will
suffice to show how little worth is the argument
based on the text before us. When we read in Prov.
viii. 10, "Receive my instruction and not silver,
and knowledge rather than choice gold," we perceive
that the two forms of expression explain one another.
Who would conclude from the phrase "and not silver"
that it was absolutely forbidden in all circumtances
to take silver? Or again, when we read, "Let a
bear robbed of her whelps meet a man in the way, and
not a fool in his folly" (Prov. xvii. 12), does any one
conclude that it was of no consequence what became of
a man exposed to the attack of a wild beast, so long
as he kept out of the way of a fool? The prophet, in
brief, says only what Samuel said long before him,
"To obey is better than sacrifice, and to hearken
that the fat of rams," though the seer of Ramah
himself offered sacrifices as a regular religious observance. What he did, no doubt his successors in
the prophetic office countenanced; and there is absolutely no proof that, up to the time of Josiah, the
Temple at Jerusalem was a place at which no purer
service was known than that practised at the high
places. The writer of the books of the Kings, though
his testimony cannot be pressed here, had *some* good
reason for singling out certain kings who introduced

heathen corruptions into the Temple service, and instancing the attempts, successful or otherwise, to abolish them by others. To suppose that he acted arbitrarily in this matter is to criticise away his accounts altogether, and would leave us no assurance of the truth of even the account of Josiah's reformation. There is no reason to doubt that at certain times, and under the more faithful of the kings, the worship of the central sanctuary at Jerusalem was observed with something of the purity and regularity which were maintained after the time at which the critics allow the reform took place. To take the case of Isaiah, can any of the modern school tell us what led that prophet to clothe the vision of his inauguration to the prophetic work (Isa. vi) in the dress which he gives to it, and why, if the Temple service was full of abominations, its furniture and arrangements should have been chosen for the imagery of one of his highest flights of prophetic inspiration? What was the altar from which a live coal was taken, the touching of his lips by which was to purge his iniquity? One would have thought there was more need—if the modern position is correct—for the purifying influence to proceed in the opposite direction, from the prophet to the altar, and that the message delivered to the prophet should have been like that of the prophet against the altar of Bethel (1 Kings xiii. 2).

But we are told confidently that Jeremiah gives conclusive proof of the modern theory when he says (vii. 22): "For I spake not unto your fathers, nor commanded them in the day that I brought them out of the land of Egypt, concerning burnt-offerings or sacrifices : but this thing I commanded them, saying, Hearken unto my voice, and I will be your God, and ye shall be my people." Well, if we are bound at all hazards to take words literally, the words are literally true ; for, according to the account of Exodus itself the command in the day of the deliverance from Egypt was not a command in regard. to burnt-offerings and sacrifices. The people at that crisis had to make the grand venture of faith and obedience; and not till they were delivered and safe in the desert was there any " command concerning " a system of sacrifices. It is this idea that is working in the prophet's mind, though I do not believe he imagined for a moment that his words would be taken as a *historical statement* of the late origin of sacrifices, or of the time of its introduction at all. The polemic was not as to the *date* of introduction of sacrifice, but as to its rightful place and meaning. Jeremiah was not opposed to all ritual service, as Graf himself admitted. His words are just an expansion of the fundamental prophetic dictum of Samuel that to obey is better than sacrifice. The thing he is insisting on, as all the prophets do, is the utter worthlessness of sacrifices and offerings without the obedience of the life and the fidelity of the heart. And to make the words mean more is to make Jeremiah declare that up to his time there was no law for worship whatever, and yet worship at that period without authorised ceremonial and sacrifice is inconceivable.

(2.) On the other hand, we are told by the advocates of the modern theory that it was through prophetic influence that the Code of Deuteronomy was brought into existence and recognition, and that the movement once set agoing, resulted also in the codification of the Levitical law; that, in fact, the prophets seeking to give permanent form and authoritative sanction to their teaching, embodied it in the form of a code; that thus prophecy had its final development, but in reaching this development destroyed itself. Speaking of the manner in which the Deuteronomic Code was brought in, Wellhausen says : " With the tone of repudiation in which the earlier prophets, in the zeal of their opposition, had occasionally spoken of practices of worship at large, there was nothing to be achieved; the thing to be aimed at was not abolition but reformation, and the end, it was believed, would be helped by concentration of all ritual in the capital " (p. 26). He admits, indeed, that merely to abolish the holy places, and only to limit to one locality the cultus, which was still to be the main concern, was by no means the wish of the prophets—though it came about as an incidental result of their teaching (p. 23). This, however, seems to be hardly consistent with the preceding position; nor do I think it is reconcilable with a fair interpretation of the declarations of the prophets on the subject. The influence of the prophets cannot be said to have been at any time in the direction of the enforcement of external observances, except in so far as they urged the people to that change of heart which would result in such observances; and there is no proof from their own writings that they knew of any way of curing the **people's** godlessness but the exercise of repentance and **the** return to heart religion.

If there is any one class in the Old Testament history to whom we must accord the title of earnestness and sincerity of purpose, it is the prophets. The most superficial reader must perceive their deep religious devotion, their freedom from self-seeking and time-serving. It is difficult, however, to reconcile the admission of these qualities with the characters they exhibit and the parts they are made to play on the modern theory. Wellhausen, for example, attempts to prove that Isaiah never laboured for the removal of the Bamoth, but only for their purification;[1] although he himself tells us that all writers of the Chaldean period associate monotheism in the closest way with unity of worship (p. 27), and admits that Isaiah himself gave a special pre-eminence in his estimation to Jerusalem, and that "even as early as the time of Micah the temple must have been reckoned a house of God of an altogether peculiar order, so as to make it a paradox to put it on a level

[1] The reason given for this statement should not be passed over; it is characteristic of Wellhausen's method of proof: "In one of his latest discourses his anticipation for that time of righteousness, and the fear of God which is to dawn after the Assyrian crisis, is: 'Then shall ye defile the silver covering of your graven images, and the golden plating of your molten images; ye shall cast them away as a thing polluted: Begone! shall ye say unto them' (xxx. 22). If he thus hopes for a purification from superstitious accretions of the places where Jehovah is worshipped, it is clear that he is not thinking of their total abolition" (p. 25 f.) We will leave the circles in which " appreciation of scientific results can be looked for at all " (p. 9), to determine here whether the " accretions " are merely the plating of the images—as those who believe image-worship was the authorised religion would no doubt say—or the images themselves, as Wellhausen himself seems to imply (p. 46), in which case one would suppose there would be little use of these places of worship at all. Pyramids of "scientific results" are poised upon such precarious points, but I take it that Isaiah was not one to concern himself, like the scribes and Pharisees, with such distinctions (Matt. xxiv. 16-18). See before, chap. ix. p. 228; comp. p. 235 f.

with the Bamoth of Judah."[1] And yet these two
prophets are relied upon as leading witnesses to
prove that the whole ritual system was not only
without authority, but positively displeasing to God.
The question is whether the inconsistency is to be
attributed to the prophets or to be charged against
a vicious theory; for other prophets fare no better
at the hands of the critics.   For, let us come down
to Jeremiah, who was contemporary with the Deuteronomic reformation, and who has even been supposed to have had a hand in the composition of the
book or the Code.   We find that prophet, so far
from trusting to the mere acceptance of a written
code for reformation, going beyond any of his predecessors in the inwardness of his teaching.[2] He
has reached, finally, the conception of personal
heart religion as a thing far before a mere national
adoption of a national God, and speaks of the law
written in the heart.   How a person with such
views—not to speak of his conviction that law had
no divine sanction—should labour to elaborate a
book like Deuteronomy, and trust to its reception
to bring about the state of things he desired, it is
very hard to understand.   Or if Jeremiah did indeed help the introduction of Deuteronomy, he at
the same time went far beyond it in the unfolding of
its teaching; and what then becomes of the assertion, that the codifying of the law put an end to
the free activity of the prophets?   No wonder that
prophecy, in reaching this position, destroyed itself,
for the prophets had stultified themselves.   There is

[1] Wellhausen, p. 25.   [2] Jer. iii. 16; xxxi. 31 ff.

here an exhibition of inconsistency which requires explanation, and the explanation that is given is peculiar. "In his early years," we are told,[1] "Jeremiah had a share in the introduction of the law; but in later times he shows himself little edified by the effects it produced; the lying pen of the scribes, he says, has written for a lie (Jer. viii. 7-9)." To say nothing of the very doubtful determination of early and late in Jeremiah's utterances on this subject, we are asked to believe not only that the prophet had a share in the introduction of a code which pronounces a curse on those who shall not observe it, and afterwards turned his back upon all ritual law, but also that he allowed the book of his prophecies to go forth (Jer. xxxvi. 4, 5, 32) with the record of his inconsistency on its face. Had not the prophet of Anathoth trouble enough in his lifetime that he must be thus tortured in modern days? Or are we to say that a character so vacillating deserved all that he suffered? Yet Vatke would build him a sepulchre, by claiming him as the earliest witness for the late origin and unhistorical character of the Mosaic law.[2] It will hardly be denied that the prototype of modern critics is made to appear in rather a sorry character; for, if all this is true, he utters his own condemnation (Jer. xiv. 14). Again, it is not easy to comprehend how Ezekiel, pining over the low condition of his countrymen in exile, and reaching those spiritual intuitions expressed in his vision of the dry bones, and the

---

[1] Wellhausen, Hist. of Israel, p. 403.

[2] Bibl. Theol., p. 220 f.; Bredenkamp, Gesetz und Propheten, p. 106.

waters issuing from the sanctuary, should at the same time believe that the remedy for his people's misfortunes was to be found in a minute observance of ceremonial ordinances, and occupy himself with a codification—on a limited scale—of Temple ritual, as if the putting down of Levites and the putting up of priests was to bring about a national revival. Nor does he, in point of fact, represent things in that order. All these things are good enough when the people are of one mind in serving their Lord, and desire to give expression to their active religious life: they are absolutely powerless to produce such a life, as all the prophets well knew.

In order to perceive how the prophets stood to the law, we must take into account their whole position as religious teachers, and their relation to the religious movement of the nation. Kuenen, as we have seen in another connection,[1] insists upon the common ground on which people and prophets stood —viz., that Jahaveh was Israel's God, and Israel Jahaveh's people. This, he says, can be traced back to Moses himself, whose "great work and enduring merit" it was "not that he introduced into Israel any particular religious forms and practices, but that he established the service of Jahveh among his people upon a moral footing. ' I will be to you a God, and ye shall be to me a people.' So speaks Jahveh, through Moses, to the Israelitish tribes.[2] This reciprocal covenant between Jahveh and His people, sealed by the deliverance from Egyptian bondage, is guaranteed by the fact that the ark,

[1] See chap. xii. p. 307.   [2] Exod. vi. 7; Levit. xxvi. 45; Deut. xxix. 13.

Jahveh's dwelling-place, accompanies the Israelites on the journey in the desert, and afterwards remains established in their midst." [1]   Kuenen thus admits that there was a "reciprocal covenant between Jahveh and His people," sealed by a historical occurrence, and vouched for by the existence of a religious symbol. We have already argued (p. 338 f.) that such a covenant is inconceivable without some attendant ceremonial institutions; and at this initial point, it seems, we may find the explanation of the real attitude of the prophets to the law. Kuenen himself hints at it when he says, "On their part the people must remain faithful to the conditions of the pact concluded with Jahveh. These conditions are principally moral ones. This is the great thing. Jahveh is distinguished from the rest of the gods in this, that he will be served, not merely by sacrifices and feasts, but also, nay, in the first place, by the observance of the moral commandments which form the chief contents of the ten words." [2]   Quite so; and this is just what all the Biblical writers say. But why slip in this, "not merely by sacrifices and feasts," if these are not only not commanded, but actually wrong? There can be no doubt whatever that the people regarded sacrifices and ceremonies as observances well-pleasing to God, and signs of their adherence to the Covenant. It is doubtful how a people, situated as they were, could have kept up their recollection of the Covenant relation without outward service and ceremony. Have we, in this

[1] Relig. of Israel, vol. 1. pp. 292, 293.
[2] Ibid., vol. i. p. 293. Cf. Allan Menzies, p. 24.

nineteenth century, got so far that we can dispense with outward observances which we regard as divinely appointed or divinely approved? Or if the prophets disagreed with this deeply rooted feeling in the popular mind, inseparably linked with that conviction which Kuenen says prophets and people held in common, they not only fail to give us clear indications of the fact, but they are in opposition to the writers of prophetic spirit and to the prophetic men who guided the nation in early times. For from the very beginning sacrifice appears as a regular and acceptable expression of devotion. The earliest of all the codes, the book of the Covenant, occurring in a prophetic writing, and containing prescriptions of a ceremonial as well as of a moral kind, proves the close union of morality and observance from the first, and shows that, in the constitution of Israel, and in the conception of the nation, the two are inseparable. And if, according to Kuenen, the people were right in the matter of fact as to a covenant dating from the time of Moses, and had, from that time onwards, practised sacrifices and other observances as marks of their allegiance to their covenant God, it will require more than the citation of a few rhetorical passages to prove that the prophets regarded sacrifice and observance in themselves as wrong, or of mere human device. Kuenen himself, in the passage quoted from him, gives the key to the true exegesis of such passages : "Not merely by sacrifices and feasts, but also, nay, in the first place, by the observance of the moral commandments." The prophets are, in fact, in all such polemic, combating the germ of what became the monstrous doctrine of Rabbinism, that Israel was created in order to observe the law.

This attitude of the prophets to the law is exhibited in the circumstances of the time of Josiah which culminated in his reformation. When it is said that the worship of the high places had become so corrupt that a reformation was felt to be necessary, let us be careful to understand what that means. It was not that at many high places there was rendered to Jahaveh a worship which should have been rendered to Him at one central sanctuary. The worship of the Bamoth was part of a great national defection. The needed reformation had much more to do, as Wellhausen admits, than to gather into one central place all the abuses of many high places; and it is altogether a weak understatement of the case to say that "even Jerusalem and the house of Jehovah there *might* need *some* cleansing, but it was clearly entitled to a preference over the obscure local altars."[1] There was required above all things a reformation of *religion*, not merely of worship; and the prophets were not the men—Jeremiah certainly was not the man—to rest satisfied with anything else. The message of Huldah the prophetess, on the occasion of the discovery of the law-book, foretold "evil upon this place," "because they have forsaken me and have burned incense unto other gods, that they might provoke me to anger with all the work of their hands" (2 Kings xxii. 17). And so we see that the work done by Josiah was of a thorough kind; the co-operation of priests, prophets, and

[1] Wellhausen, p. 27.

people was indicative of a movement of the national conscience; and the evils put away are of a much more serious kind than merely the worshipping of Jahaveh at various high places. "The king commanded Hilkiah the high priest, and the priests of the second order, and the keepers of the door, to bring forth out of the temple of Jahaveh all the vessels that were made for Baal, and for the Asherah, and for all the host of heaven," &c., &c. (2 Kings xxiii. 4 ff.), beginning with a cleansing of the central sanctuary itself. And let it not be supposed that these were recognised up till this time as elements of the national worship. The book of the Covenant itself—which is supposed to have been in existence for two hundred years—had said, immediately before the words relied on as allowing the multiplicity of sanctuaries : "Ye shall not make other gods with me; gods of silver or gods of gold, ye shall not make unto you" (Exod. xx. 23); and had reiterated the warning against making "mention of the name of other gods" (Exod. xxiii. 13), and bowing down to the gods of the nations, or serving them, or doing after their works, but "thou shalt utterly overthrow them, and break in pieces their pillars" (Exod. xxiii. 24). These things were indeed thoroughly inconsistent with the whole position which—by the confession of the nation as implied in the prophetic utterances—Israel sustained to Jahaveh; and if the sin of them did not come home to them through prophetic rebukes or through their knowledge of the book of the Covenant, the discovery of a hundred other codes could not have convinced them. The truth is that the evils had pressed upon the hearts of good men for long before: Hezekiah had partially done what Josiah now did more thoroughly; and the powerful upheaval of public sentiment that was produced cannot have an adequate cause in a mere, or in a primary, desire to centralise the worship. In a word, the idea of worship in one place cannot be taken by itself and apart from the nature of the worship which Jahaveh claimed. The tendency towards reform was there before the alleged contrivance of producing a code was resorted to. The book did not produce what was the essential part of the reform; and the reform is quite conceivable on the supposition of the discovery of any code, and had already proceeded a great way before the book of the law was brought to light.

Nor were the circumstances materially different when the later reformation took place after the exile. The little community under Joshua and Zerubbabel had returned to Jerusalem, and held a struggling existence for more than half a century [1] before Ezra made his appearance with his book, which is said to have been the Pentateuch law now first come into existence. It was the sense of their national position and national calling that had brought them thither; they did not come for the purpose of observing a ritual law, but for the purpose of keeping alive a nationality and exhibiting their faith in the divine promises. This much the teaching of the

[1] Edict of Cyrus, 538. The return of exiles under Zerubbabel and Joshua was in B. C. 536, and twenty years later (Haggai and Zechariah) the Temple was consecrated. The arrival of Ezra was in 458. Law promulgated, 444. Cf. Wellhausen, p. 492 ff.

prophets had effected, though the fruits of prophetic teaching were tardy, and brought to maturity by the sufferings of the exile. I am willing to admit that the influence of Ezekiel was a powerful factor in leading to the restoration, but I see another direction of his influence than that of codification of law. As in a former chapter I maintained that the doubtful or figurative language of a writer should be interpreted by his clearer and more unequivocal utterances, so I should say here that we are to look not to the programme of legislation which Ezekiel saw in vision, but to the reviving Spirit, breathing upon the dry bones, as the motive power which was uppermost in the mind of the prophet of the exile.

The more closely the matter is looked at, the more clearly it will appear that it is impossible to dissever the moral from the ceremonial part of the law of Israel. Moses himself is represented as a prophet;[1] and prophecy has its legal, just as the law has its prophetical, side. The idea of holiness is common to both. The law links even the meanest ceremonial observance with this moral attribute: " Ye shall be holy men unto me, neither shall ye eat any flesh that is torn of beasts in the field; "[2] and prophecy recognises a clean and an unclean land and offerings.[3] Even the prophet who speaks most exclusively of the Holy One of Israel (Isa. lv. 5) expresses abhorrence of the eating of swine's flesh and so forth (Isa. lxv. 4; lxvi. 17). The rules for purifica-

---

[1] Deut. xviii. 15; Hosea xii. 13.
[2] Exod. xxii. 31. Comp. Levit. xi. 44-47; xix. 2, 15-19,
[3] Amos vii. 17; Hosea ix. 3-5,

tions and sacrifices indicate clearly, not only that these observances were of an educative character, but also that they did not come in the place of moral requirements, as if they were ends in themselves. The sacrifices and offerings do not effect atonement for moral offences, nor do they constitute the whole religious service of Israel. The sins atoned for are those that affect the theocratic relation of the people, the offerings are the outward signs of the inward homage due to Jahaveh. We need not, indeed, wonder that the prophets, in the situation in which they found themselves before the exile, laid so little stress on the ritual worship, for it was powerless to cure the evils which they deplored. To what purpose, indeed, would it have been for a preacher of righteousness like Amos, addressing a people who trampled on the most fundamental laws of humanity, to urge to the more sedulous performance of outward acts of worship; or for a prophet with insight into God's love such as Hosea enjoyed, to direct a people openly apostate and idolatrous in heart to begin with a mere reformation of cultus? Isaiah again and his fellow-prophets of the south had before them a people—such as all ages and all countries have produced—who thought to make up for wickedness of life and hollowness of heart by loud-sounding devotion and ostentatious worship; and it is no wonder that such men contemptuously scouted the whole system of outward observance, which was that and nothing more. It was needless to insist upon the sign when the thing signified was wanting —for the outward form was then a gross lie; and just because the mission of the prophets was to insist upon the underlying moral requirements of the law, for that reason they made light of its ceremonial elements, which had no basis nor reason for existence apart from these moral requirements. On the other hand, we find the prophet Haggai, when his contemporaries in the coldness of their devotion committed the opposite mistake from pre-exilic Israel, reproving them for the scantiness of their offerings; although both he and Zechariah, who laboured for the restoration of the Temple and its service, are quite clear as to the supreme duty of heart religion and the inutility of a mere *opus operatum*.[1] The position of Malachi is to be particularly noted, because in him we find a distinctly ceremonial tone (chap. i.), and because he belongs to the time of the alleged introduction of the Priestly Code. It is very hard to believe that a priesthood such as he chides (in chap. ii.) was fit to be trusted with the task of elaborating an authoritative code.[2] It is much more likely that the prophet reproves them for deviation from a standard that was far older and much higher. In any case it is to be observed that this prophet, though technical as any priest could be, is at one with all the prophets as to the essentials of religion.

It is inaccurate, therefore, to represent the prophetic and priestly classes as opposed, and to make the history turn upon the preponderance of the one over the other. There was no greater antagonism

[1] Haggai ii. 12 f.; Zech. vii. 6, 9, 10.
[2] Bredenkamp, Gesetz und Propheten, p. 120.

than that which in a normal condition of things exists between the inner truth and its outward manifestation—which, however, becomes pronounced
when the outward expression is made the whole, or
is represented as having the vitality and the importance of the inner truth. Such times there were in
the history of Israel, as in the religious history of all
nations, when the priesthood, peculiarly liable to
settle down to formality and routine, and peculiarly
liable to the temptations besetting any privileged
order, encouraged the people to boast, saying, " The
temple of the Lord are we," or even exercised their
office for their own gain. At such times the prophetic voice was raised in scathing rebukes, whose
terms almost lead one to conclude that in the prophetic estimation the whole priestly order, and all
the ceremonies over which they presided, were in
their essence wrong. Yet even in the midst of such
rebukes there is a tone of respect for the law, and a
recognition of the sacred function of the priest. So
also when we come to any crisis in the history in
which a positive advance is made, we perceive that
it is not by a conquest of one party over the other,
but by the hearty co-operation of both, that the
movement of reform or advance succeeds. Moses,
the forerunner of the prophets, has Aaron the priest
beside him; and Joshua is still surrounded by priests
in the carrying out of his work. Samuel is both
priest and prophet; David and Solomon in the same
way are served or admonished by both. In Josiah's
time we see the priest Hilkiah as eager for the introduction of reform as the prophet or prophets who

prepared—as is alleged—the Code which was to be recognised;[1] although the Code was not to be to the advantage of the Jerusalem priesthood, according to the modern view of it, for it was to bring to the capital all the priests of the high places who should so desire, and thus reduce the emoluments and lower the prestige of the ministers of the central sanctuary. Jeremiah was of the priests of Anathoth, and Ezekiel, too, was a priest-prophet. So that at every turning-point in the nation's life, when an advance was made, or a return to a better mind, the two classes are seen working in harmony. Which is just saying in other words that the better mind resulted in a better life, and that faithfulness of heart was expressed in the better observance of the authoritative forms of religion.

On this subject, as on many others connected with the history of Israel, we must beware of concluding that distinctions which we can abstractly draw, and of which the history shows the possibility, were actually drawn at the time. "The passion of the human mind," says Dr. A. B. Davidson, "is for distinctions and classification. Broad distinctions are rare in the Old Testament. The course of revelation is like a river, which cannot be cut up into sections. The springs at least of all prophecy can be seen in the two prophets of northern Israel; but

---

[1] And so some would have it that the Code is a composite work. "The Deuteronomic *torah*," says Cheyne, "is in fact the joint work of at least two of the noblest members of the prophetic and the priestly orders."—Jeremiah, His Life and Times, p. 63 f. One may obtain, from this, some idea of the critical principles on which the separation of sources is effected, and may be inclined to ask, if two writers of different tendencies could work so harmoniously here, why similar tendencies should be put so far apart elsewhere.

the rain which fed those fountains fell in the often unrecorded past." [1] On reviewing the history we may perceive the two currents of influence, the priestly and the prophetic, and in analysing the combined stream of national life we may be able to separate them in thought and assign different effects to them respectively. But we are not for all that to jump to the conclusion that priests and prophets were arrayed in hostile camps, and existed like two parties in a modern state. The prophets are as free in their denunciations of prophets when these are unfaithful, as they are in their rebukes of the excesses of the priests. The truth is, that on this low view of a struggle of parties, the history of Israel is as devoid of interest, as it is incapable of explanation. When it did come to a struggle of parties in Israel, in the later stages of the history, when some leaned to Egypt and some to Assyria, the days of Israel's independence were numbered. The thing that made two parties in *ancient* Israel was not the question of ritual or no ritual, not the question of written Torah or oral Torah, but the question of fidelity to their national God, and purity from heathen contamination. The daily observances of the Temple might go on unrecorded for years— as I believe they went on far more regularly than is now supposed—and call for no remark. But as soon as these were rested in as the essentials of religion, or improved and adorned by a tampering with heathen ways and an aping of idolatrous rites, then the prophetic voice was raised, and in such

[1] Expositor, third series, vol. vi. p. 163.

terms that we perceive how all the time these men knew wherein the essentials of true religious worship consisted.

Though, therefore, the legalistic tendency set in after the great prophets had done their work, the two things were not cause and effect. It was not the " prophets that were the destroyers of old Israel," but it was Israel that destroyed itself. A mistake may be very readily committed from taking too narrow a view of development, and assuming that what is immediately subsequent to something else results naturally from it. There are *re*-actions and recoils as well as direct influences in the same line. The true succession of Old Testament prophets is found in the Gospel, not in the scribes. Though Jesus Christ followed the scribes, He did not develop their teaching. He did not, however, deny its historical basis. He was the direct successor of the prophets, but He assumed and took for granted that law preceded prophecy, and that law was also of divine authority. From His polemic with the scribes and Pharisees of His day, one might hastily claim Him as maintaining the human origin of the Codes, and the natural basis of sacrifice. Yet, though He rejected the traditions and commandments of men, He attended even to the ceremonial of the law, and in His life and teaching treated the law as given through Moses by divine authority.

CHAPTER XVIII.

CONCLUSION.

*The modern theory is "thorough-going," but does not do jus-
tice to the facts of the case—Its arbitrary treatment of the
writers and books of the Old Testament—Its weakness
"as a whole," when great crises and turning-points are
to be explained—Does not go to the core of the religion,
but dwells on external details—Rejecting the supernatural,
it is itself unnatural—Even on its literary side, not so
strong as it seems—Objection to the Biblical theory that it
does not make room for development—Objection answered:
true development exhibited—The appeal to religions of
"primitive peoples" considered—The Semitic disposition
to religion—Reference to early chapters of Genesis—Comparative religion—Bearing of the whole subject on Inspiration.*

WE have thus endeavoured to estimate fairly the
two theories of Israel's earlier religious history.
No attempt has been made to present all the details
in which the theories are opposed; but consideration
has been fixed on the fundamental lines and underlying principles. Our conclusion has been, that the
Biblical theory, when not burdened with assumptions
with which it has been often "traditionally" encum-
bered, will stand the test of a sober and common-
sense criticism, as an account of the existence in

Israel, in early or so-called pre-prophetic times, of very distinctive religious conceptions and religious ordinances, obtained in connection with well-marked historical events and under well-determined historical conditions.

The modern critical theory, if it has been able to point out difficulties connected with the Biblical theory, especially as it has been traditionally maintained, raises difficulties of a much more serious kind in the way of its own acceptance. At first sight, it has all the attractions of a "good-going" hypothesis; for it promises to exhibit the growth of religious conceptions and religious observances from the lowest stage to their finally developed phases; and, considering the long course which Israel's history ran, and the broad field available for observation, this is what we should expect to find practicable. But the theory is too thorough-going, for it goes in the teeth of evident obstacles, and refuses to bend its way to embrace plain facts; and what we want is a theory that will give the best explanation of things that cannot be disputed. Were it the case that we knew practically nothing of the development of Israel's religion in Palestine, it might be very well for a theory to sketch a scheme which would be another contribution to the histories of religious thought. But there are books, there are men, there are abiding effects to be accounted for; and in face of these the modern theory shows its weakness. We have conducted our inquiry on the narrowest possible grounds, by restricting ourselves to compositions whose dates are assigned by the critics

themselves;[1] and on that narrow ground I am prepared to rest my objections to the two cardinal points
of the theory.   On the one hand, I maintain that the
earliest writing prophets, Amos and Hosea, give
clear evidence that the ethic and spiritual nature of
the religion was apprehended and firmly possessed
in their day, and long before it—evidence which can
only be set aside by a forced interpretation of some
passages and an excision of others.   On the other
hand, I maintain that the existence, at what is
called the earliest literary age, of these same books
and likewise of the book of the Covenant in the
heart of a Jehovistic writing, ascribing to Moses
authoritative and specifically religious institutions,
relating to sacrifice and ritual as well as idolatry
and morals, is irreconcilable with the fundamental
positions of the modern theory on the subject of law.

Wellhausen, in one place, says it would not be
surprising, considering the whole character of the
polemic against Graf's hypothesis, if the next objection should be that it is not able to construct the
history.[2]   My great objection to the theory is, not
that it cannot construct a history, for the ingenuity
of critical writers is equal to that, but that it does
not leave sound materials out of which a credible
history can be constructed.   The hypothesis of Graf
carries with it the assumption that the narratives
accompanying the laws of the Pentateuch are not
history in the proper sense of the word at all, but
the product of late imaginative writers, and, in
short, fictitious.   And not only are the narratives of

<hr>

[1] See Note XXXI.   [2] Hist. of Israel, p. 367, footnote.

the Pentateuch so treated; the historical and prophetical books are in a similar manner discredited,
so as to be admissible as testimony only after they
have been expurgated or adjusted on the principles
of the underlying theory. The historical books, we
are told, were written long after the events they
relate; and even when they contain the records of
historical facts, these records are overlaid with later
interpretations of the facts, or even glossed over to
obliterate them. Even the prophetical books are not
to be relied upon to determine the religious history;
for the books, in the first place, have undergone
great alterations in the process of canonisation—and
in the second place, even where there is an unam-
biguous declaration of a prophet as to a certain sequence of events, it is open to us to accept or reject
his statement on "critical" grounds. Modern critical writers, in fact, can scarcely lay their hands on
a single book and say, Here is a document to be relied upon to give a fair, unbiassed, untarnished account of things as they were. The blemishes that
criticism seeks to remove are not such as may be
contracted by ordinary ancient documents in the
course of their literary transmission. They have
come into the documents in the interests of a theory
(and indeed they have a wonderful coherence in
tenor), and by another theory they are to be eliminated. The literary task of critical writers, therefore, is not so much to discover and account for
facts of a history long past, as to account for the account which later writers give of them. The history
which Wellhausen constructs is in fact a "history of

the tradition "; and in many cases it seems a laborious endeavour to show how something very definite grew out of nothing very appreciable.   The further one follows the processes, the more apparent it becomes that the endeavour is not so much to find out by fair interpretation what the writer says, as to discover his motive for saying it, or what he wishes to conceal.   He belongs to some class, or has some political expediency to serve; or he lives in a circle of certain ideas, and these *tendencies* are made to give birth to the facts, instead of being, as is more likely, the result of the facts.   " The idea as idea is older than the idea in history," says Wellhausen;[1] and he is continually applying this maxim in the sense that when an idea takes possession of the leading men of a certain time, they straightway proceed to invest it with a historical character, by placing its exemplification or embodiment back at some remote period of the history.   I think the maxim is better illustrated im the processes of Wellhausen and his school, who first find an " idea," and then seek by main force to read it into the unwilling documents. In this way a history is no doubt constructed, but the supporting beams of it are subjective prepositions, and the materials are only got by discrediting the sources from which they are drawn.

I say this is a very serious attitude to assume towards the writers of the Old Testament books, if it can in any degree be justified; and if it is not well justified, it is a very serious objection to any theory that requires it.   The men who moulded the

[1] Hist. of Israel, p. 36.

history of Israel were the men who had most to do
with the production and preservation of the national
literature. We know what sort of men they were.
But, on the modern theory, the greatest characters
in Israel's history, instead of being spontaneous actors in a great life-drama, are merely posturing and
acting a part on a stage. What they give us as history is merely their fond idea of what history should
have been; in many cases it is not even so much, but
pure invention to give a show of antiquity to what
had to be accounted for and magnified in their own
day. History was never made in this way. Men
that make history such as Israel's history was, are
intent on great purposes, moved by noble ends; but
what we are asked to contemplate at the great crises
and turning-points is a set of men thinking how
they will elaborate a scheme of history. Fictions
become the greatest facts, and the French critic has
carried out the theory to its true conclusion when he
ascribes the great bulk of the Hebrew literature to
the free creation of a school of theologians after the
exile. "The theologians and writers of that time,"
he says, "have been able to give such a character
of life to the creations of their genius that posterity
has been thereby deceived, and has believed in a
Moses living 1500 years before our era, whereas
this Moses was only created in the fourth century,
and had no more reality than an incomparable fiction." [1] And thus the great merit of the Hebrew

---

[1] Maurice Vernes, Résultats de l'Exégèse Biblique, p. 227. Of course
the conclusions of Vernes are disowned by the prevailing school, but
the *principle* of his criticism, the imagination of writers of the exilian
age, is frankly avowed by Wellhausen, p. 419. See Note XXXII.

race, the great quality for which they have distinguished themselves in the world, is their power of imagination! Such a mode of viewing the Old Testament writings, as the conduct of the critics shows, leaves individual critics to construct each his own scheme of the history. To most people it will appear that, if such a mode of treatment is once introduced, the inquiry into the true course of Israel's history is a matter of the utmost uncertainty; to many the inquiry would probably cease to have much practical interest.

It is to be lamented, I think, that now at the very close of the nineteenth century a tone of criticism should reassert itself which is out of harmony with the liberal views with which we have been priding ourselves we had learned to regard all nations. So much has our knowledge of the religions of the world extended, and our sympathy for the struggles of the religious instinct been stirred, that we might expect from leaders of investigation in these subjects a disposition to look for the best side of all religions, and to put the most favourable construction on the efforts of their founders. It is not so long ago that it used to be the orthodox thing to characterise the prophet of Arabia as a designer, a schemer, an impostor; but it had come to be generally admitted that, in his early struggles at least, Mohammed was a sincere inquirer, following out lines of thought and belief that existed in a somewhat narrow circle before him. Kuenen, however, has practically come back to the old position. According to this view, Mohammed had an eye to

Christians and Jews, and counted upon the latter particularly for recognition of his teaching. And so he framed his device of that *milla* of Ibrahim, of which at first he never thought, for " the opinion that Mohammed came to awaken and to restore what already existed amongst his people, if only as a faint reminiscence of a distant past, finds no support in the Qoran when read in the light of criticism." [1] Great is criticism of the modern critics! It has discovered another *scheme*, like the schemes and programmes and fictions of the Hebrew writers. And so the boasted enlightenment and toleration of the nineteenth century comes round again to explain the origin of religions by the fanaticism of prophets and the frauds of priests. [2]

But, it is said, the theory must be taken as a whole, and apart from varieties of opinion that may be held on details. It is just when thus taken that I find the greatest difficulty in accepting it, because there is so marked a disagreement between the whole and its component parts. There are certain great outstanding facts whose existence cannot be ignored,—such as the prophetic activity in Israel, the belief in one national or one sole Deity, the national testimony to an early history of great moment, the ascription of legislation to Moses; and the incompetence of the modern theory to set these in their true perspective is very striking. On the one hand, the Biblical theory gives definite con-

---

[1] National Religions, p. 19.

[2] A melancholy example is furnished in Lippert's ' Allgemeine Geschichte des Priesterthums,' published as recently as 1884. König, Falsche Extreme, p. 2.

nections for events, and historical occasions for transitions and advances. On the other hand, the modern theory is strong in minute analysis, but weak in face of great controlling facts. It will laboriously strain out a gnat in the critical process of determining the respective authors of a complex passage, but when it comes to a real difficulty in history it boldly swallows the camel and wipes its mouth, saying, "I have eaten nothing." Nabiism, or the prophetic activity, even Jahavism itself, are borrowed from the Canaanites or Kenites; and when it is asked why the Canaanites or Kenites did not reach the same truth that Israel attained, we get no answer. And when we ask what then had Israel to distinguish it, the feeble answer is returned that when Israel (for no reason stated) assumed Jahaveh as their national deity, they also resolved and were told that He only (for no reason assigned) was to be their only God. And when the undoubtedly pure and high conceptions entertained by the prophets are pointed out, and an explanation demanded of their origin, we are told that a "conception" was "absorbed" by the prophets and came out in this purified form; but we get no sufficient account of the faculty that enabled the prophets to absorb this and that, and give forth a product which is entirely unlike the thing absorbed. In the same way no satisfactory account is given of the ascription of law to Moses, and no firm basis for the various Codes. The theory is, again, strong in details of analysis, but weak in face of a historical event. No explanation is given of the origin of what is de-

clared to be the first of all the Codes. When a
great reform of religion such as took place in Josiah's
days has to be explained, instead of historical criticism reconstructing an intelligible historical situation, we are shown how a book was constructed
which brought it about. Though all the scathing
rebukes and denunciations of the prophets up to
this time had been powerless to wean the people
from their idolatries, the production in some secret
conclave of this book, telling unheard-of stories
about Moses, and laying down on his authority laws
which were then partly impracticable, rouses a
whole nation. And again, in the captivity, after the
Temple had been destroyed and the people scattered
for their sins, the main thing the best of them
think about is the gathering together of the ritual
practices of the priests, and, instead of being hum-
bled for their transgressions, imagining ever so
many great things their nation had been and done
in the early ages. Upon the strength of this a
colony braves the hardships of a long journey from
Babylon to Jerusalem to set up the worship which
they had agreed was the right ritual to practise.
This falling back at every stage upon the introduction of some new factor, which does not grow out of
the history itself, but is made to give a turn to the
whole history, is artificial. Jahaveh, introduced
from the Kenites, becomes the distinctive deity of
Israel. Prophetism imitated from the raving of
Canaanites becomes the glory of Israel. Codes of
laws, gathered up from a haphazard praxis or devised as reforming schemes, become so sacred that

the nation will battle for them as for existence. In short, we are promised the exhibition of a course of development, and at decisive turning-points the theory of development fails. It may seem at first sight remarkable that there should be so much consensus of critical opinion in regard to these outstanding and testing points of the history. But if we look more closely we shall observe that, after all, the consensus is confined to the underlying postulate, which of course controls all the details. The theory itself is clear and thorough enough, and of course it hangs together as a whole. But it does not hold the parts together, because it does not supply the proper nexus that unites them in an orderly historical development. There must be a bond of a more vital fibre, a force more deeply inherent, which the modern theory has not penetrated to nor unfolded, to account for a religious and spiritual movement, which, looking to the broad field on which it is displayed and the diversified circumstances under which it took place, is nothing short of majestic. The self-styled "higher" criticism is indeed not high enough, or, we should perhaps more appropriately say, not deep enough for the problem before it.

The strongest objection, in fact, to the theory "as a whole" is, that it hardly at all touches the religion round which the whole history properly turns. Superstition there has always been among all peoples, and no doubt there was much superstition mixed up with the popular religion of ancient Israel. But religion is not necessarily superstition, nor does it necessarily flow from it in natural development. Unquestionably there was among the best souls of the nation of Israel in early times—and these may have been a larger proportion of the people than we generally suppose, as the answer to Elijah (1 Kings xix. 18) in his day indicated—a strong current of true religious life, to the fountains of which we must reach, if we would understand this wonderful history. To this aspect of the subject, however, the modern theory pays far too little regard. Take, for example, the treatment of the book of Psalms now in vogue in the higher circles of criticism. One would have thought that if anywhere the inquirer into the history of religious thought and life would find valuable "sources," it would be in this collection of the sacred and national songs of Israel. But Wellhausen, for example, who boasts that he could understand the history of Israel without the book of the Law, can also dispense with the book of the Psalms. In the "index of passages discussed" appended to his 'History of Israel,' there is only one reference to one psalm (Ps. lxxiii.), which too, of course, is placed very late in date. I think it a positive objection to the theory, not so much that it brings down the bulk of the psalms to post-exilian times, but that it is able to dispense with them as materials for a history of the older religion of Israel, and to relegate them to a time at which, according to its own showing, the religion had taken a more mechanical and formal phase. It is now the fashion to speak of the Psalter as the psalm-book of the second Temple, in the sense, not that it is a collection of older religious compositions brought together by the piety of a later generation, but that they were composed purposely for use in public worship. Thus, by one stroke, the tongue of ancient Israel is struck dumb, as the pen is dashed from its hand, these art-less lyrics are deprived of their spontaneousness, and a great gulf is fixed between the few which a nig-gardly criticism admits to be of early date, and the full volume of devotional song which in many tones was called forth by the shifting situations of olden times. Of course the hypothesis of a low religious stage in pre-exilic times demands this, but it is an additional difficulty which the theory raises in the way of its own acceptance; for even if the psalms are late, the influence that started and produced them must lie early and must lie deeper than in legal ordinances and formal ceremonies. So far as concerns their higher tone, which is supposed to mark a late date, it is not higher than what we meet with in the very earliest writing prophets. In the glowing periods of these prophets we have unmistakable evidence of the deep religiousness that suffused the minds of those who from the first guided the religious life of the nation. But all that side of the early religious history—and how much is that all!—might almost as well never have existed, for all that the modern his-torians make of it. The deep spirituality of Hosea, who stands, like the Saviour of mankind, weeping over Jerusalem, full of the very love of God; the strong ethical tone of Amos and his enthusiasm for God; the lofty aspirations of Isaiah for righteous-ness, and his rapt visions of future glory,—these

surely are not isolated phenomena in the centuries
that rolled over Israel when all that is best in the
history was being achieved, but indicate a strong
under-current of perennial religious life. Yet for all
these, even taken in their isolation, how little sympathy do our modern critical historians exhibit!
Whereas Ewald, in a past generation, came to the
Old Testament books with a sympathetic spirit, and
Delitzsch in our own generation, with a piety par-
donable in the circumstances, heard in these prophetic voices the echo, thrown backward over the
centuries, of the Gospel of Christ, we get nowadays
some dry analysis of the "idea" and the "conception" of each prophet, and a grudging doling out of
the attributes of might and holiness in the character
of God, and reluctant admissions of nascent monotheism here and there, but we catch no fire from the
prophetic words as they are weighed and measured
out in the scales of the critics.[1]   These men, whose
words are the fittest found even yet to express all
that we can think loftiest of God, are represented as
groping after the idea of one God, contending for
the honour of a deity that is little better than a
Chemosh or a Moloch; and when they cease to
write and become men of action, they are set before
us as moved by paltry motives of expediency, up-
holding the dignity of their order against the priest-

[1] Wellhausen must needs even belittle the impression of sublimity
produced by the account of the Creation in the first chapter of Genesis.
He is generous enough to admit that "the beginning especially is incomparable." But "chaos being given, all the rest is spun out of it:
all that follows is reflection, systematic construction; we can easily
follow the calculation from point to point" (Hist. of Israel, p. 298).   He
could have done it himself in short.   Instead of the artless gestures
of a child we have the stiff movements of a Dutch doll.   But is it the
Hebrew writer or the modern critic that is wooden-headed?

hood, or conspiring with them to bring about a masterly movement for the concentration of religious worship directly under their own supervision. Feasts, sacrifices, incomes of the clergy, in such things, and in the centralisation of the worship at Jerusalem, the history of religion is made to consist;[1] but the *heart* of the religion is hardly looked at, or rudely torn out of it.

So that, when all is said and done, the impression on the mind of an unprejudiced reader certainly is that there is more in the religion of Israel than the modern historians are able to see or willing to acknowledge. Let their literary analysis be ever so thorough, one who will read the Old Testament books as he would read any other ancient documents, must remain convinced that justice is not done to them by a criticism which ignores their most characteristic element. The critics object to the Biblical theory that it relies so much on the supernatural: the characteristic feature of their own is the unnatural. The Biblical theory says there was a course of history quite unprecedented, or certainly most extraordinary; the modern theory says that the history was nothing remarkable, but there was quite an unprecedented mode of imagining and writing it. There have to be postulated miracles of a literary and psychological kind, which contradict sound reason and experience as much as any of the physical miracles of the Old Testament transcend them.

Even in what is its strong point, literary analysis,

[1] See Wellhausen, pp. 13, 27.

I do not know that the modern theory is very for-
midable if the underlying historical postulates are
not granted. Let us suppose for a moment that it
is possible on purely literary grounds to separate
different portions of the Pentateuch books, and
pronounce them to be from different hands. It is
still confessed [1] that the relative positions and dates
of these portions cannot be determined from themselves. Only when the theory of the historical development is introduced do the original sources or
diverse components fall into the places assigned to
them in the scheme. But if the theory of the development can be shown to be so far untenable that
what is pronounced by it late may well have been much
earlier, then the arrangement and dating of the
parts are open to revision. As to the critical process of separating the sources as literary products,
I regard it as a matter of secondary importance, so
long as we are able, by the help of the prophetic
writers, to determine in a general way that the
books in their combined form are trustworthy documents, and that the views they set forth are not unhistorical. It may be open to question, however,
whether the separation has not been carried too far,
and in a manner somewhat arbitrary and artificial.
When we find a real character in flesh and blood in
Hebrew history, we find him capable of entertaining
more than one idea in his mind, and even sustaining
apparently incompatible relations, as Samuel, who
offered sacrifice, and yet seems to scout it as useless.
I think it is most probable that the men who wrote

[1] Wellhausen, History, p. 10.

the component parts of these books were representative and public men, not mere "priests" here or "prophetic men" there. I do not know, indeed, that the main "sources" of the Hexateuch differ more in style or substance among themselves than do the synoptic Gospels. And most certainly there is an over-driving of critical processes in the historical books when narratives are cut up into contradictory parts, because some character in the story is represented as actuated by different motives at different times, or playing parts which either are or seem to be inconsistent.

But let it be granted that the "sources" of the Pentateuch books have been pretty accurately determined, or let the very highest value be given to the results of critical analysis, there is one remark that occurs in regard to them. We have seen good reason for believing that the art of literary composition does not begin about the time of the first writing prophets, but was then well advanced. It seems to me that the existence of these "sources" of the critics proves the same thing and proves more. There they are, combined, at a very early period of literary composition—J and E at least—so inextricably that they cannot be separated, to say nothing of the redaction, whether by the Deuteronomist or another. Now we are continually being told that in ancient times there was no literary copyright, and that the possessor of a book considered himself entitled to treat it as his own, by adding to it or incorporating his own materials with it; and that in this way we might get such combinations as these books exhibit. It is said also that the earliest writings must have been of a private or personal character—*i.e.*, not stamped with such authority as canonical writings came to possess. Now, when we look at the component parts of the Old Testament writings, as the analysis of criticism exhibits them, there is nothing that strikes us more forcibly than the care that was evidently bestowed in preserving even minute parts of separate documents. It may be, as is generally supposed, that when, *e.g.*, J and E had a passage in common, the redactor who combined them adopted the one and excluded the other; but the obstinate way in which minute fragments, even single words, of the one intrude into the other, where presumably there was some slight divergence or additional detail, and this in the case of all the sources or redactions, leads us to the conclusion that even at that early time when these sources were combined, there was a regard for literary copyright.[1] Whether this is consistent with the idea that these sources were private documents is not very certain. One would think that the writing of the history of the nation on the broad scheme (comparatively) on which these writers proceed, was not left to private and irresponsible men—at least was not undertaken by any or every one who cared to do it. We should most naturally look for the authors of such writings, when great writers were rare, among outstanding and responsible men.

---

[1] Horton, in speaking of one so late as the author of the books of Chronicles, says, when he had different authorities before him, he " preferred leaving them unharmonised to tampering in any way with the facts. "—Inspiration and the Bible, third edition, p. 160.

This whole aspect of the matter would almost lead
to the conclusion that the germ of a canon existed
much earlier than is generally asserted. Especially
if, for J and E and the like, we substitute the
names of prophets or theocratic men, who guided
the nation's religious life and interpreted its history,
it will not be so evident that our earlier Scriptures
were left to the haphazard emendation of every
private hand into which they came.

But now, if the knowledge of God in a pure form
is to be placed so far back in history, and made to
start with a simple revelation to Abraham, what becomes of development? Well, in the first place, the
modern theory also has to postulate a starting-
point; and, we have seen, its difficulty is marked
when it seeks to place the absolute commencement
of a spiritual religion at a late period. But, in the
second place, the Biblical theory is more conspicuously a theory of development than the modern one.
It makes the advance of the religious idea really an
unfolding of a germinal conception, not an advance
from one attribute to another, as from might to holiness, but an expansion of one fundamental conception into wider references and application. And it
is a development marked by historical stadia. From
the Being who made Himself known to the soul of
Abraham, and from that time onward was the covenant God of one nation, faithful to His word, even
though His people should be unfaithful on their part,
we can trace an unbroken development to the God of
all the families of mankind. For if He defends His
own people from their enemies, and is at the same

time a merciful God to His own, the idea follows, and we see it early, that His enemies, by submitting to Him and casting in their lot with His people, will share in His people's blessings, and thus the God of Israel will become, in fact as well as of right, the God of all. Strictly speaking, the Old Testament writers never got beyond the idea of national religion. Though they perceived that Jahaveh ruled all nations, and acted on strictly moral and just principles towards all, they never conceived that there was no difference between His relation to Israel and His relation to the nations. In point of fact there was a difference, as history has proved. Even in New Testament times, we see how hard it was for the apostle Peter to perceive that God was "no respecter of persons, but that in every nation he that feareth Him and worketh righteousness is accepted with Him" (Acts x. 34, 35). St. Paul also had to fight hard for the position that "circumcision is nothing, and uncircumcision is nothing, but the keeping of the commandments of God" (1 Cor. vii. 19), and to the last had to contend for the truth that the God whom he preached was not the God of the Jews only, but also of the Gentiles. The highest that the Old Testament prophets attained to was an anticipation of a condition of things under which, through Israel, blessing would come to the whole world; it was again an expansion of this when, in the New Testament, the middle wall of partition was broken down, and all who have the faith of Abraham, whether they be his seed or not, shall share in his blessing. The devel-

opment here is unbroken; and though the history
shows, as all history does, action and reaction, yet
there is an onward advance from beginning to end.

Thus from Abraham on to the close of national
independence there was a regular and steady development, the idea of Jahaveh and the conception of
what His religion implied undergoing a steady expansion in the prophetic teaching, aided by the political events through which the nation passed. The
revival of the time of Ezra was a new starting-point,
or, as we may better express it, the course of development had come round by a wide cycle to a new
starting-point; for all historical movement is of this
kind, in cycles which come back again upon themselves and follow apparently the same path, though
on a higher plane. What happened in Ezra's time
was this: An attempt was made, on the basis of the
experience of the past, to live the national life over
again under new conditions. What had been already
achieved was gathered up; the national life, instead
of having primarily a promise of a future, fed itself
on the recollections of the past; it closed around the
results of the former prophetic activity, and sought
to conserve what had been attained, as the starting-
point for a new round of experience. There is in the
plant a similar cycle of life: the flower blossoms and
then decays; but before it has fallen, it has developed the seed which is to be the life of a coming
season; and though we may think that the plant has
completed its period of life, this is not so if it has
matured the seed which has vitality in itself for future growth. The hard and dried seed-pod is not so

attractive an object as the fair blossoming flower, but it not only is the result of the past, but has also promise for the future. And if, to preserve the figure, the period of the Talmud exhibits men amusing themselves at play with dried peas, yet these seeds were not dead, and many even in the Talmudic period recognised their vitality. And when, finally, the fulness of the time was come, the seeds which had fallen on dry ground shot forth with new and more beautiful life: the truths reached by men of old time, which had been treated as so many dogmas or formulæ, were seen to be truths endowed with perennial life. The teaching of the prophets, and the fond beliefs of the people, that Jahaveh would ever be Israel's God, were illustrated in a new and striking manner in Him who was raised up an horn of salvation in the house of David, and the anticipations of the time when Gentiles should come to the light of Israel, were fulfilled when the wall of partition was broken down, and it was shown, in the light of the Gospel, that Abraham was father of all that believe, whether they be Jews or Gentiles.

But M. Renan objects: This makes the religion of Israel a thing that has no beginning—a thing as old as the world—a supposition which, from his point of view, is not for a moment to be entertained. And from him and from others we hear the reiterated appeal to "primitive peoples," "rudimentary ideas," and so forth, with the implication that the progress of Israel's religious life must be made to square with the progress found in other nations. To all which our simple reply is—In point of fact it was not the same; the modern theorists themselves are bound to admit as much within the sphere of which they say we have authentic information. And there is the other fact, patent in history, that other primitive peoples, and even peoples of the same Semitic race, never got to the stage, or anything approaching the stage, that the Hebrews reached. In view of these plain facts in the world's history, it is simply trifling to insist upon making Israel's history square with that of all other peoples. The Oriental of the present day has a very expressive answer to all such arguments. He simply extends his hand, and says, " See; are the fingers of the hand all of one length?" In the matter of religion we are not to be guided by the degree of " culture " to which a nation has attained, or justified in speaking of early and late at all. The Egyptians and Assyrians were far in advance of the Israelites in civilisation and outward culture, but they are not to be compared with them in the sphere of religion. Renan himself has pointed out how the simple nomad is far in advance of the settled inhabitant of the city in religious experience. The history of the world would seem in a striking manner to confirm the Biblical statements that man cannot by searching find out God; that the world by wisdom knew not God. While the most acute philosophers and thinkers of Greece were reasoning about these things, the simple-minded Hebrews had reached a firm position from which they never receded, and from which the whole thinking world, as from a starting-point, has had to advance.[1] It is all

[1] Bredenkamp, Gesetz u. Propheten, p. 13.

very well for us *now*—when the light shines—to formulate our arguments for the existence and character of God; for we know what we want to prove. But the fact that reasoners by reason did not succeed in proving it till the Hebrew race had made it known to the world, and the other fact that *they* did not reach it by a process of reasoning or reflection, or adding on of one attribute to another—these facts show that such a knowledge is given with more direct force, and in a more complete form. What seems, in fact, hard and laborious to us with our logical categories and subjective processes, seems to have come instinctively to the Abrahamic race; and even Stade has admitted that if there was not precisely an instinct of monotheism in the Hebrews, they, above all others, showed a predisposition to it.

In this connection it is interesting to recall an incident mentioned by F. W. Newman,[1] from his own experience as a missionary. "While we were at Aleppo," he says, "I one day got into religious discourse with a Mohammedan carpenter, which left on me a lasting impression. Among other matters, I was peculiarly desirous of disabusing him of the current notion of his people, that our Gospels are spurious narratives of late date. I found great difficulty of expression; but the man listened to me with great attention, and I was encouraged to exert myself. He waited patiently till I had done, and then spoke to the following effect: 'I tell you, sir, how the case stands. God has given to you English a great many good gifts. You make fine ships, and

[1] Phases of Faith, second edition, 1853, p. 32 f.

sharp penknives, and good cloth and cottons; and you have rich nobles and brave soldiers; and you write and print many learned books (dictionaries and grammars): all this is of God. But there is one thing that God has withheld from you and has revealed to us; and that is, the knowledge of the true religion, by which one may be saved.'" Newman adds: "When he had thus ignored my argument (which was probably quite unintelligible to him) and delivered his simple protest, I was silent and at the same time amused. But the more I thought it over, the more instruction I saw in the case." For my own part, I have much sympathy with the opinion expressed by the Moslem carpenter. He is a type of many that are to be found in the humbler ranks of society in the East at the present day, who are little qualified to follow a connected argument, but to whom religious conceptions of a high order come as a matter of course. Such men, doubtless, were those who wrote and who read many of the books of the Old Testament; and hence the books themselves, though subjected to the most harassing criticism, and characterised as "spurious narratives of late date," smile at all such criticism, and give forth with confidence their testimony to a faith, which is independent of time, and indifferent to modes of literary composition.

Our investigations have been confined to the history of Israel as *a nation*, and the conclusion I have come to is that the history, as told by the Bible historians, is credible in all the essential points at which we have the means of testing it. The Biblical view carries back the national life and the national religion to Abraham, and so far as we are able to check the accounts, we have found that without this assumption the history cannot be explained. In other words, from the 12th chapter of Genesis onwards, we conclude that we have a credible and trustworthy account of the leading events and crises of the history of Israel. As to the antecedent eleven chapters of Genesis, the matters therein treated do not fall properly within the scope of our present inquiry. They do not constitute part of the history of Israel, strictly speaking, though in the Biblical writings they are made to lead up to it and give a basis for it. These accounts of primitive and primeval times, if we place them, simply as ancient documents, side by side with the early traditions and cosmogonies of other nations, are, as has been universally admitted, characterised by a sobriety, purity, and loftiness of conception which render them altogether unique. If we should set them down as merely the attempts on the part of the Hebrew writers to give an account of origins of which no historical record was in their hands, merely the consolidated form of legends and myths handed on from prehistoric times, we cannot but recognise the singular line that myth-making took in this particular case, as distinguished from the cases of polytheistic Semitic and non-Semitic races. Such myths, if they are to be so described, are not born in a day; even if the writer of the earliest of them is set down as late as the eighth or ninth century before Christ, the folk-lore, if you will, of his people was of quite a unique character before it could furnish such materials; and the writer of them must already have formulated to himself, to say the least, a very definite philosophy of history, and had a much broader conception of the world and of its relation to God, than we should expect from one in the primitive stage of religion. As compared with the earliest formulated accounts of creation and primeval times contained in Assyrian literature, they are pervaded by an entirely different spirit, emancipated from bonds of polytheistic notions, and moving altogether on a higher plane. If we find, as have been found, correspondences of a remarkable kind in the Hebrew and other early accounts of the creation, and so forth, we must not, as has too often been the practice, jump to the conclusion that everything which Hebrew literature and tradition have in common with those of other nations must be borrowed by the Hebrews. Why should the Hebrews borrow from every side, and yet retain something so clearly distinguishing them from each and all of the others? Why should we not admit a common primeval tradition, when it is thus attested by independent witnesses? Nay, seeing that the Hebrew tradition, at the very earliest point at which we can seize it, is purer and loftier than any other, why should it be at all incredible that in that race, from pre-Abrahamic times and in the lands from which the faith of Abraham was disseminated, there were found purer conceptions of God and deeper intuitions into His character and operations than we find elsewhere— glimmerings of a purer faith which had elsewhere

become obscured by polytheistic notions and practices? Do not the results of the study of comparative religion tend to show that even polytheism is an
aberration from a simpler conception, and that the
lowest forms of nature-religion point to a belief in a
Being whose character always transcends the forms
in which the untutored mind tries to represent Him,
and is not summed up in all their attempts to give
it expression? That being so, why should it be a
thing incredible that in one quarter, a quarter which
in the clear light of history is found to stand sharply
defined from its surroundings, the souls of the best
should have kept themselves above these degrada-
tions, and nursed within themselves the higher,
purer, more primary conception; and that this
should have taken shape in the faith of Abraham, or,
if we state it otherwise, formed the basis on which
the purer faith of Abraham was reared? This will
not seem incredible to any who believe that there is
but *one* God, and that He has been the same from
the beginning. It is only a statement in another
form of St. Paul's words, that God has never left
Himself without witness; and it is quite in keeping,
I believe, with the best results of the comparative
study of religions.

In the foregoing chapters, I have carefully ab-
stained from making any appeal to the authority of
New Testament Scriptures. The first and fundamental question is, not whether the modern theory
agrees with our Christian religion and our Confession, but whether it agrees with sound sense and
sober reason. If the theory is to be held as proved

on these solid grounds, our views must be adjusted
in regard to it.   I cannot help adding, however, that
if the postulates and methods of this kind of criticism are to be admitted, a good many other things
besides our views of Old Testament history will require to be readjusted.   The question may be put to
a good many who seem disposed to accept the
modern critical treatment of the Old Testament,
whether they are prepared to allow the same processes to be applied to the New.   I would seriously
ask those Christians who regard Stade's ' Geschichte'
as a successful exhibition of the religious history of
Israel, to ponder the application of the *same principles* of criticism to the life of Jesus Christ in the second volume of that work.   So far as I can see, the
arguments used in the one field may be employed
equally well in the other, and the Gospel history be
critically reconstructed out of the tendencies and
views of the second century, just as the account of
the pre-prophetic religion given by the Hebrew
writers is made the result of the projection backward of later ideas.

Just because the issues in this controversy are so
far-reaching, is it necessary to meet the critical view
on its own ground, and to examine the foundation
on which it rests.   Questions are involved that lie
much deeper than those of the verbal inspiration or
the so-called " inerrancy " of Scripture.   It seems
to me vain to talk of the inspiration and authority
of books till we are sure that they are credible and
honest compositions, giving us a firm historical
basis on which to rest.   My whole argument has

been to show that, examined by the light which they themselves furnish, these books are trustworthy documents; that the compositions which are un-doubted and accepted give their testimony to those that are questioned or rejected; that the books as they lie before us, so far as they can be tested by the only tests in our possession, and making all allowance for the ordinary conditions of human composition and transmission of books, give us a fair and credible account of what took place in the history and religious development of Israel. If that point is allowed to be in a fair way established, I leave the argument for inspiration and authority to take care of itself. The picture which the books present, if it is admitted to be in any sense an adequate representation of fact, will probably be sufficient to convince ordinary Christian people that in ancient Israel there was a divine control of events, a divine guidance of the best spirits of the nation, a divine plan in the unfolding of the history, which we may sum up by saying there was a divinely guided development, or, as it has been expressed,[1] that the history itself is inspired. How far such a description, in any specific sense, may be given of the history as it is represented by the theory I have been combating, I leave its advocates to determine. I should think, however, that that is the very *mini-mum* of any theory of inspiration worthy of the name. I should think, moreover, that those who do regard the history of Israel as divinely guided and inspired in a sense altogether different from other

[1] Horton, Inspiration and the Bible, p. 171.

ancient history, instead of underrating as a vague
or negative result such a conclusion as it has been
my endeavour to establish on the bare ground of
historical criticism, ought to rejoice if, with even a
degree of probability, it can be made out.   **M.**
Renan would indeed have us believe that the idea
which animated ancient Israel, and was carried
over into Christianity, is played out, having received
its death-blow at the French Revolution, when certain thinkers came to the conclusion that there was
no Providence controlling the events of man's world,
no God who is to be the judge of man's actions.[1]
Instead of hailing with pleasure such an emancipa-
tion of the human spirit, we ought gladly to wel-
come any help that comes to the aid of faith in such
a God as the patriarchs and prophets are represented as making known—a God whose revelation
of Himself has been advancing with brighter radi-
ance, till it culminated in the manifestation of His
Son Jesus Christ, who was the "light to lighten the
Gentiles, and the glory of His people Israel. " Such
a faith as Old Testament prophets possessed has
been the blessing and the guide of the best of mankind in their achievement of the best up till this
hour; such a faith is more than ever needed just at
the present moment, to save the human race from
losing respect for itself, and to rekindle hope and
aspiration for the future.   The choice has to be
made, in the last resort, between such a faith and
"the divine pride of man in himself," which, we

[1] Souvenirs d'Enfance et de Jeunesse, p. 337; Histoire du Peuple
d'Israel, tome i. pp. 27, 40, 41.

are told, is to be "the radical foundation of the new religion. "[1]   And even the volatile Frenchman himself has said: "It is not impossible that, wearied with the repeated bankruptcies of liberalism, the world may yet again become Jewish and Christian."[2]

[1] Walt Whitman, Democratic vistas (Camelot Series), p. 65.
[2] Histoire du Peuple d'Israel, tome i. p. vii.

NOTES.

Note I. vol. i. p. 7.—English readers naturally expect that scholars should be able, by mere linguistic features, to arrange the Old Testament books in chronological order; and find it difficult to understand how, in the matters of language and style, there should be so little appreciable distinction between books dating centuries apart. That the fact is so, is sufficiently proved by the various dates assigned by different critical scholars to the same compositions. What used to be regarded as the earliest of the (large) components of the Pentateuch, is now by the prevailing school made the latest, and the linguistic features have not been considered a bar to either view (see p. 46). The uniformity of the language of the Old Testament is partly explained by the fact that the ancient mode of writing only the consonants did not provide for the preservation of those variations in vowel-sounds which usually mark the history of languages; and when, at a late period, a system of vowel-points was adopted, a uniformity in this respect would be the result. The English reader must not, however, conclude that there is no difference observable between early and late productions. The books of Daniel, Ezra, and Nehemiah betray their later date by the presence of the so-called Chaldee portions; and the book of Ecclesiastes, as Delitzsch has said, must be placed late, else there is no history of the Hebrew language at all. The books of Chronicles indicate their lateness even by the matter. Still, in the great mass of the Hebrew literature there are no sure linguistic landmarks denoting definite literary periods. It must be admitted that in this, as in other respects, the East is more stationary than the West; and it is therefore somewhat misleading to compare long periods of our own history with the same number of *years* in Hebrew history (as is done, *e.g.*, by Horton, in 'Inspiration and the Bible,' third edition, p. 143). A modern Arabic author will write in the style of an ancient classic, without subjecting himself to the charge of pedantry; and the uniformity of the style of Assyrian documents is remarkable. When once a certain style for a certain subject is fixed, it tends to stereotype itself; and one author may be master of more than one style. At all events, the determination of separate authorship does not, as a rule, go far to the determination of date. Cf. below, Note XXVI.

Note II. vol. i. p. 23.—M. Renan's estimate of the historical sciences, to which his life has been devoted, is not very high: "Little conjectural sciences, which are unmade as fast as they are made, and which will be neglected a hundred years hence." With his sneer at the "ugly little Jew" (St. Paul) who was unable to understand the goddess whom Renan on the Acropolis addressed, may be contrasted the declaration of Heine in his 'Confessions': "Formerly I had no special admiration for Moses, probably because the spirit of Hellenism was dominant within me, and I could not pardon in the lawgiver of the Jews his intolerance of all types and plastic representations. . . . I see now that the Greeks were only handsome youths, while the Jews were always men, powerful, indomitable men." See 'Wit, Wisdom, and Pathos from the Prose of Heinrich Heine,' by Snodgrass, second edition, p. 256 f.

Note III. vol. i. p. 25.—Tiele in his 'Kompendium der Religionsgeschichte,' § 3, thus lays down the fundamental lines of the whole subject: It is probable for various reasons that *primitive* religion, which has left but few traces, was followed by a prevailing period of animism, which is still found in the so-called *nature-religions* (or, as he prefers to call them, "polydemonistic-magical tribal religions"), and which, at a still early period among civilised peoples, was developed into *polytheistic nation-*

al religions, resting on traditional teaching. At a later time there arose out of polytheism, here and there, *nomistic* religions, or religious communities based on a law or sacred writing. In these polytheism was more or less overcome by *pantheism* or *monotheism*, in the last of which are found the roots of the *world-religions*. All this, as is pointed out by Tiele's French translator (Maurice Vernes, L'histoire des Religions, p. 42), is very much a repetition of Auguste Comte's famous trilogy, fetishism, polytheism, monotheism; with this difference, that Tiele and his followers regard monotheism as a permanent religion, while Comte and his school regard it as destined to give place to positive philosophy. It is plain, moreover, that, starting with a determination of what is to be found, the inquirer will be strongly tempted to find it, at the expense, it may be, of sober interpretation of facts.

Note IV. vol. i. pp. 30, 47.—Writers of the critical school are in the habit of attacking what they call the "traditional theory." With this, however, we need not concern ourselves, except in so far as it is found in the Biblical writers. The O. T. writers have a theory, and it is enough that we examine it, especially as the advanced critics tell us plainly that it is erroneous. (See Kuenen, National Religions, p. 69 f.) Whether Robertson Smith gives an exact statement of the traditional theory (O. T. in Jewish Church, p. 208 ff.) I am not prepared to say. I agree with him, however, that the position assigned to the prophets, in the theory as he sketches it, is not consistent with the declarations of the prophets themselves (p. 216). My whole contention is, that the Biblical writers do not bind us to any theory or view of the mode of composition of books, whatever may have been "traditionally" inferred or taken for granted in the matter; but as to the sequence of events, and the religious significance of events, their language is plain and emphatic. It is with that language, and the view it expresses, not with traditional interpretations of it, that we have to deal.

Note V. vol. i. p. 37.—Vatke, from whom Wellhausen "gratefully acknowledges himself to have learned best and most" (Hist.

of Israel, p. 13), says that Moses must be measured by his time, and that it is impossible that an individual should rise suddenly from a lower to a higher stage and raise a whole people with him; so, though an individual may out of weakness fall back to a lower level (as to idol and image worship), yet this is impossible in the case of a whole people, if the consciousness of the unity of God was actually alive. As to the age of Moses, according to whose standard the lawgiver is to be measured, Vatke denied to it even the knowledge of writing (Bibl. Theol., 179-183). Ewald, on the other hand, speaking of the time of Moses, says: "A new power was in that distant age set in motion in the world, whose pulsations vibrated through the whole of antiquity," &c. (Hist. of Israel, Eng. transl., vol. ii. p. 169); and F. C. Baur says that Mosaism must ever be regarded as a great religious reform, a renewing and restoration of a purer religion, periodically obscured and threatened with a still deeper obscuration (in Studien und Kritiken for 1832).

Note VI. vol. i. p. 47.—The classical passage in the Talmud (Baba Bathra, 14 b.) contains really all that the rabbins had of tradition on the subject of the authorship of the Old Testament books; and it is so obscurely expressed that it is evident the tradition, whatever it was, was mixed up with crude guesses of their own. The passage is given by Strack in the Herzog-Plitt Encyklopädie, vol. vii., art. "Kanon des Alten Testaments." It is also given in English, and discussed by Briggs, Bibl. Study, p. 175 ff.

Note VII. vol. i. p. 51.—During the Egyptian war of 1882 there was a newspaper edited by an intimate associate of Arabi, and circulated widely among the *fellahín* and those favourable to Arabi's cause. It gave most circumstantial and minute details of his operations and glowing accounts of his victories. The readers of this paper believed, for example, that a midshipman who lost his way on the sands somewhere near Kefr Dawár, and was taken prisoner, was the admiral of the British fleet; and their belief was encouraged by the attention bestowed on the prisoner, and the state in which he was made to live in one of the palaces. They also believed that Arabi's troops had many successful engagements with the British; and, as a native writer says, had the sum of the British reported as killed been added up, it would have amounted to ten times their whole actual number (Scottish Review, April 1887, p. 386). A copy of this paper, dated a day or so before the battle of Tel-el-Kebir, was picked up in the trenches by a British soldier, and used as letter-paper to write to his friends at home. I had the good fortune to see it, and I found it full of the most extravagant accounts of the doings of the rebel army on the very eve of its discomfiture. What would a future historian make of a complete file of this paper?

Note VIII. vol. i. p. 59.—It is not necessary for us to enter into critical questions as to the composition and the original "sources" of the various books; but a brief statement of the chief critical conclusions and designations is here desirable. The oldest of all the historical authorities recognised by critics are those songs, or poetical pieces, which presumably had their rise in connection with stirring events, and were, in the first instance, handed down orally. The song of Deborah, says Stade, bears traces of having been composed under the immediate impression of the victory it celebrates, and it is usually appealed to as one of the oldest sources of historical information. The Hexateuch (*i.e.*, the six books Genesis to Joshua) is regarded as one great composite work, within which several large component parts (to say nothing of redactional matter) of different dates are distinguishable. The book of Deuteronomy may be set aside as a part by itself with well-marked features. There remain two larger sources, capable again of minor subdivision. The first of these in historical order is a story-book, now usually designated (after Wellhausen) J E, having been originally two books, one (J) characterised by the use of the name Jahaveh, the other (E) by the use of the name Elohim, the former belonging probably to the southern kingdom, the latter to the northern. They are both of prophetical or popular character. Wellhausen's school makes J the earlier, placing it in the middle of the ninth century B.C., while E would fall not later than 750 B.C. Both of these may have incorporated older sources, and may both have been originally of larger compass; they are now so closely joined together that a separation of them in their original entireness may be considered impossible. This combined source J E is often designated the Jehovist, to distinguish it from J, the simple Jahvist. The other great component part of the Hexateuch used to be called the Grundschrift or Fundamental Writing, because it was regarded as the earliest main source, a sort of backbone about which the other parts were grouped. Its first portion is the opening chapter of Genesis, and in the remainder of that book those portions that are headed "these are the generations," &c., belong to it, and hence Ewald called it the "Book of Origins." It was also called the "Older Elohist," to distinguish it from the Elohistic story-book, now called E. The main portion of it lies in the middle books, particularly in Leviticus, and from this part, which is its most striking feature, this source is now usually denoted by P.—*i.e.*, Priestly source. Wellhausen thinks that the kernel of this work was, what he designates Q (=*quatuor*, four), a work containing the four covenants (Gen. i. 28-30, ix. 1-17, xvii.; Exod. vi. 2 ff.) This great source is now regarded, not as the underlying fundamental document, but, so to speak, the final encircling framework, which held all the others together in a systematic scheme, and in date it is declared to be exilic. Some critics recognise more, some less, pre-existing material within its own proper domain; and it need not be said, the views as to the processes by which the whole composite Hexateuch grew to its present form, vary considerably (see chap. vi. p. 155 ff.) As to the other historical books, the books of Kings bear on their face that they were composed in the time of the exile (whatever earlier materials they may embody). In 1 Kings vii.-viii., Wellhausen recognises marks of the influence of the (still later) Priestly Code (Hist. of Israel, p. 280). The book of Judges, besides an introduction (i. 1-ii. 5) and an appendix (xvii.-xxi.), is made up of a number of stories, recounting the exploits of local heroes. These stories, however, are set in a framework, said to be from a different hand, explaining in stereotyped phrase how the various oppressions came about, how the deliverer was raised up, and how long the effects of the deliverance lasted. The chapters at the end (xix.-xxi.) Stade calls a "tendency romance," fully in accord with the Priestly source (Gesch., i. p. 71). Wellhausen, however (Hist., p. 237), does not make this portion so late as P. C., with the exception of one reference to the "congregation," and the mention of Phinehas. So he says (Hist., p. 256) that 1 Sam. vii., viii., x. 17 f., xii., betray a close relationship with those chapters of the book of Judges.

Note IX. vol. i. p. 85.—The hieroglyphic system is found in perfection on the monuments of the 18th and 19th dynasties—*i.e.*, earlier than the exodus. But by that time it was a venerable system; for remains of monuments from even the 4th dynasty exhibit a character essentially identical with that found in the inscriptions of Thothmes and Rameses. Budge, in speaking of the cover of the sarcophagus of Menkau Ra (or Mycerinus), of the 4th dynasty (dated by Brugsch, 3633 B.C.), says: There is little difference between the shape of the hieroglyphics of those days and those of a much later date; and however far we may go back, we never come to an inscription belonging to a period in which we can see that the Egyptians were learning to write (Dwellers on the Nile, p. 63). In 1847 was published by Prisse a facsimile of a papyrus found in a tomb of the 11th dynasty (*i.e.*, some centuries earlier than Moses). Old as it is, it is a copy of an original work composed by a writer of the 5th dynasty; and, to crown all, the original author, who is an old man, laments over the good old times that are gone. A translation of Pentaur's poem by Professor Lushington is contained in Records of the Past, first ser., vol. ii. p. 65 ff. Comp. Budge, Dwellers on the Nile, chap. v. It is interesting to note that it exhibits the system of parallelism which is so characteristic of Hebrew poetry, and has other resemblances to the lyrical and prophetical style of the Old Testament.

Note X. vol. i. p. 129.—How very early the Messianic expectation had taken a precise form may be gathered from the way Amos speaks of the "day of Jahaveh" (v. 18-20.) This expression, which appears so prominently throughout prophetic literature, was evidently by his time in common use to denote "a good time coming." The polemic of the prophet implies this, as it also teaches the fundamental conception of the "cycle" of history to which reference is made above, vol. i. p. 130.

Note XI. vol. i. p. 138.—Robertson Smith says: "That the division of Israel into twelve tribes did not assume its present shape till after the conquest of Canaan, is recognised by most recent inquirers" (Kinship and Marriage in Early Arabia, p. 219). Stade tells us that no historical recollection goes back to the time of the entrance of the Israelites into Western Palestine (Geschichte, i. p. 147); that there were never twelve tribes at one and the same time, but sometimes more, sometimes fewer, and that only by artificial means was the number twelve made out (a number found in the similar legends of other peoples), either by leaving out Levi, or by making Ephraim and Manasseh one. The system, he says, is due to the priests, and grew up at the sanctuaries to confirm the general system of patriarchal legends (p. 145). We may conjecture, he says, that a system once prevailed, according to which the tribes were represented as the *wives* of Jacob, for the names Leah, Rachel, Zilpah, Bilhah, are to be taken as names of Hebrew tribes. Independent of this there must have been a genealogy representing the tribes as *sons*, as is apparent from the fact that Leah is just another form of Levi; but the legendary cycle which knew the tribe of Levi in the form of Leah, wife of Jacob, knew nothing of the legend which represented it as Levi, the son of Jacob, and *vice versâ* (p. 146). Moreover, the principle of genealogy must have crossed other systems of division, particularly the geographical system, by which tribes contiguous in situation were represented as consanguineous. Yet, after allowing himself all this latitude and choice of explanations, Stade cannot, *e.g.*, account for the fact that Reuben, an insignificant tribe, was made the firstborn (unless, perhaps, as he suggests, it was just *because* this was an insignificant tribe, put forth, so to speak, as a neutral-coloured figure-head to allay the jealousies of the two great rival tribes, Judah and Ephraim). Nor can he explain why Zebulon and Issachar (northern tribes) are grouped with Judah under Leah, and Asher (west) with Gad (east) under Zilpah. It seems also an extraordinary statement to make, that the circles which knew of Levi and Leah as the son and wife respectively of Jacob, knew nothing of the legendary beliefs of one another; for one would suppose that if the tribal genealogies were preserved anywhere, it would be in the tribe concerned; and yet one part of the tribe, on this supposition, would not know what the other part thought of themselves. It seems to me, that to place the formation of all this legendary matter, as Stade does, in the time of the divided monarchy (p. 147), is not justifiable in the face of the song of Deborah, nor consistent with his own position stated elsewhere (p. 396), that the monarchical system, by concentrating power, struck at the religious system on which tribal formation rests, not to speak of the opposition of the Jahaveh religion to the same ideas. In other words, the system requires longer time to grow, and presupposes a much more primitive condition of society than his assumption implies. Much more may this be said of the explanation, favoured by Robertson Smith, of the tribal system by the belief and practice of totemism, on the ground of the animal names of some of the tribes (Kinship, &c., *l.c.*) The last-named writer claims to have pointed out that the name Sarah or Sarai corresponds as closely with Israel as Leah does with Levi; and argues hence that, as Abraham was originally a Judæan hero, we have an explanation how Sarah (= Israel) was Abraham's sister before she came to be called his wife and the mother of Israel and Judah alike (ibid., Note XI. to chap. i., p. 257). The great difficulty is to find *room* for the development that all this implies within the firm historical limits prescribed by our written documents. The personality of the patriarchs, as tribal heads, is not inconsistent with a growth of tribes by accretion, as modern Arab practice shows. The Biblical theory, placing a long period between the patriarchs and the exodus, allows room for this; but Stade does not, by ascribing the tribal formation and the growth of the legends to the times succeeding the invasion of Canaan. As to a tribe not knowing its father, as he asserts, see an article by Curtiss in Expositor, third series, vol. vi. p. 328 f. Stade's assertion that no historical recollection goes back to the time of the entrance into Canaan, is met by the concurrent testimony of all the sources, and the clear voice of the earliest writing prophets, to the effect that Israel came out of Egypt.

Note XII. vol. i. p. 142.—Yet the only passage in which Abraham appears as a warrior (Gen. xiv., in which the rescue of Lot is described) is relegated by Wellhausen and Kuenen to post-exilic times, and declared to be quite unhistorical. The chapter is a veritable *crux* for modern criticism; it will not allow itself to be classed with any of the main sources, and so Kautzsch and Socin print it in a type by itself (Die Genesis, mit äusserer Unterscheidung der Quellenschriften). Wellhausen declares that it may be described, like Melchizedec, as "without father, without mother, without genealogy." Critics of a more moderate type (as Schrader, Dillmann, and Kittel) regard it as an old independent piece (perhaps borrowed from a native Palestinian source) taken up by E. To which Wellhausen replies that this is the last document to which it should be assigned, since in E Abraham is represented as a "Muslim" and a prophet, but never a warrior. Neither, says he, does the glorification of Jerusalem (the southern sanctuary) suit E, a northern story-teller. Most probably, he concludes, the final redactor who united J E with Q, took up this recital, which had no connection with the antecedent and subsequent context (Composition des Hexateuchs, pp. 26, 310). So Kuenen calls it a 'post-exilic version of Abram's life, a Midrash (Hexateuch, sect. 16).

Note XIII. vol. i. p. 149.—H. G. Tomkins, in his 'Studies on the Times of Abraham' (Bagster, 1878), has brought together much interesting matter, drawn from recent archæological research. Reference may be made also to Deane's 'Abraham; His Life and Times,' in the "Men of the Bible" Series. It is time that an extreme criticism, which will persist in representing Israel as groping its way out of the most primitive ideas, while civilisation prevailed around them, should bend to the force of facts which are multiplying every day. What has been done in the field of Homeric studies should not be without its lesson to Biblical students.

Note XIV. vol. i. p. 192.—Robertson Smith (Religion of Semites, first series, p. 92 ff.) has an ingenious discussion of the original signification of *baal*, in which he relies much on the Arabic expression (baal land), which denotes land nourished by subterranean waters. Whether his conclusion be right or not, it is evident that a good deal must have happened before a god under the earth beneath became the chief god in the heaven above; and also that by the time we reach the stage of conception of the earliest Hebrew writing (not to say language), in which "baal means the master of a house, the owner of a field, cattle, or the like," we are very far indeed from the original Semitic conception, if, indeed, that order of development took place at all. In this very learned work there are too many sudden leaps from primitive notions of Semitic peoples to such an advanced stage of thought as is represented by the prophets. In my opinion, the work would have been as valuable a contribution to our knowledge of the *common* Semitic religion, and much less confusing and inconsequent, had the author not proceeded on the assumption that the theory of the history of Israel set forth by Wellhausen and Kuenen is established, or, as he states the matter, that the researches of writers of that school have "carried this inquiry to a point where nothing of vital importance for the historical study of the Old Testament religion still remains uncertain" (Pref., p. vii.) The precariousness of the philological argument, so much employed by him, is seen in the fact that expressions illustrating what are claimed as primitive beliefs are found as frequently in undoubtedly late as in early writers. In the Archæological Review (vol. iii., No. 3, 1889) there is an article on Totemism by Jos. Jacobs, who comes to the conclusion that, although not only certain names of Edomite and even Israelite tribes, and also prohibitions of food, family feasts, and so forth, possibly allow the inference of pre-existing totemism, there cannot be a thought of "its actual existence in historic times." And it is with historic times that we are concerned.

Note XV. vol. i. p. 193.—The name Elohim, which is a plural form, has been taken by many to prove that polytheism was the original belief of the Hebrews. Baudissin (Studien zur Semit. Religionsgesch., Heft I. p. 55 ff.) says that the plural designation of God can only have arisen through the ascription to One of all the powers that resided in different deities. To which Baethgen (Beiträge zur Semitischen Religionsgeschichte, p. 132 ff. and p. 297) objects that this is to give to the word an origin in pantheism, of which we have no trace in any Old Testament writer; and that if the God of the Israelites were only the sum of all other gods, he could not be set over against them nor over them. As to the idea that the plural form may have been a summing up of all the gods or divine powers which *Israel* acknowledged, he objects that, in that case, we should have expected to find traces of the names of such other supposed gods, and also to find a singular noun to denote one of the Elohim. The singular word Eloah, which at all events is poetical and rare, he supposes to be a later formation from the plural which was in common use. Max Müller tells us (Selected Essays, vol. ii. p. 414) that no language forms a plural before a singular; but it cannot be denied that in this instance the singular form is little used, and the plural word is used not only to denote the "gods" collectively of the nations, but even to denote any one of these (see Judges xi. 24; 1 Sam. v. 7; 1 Kings xi. 5; 2 Kings i. 2, 3, 6, 16; Isa. xxxvii. 38) as well as the one God of Israel. Baethgen emphasises the striking fact that Israel, from whom in any case monotheism came, is the only Semitic people which employs this plural form of the divine name, whereas all the other Semitic nations have a singular name for deity, even though they were polytheists (ib., p. 139). If the name did not indicate from the beginning a plurality of majesty or of attributes, it can at most only be taken as a proof of primeval or primitive polytheism; but it cannot be taken as a proof of polytheism after the time of Abraham. Robertson Smith is inclined to believe that the idea underlying the plural Elohim is that of "vague plurality in the conception of the Godhead as associated with special spots, . . . and that not in the sense of a definite number of clearly individual deities, but with the same indefiniteness as characterises the conception of the *jinn*" (Religion of the Semites, first series, p. 426). This seems to be the sense attached to the word by M.

Renan, who describes the Elohim as "myriads of active beings very analogous to the 'spirits' of savages, living, translucid, inseparable in some sort the one from the other, not having distinct proper names like the Aryan gods" (Histoire du Peuple d'Israel, i. p. 30). If this be the original sense attached to the name, it is not the sense as given by the Biblical writers to their national deity within the times of which we speak; or if the Israelites at the time of the prophets or from the time of Moses believed in the existence of such beings as are here described, they evidently ranked them as very inferior to the national God.

Note XVI. vol. i. p. 203.—The expression "the Lord of hosts" (Jahaveh Cebaoth) is found in a double sense in the Old Testament writings. The "hosts," in the one case, are the armies of Israel (Exod. vii. 4, xii. 41, 51; compare 1 Sam. xvii. 45) whom Jahaveh leads to victory; and this use is found in the early historical books, having apparently arisen or been stimulated by the military experiences of the early history. In the prophets, however (see, *e.g.*, Hos. xii. 5), we see that the expression was no longer, or no longer simply, limited in reference to armies, but included the heavenly host, the stars and angels. So the LXX. often render by the word $\pi\alpha\nu\tau\sigma\kappa\rho\acute{\alpha}\tau\omega\rho$. (See art. Zebaoth in Herzog-Plitt, Realencykl., vol. xvii. p. 427.) Sayce's remark might give the impression that the latter use is the more original, and some have concluded that this reference is primitive. Against this view, however, has to be set the fact that the expression seems to have come into use in connection with military exploits. Kautzsch has pointed out (in Stade's Zeitschrift für Alttest. Wissenschaft, 1886, p. 17) that in the connections in which it occurs in the early historical books, it either is closely associated with the ark, the symbol of Jahaveh's leadership, or otherwise has a warlike reference. König has also pointed out (Hauptprobleme, p. 50) that the host of heaven is denoted by the singular word, not by the plural Cebaoth. In the prophetic (and as he concludes later) use, this plural designation embraces both the earthly and the heavenly hosts.

Note XVII. vol. i. p. 208.—For a thorough-going treatment of the Old Testament on the mythological method nothing can surpass the work of Goldziher (Mythology among the Hebrews, translated by Russell Martineau), who explains the characters in Genesis and Judges almost uniformly as sky-myths. I do not think that the myth of the dawn is now taken so seriously as it used to be. The temptation, however, seems to be strong with some minds to look for an ancient mythology underlying the primeval or even the patriarchal history. It is well known that old heathen deities survive under the guise of heroes and mythical ancestors, and it is therefore quite legitimate to examine the names and records relating to those earliest times, to see whether they rest on such a mythical basis. We can only here refer to attempts that have been made in this direction. A summary statement will be found in Baethgen's Beiträge zur Semitischen Religionsgeschichte, p. 147 ff. The conclusion to which he comes is, that any speciousness which at first sight appears in the identification of antediluvian or patriarchal names with faded deities disappears on closer inspection, either because the supposed deities are not otherwise traceable in Semitic religion, or because the names are susceptible of a much simpler explanation, or because the explanations given break down at the decisive point. As to the story of Samson, which affords such ample scope to the advocates of the sun-myth (Steinthal, Zeitschrift für Völkerpsychologie, 1862, ii. p. 129 ff., translated in Goldziher's work), it has always seemed to me that the mythological features are too strongly marked for the period at which Samson is placed—*i.e.*, he is surrounded, in the period of the Judges, by characters so thoroughly human, that he would be a glaring literary anachronism as a pure sun-myth. It may be that some traits of the story are coloured by folk-lore (though, on the other hand, there are others that will not be constrained into mythology by even the most violent methods), but that is very different from saying that he was not a hero such as the story paints him. Any traces of mythology to be found in the Old Testament are far less elaborate. They may be said to be mere traces, either remains of an extinct system or rudiments that were never developed,—such as the references to the "sons of God and the daughters of men," Rahab, Leviathan, Tannin, and suchlike. These, it should be observed, as they lie before us in the books, are handled with perfect candour and simplicity, as if to the writers they had become divested of all dangerous or misleading associations, or were even nothing more than figures of speech. They may, in part, as Flöckner and Baethgen suggest, have been adopted from non-Hebraic sources, just as classical allusions are found in modern poets. I cannot in a brief note go as fully into the question as I should like, but I have a very strong impression that in the particular of the "Dawn," which Cheyne seems to think points to a whole system of early mythology, we have a crucial instance of the different mental attitudes of the Hebrew and Aryan races. I believe there is no Semitic heathen god of the dawn, nor in the Hebrew Scriptures any hint of the contest of light with darkness. The name of the dawn in Hebrew is indubitably based on the idea of *darkness*, so that the dawn is primarily the *Morgendämmerung*, not the *Morgenröthe*. I should say that we have an undoubted instance of its use in this sense in Joel ii. 2, "dawn spread upon the mountains"—an exact picture of the gloom caused by the cloud of locusts. And I venture to suggest to scholars the possibility of giving the same sense to the word in the much-discussed passage Isaiah viii. 20, which, without the supplying of a single word or any violence to grammar, might read, "To the law and to the testimony: should they not speak according to this word, which has no dimness?" The standing phrase the "dawn went up" may thus primarily mean the rising up of the black cover of night, so that the sun, the *only* source of light, may appear; and if so, the passage in Job (xxxviii. 12 f.) would be all the more striking. The subject is worth more study than it seems to have received. Cheyne in his last commentary (The Book of Psalms) shows a growing tendency to notice myths or supposed myths alluded to or lying under Biblical expressions. When attention is at every turn drawn in this way to the eyelids of the dawn, the sides of the north, the sun as a bridegroom or strong man, the speech of the day, the gates of death, and so forth, and the mythological beliefs of other (even non-Semitic) peoples are adduced in connection, the ordinary reader can hardly be blamed for concluding that the Hebrew writers employing such expressions were on the level of heathen mythologisers. No doubt, the qualification is sometimes added that the myth is old or faded or primitive. But if so, how old is it? And what proof is there that it was ever more developed than we find it? And then, on this mode of interpretation, how much poetry will be left us? Religious language is always metaphorical; the crisis in the religious life of a people comes when either the metaphor is to run away with the thought, or the mind control the metaphor; and I maintain that the Hebrew writers, from the earliest point we can reach them, though saturated with poetry, are free from mythology in the ordinary sense. At all events, I would submit that these references are singularly out of place in a commentary, unless they are *historically* attested at the time of the writer. If it is the main object of a commentator to exhibit the mind of the writer commented on, nothing but confusion can arise from suggesting to the reader thoughts which could hardly have been in the writer's mind. It is all the more out of place when the literature under consideration is post-prophetic. Whatever may be said of the low level from which religious ideas among the Hebrews started, it will scarcely be maintained that they had a conscious belief in these nature-myths by the time of the exilic or post-exilic literature.

Note XVIII. vol. i. p. 218.—David occupies so distinguished a position in the Biblical theory of the history that heroic measures have to be taken on the modern theory to explain his true standing. His personal character and the religion of his time are described by Renan in terms which it is not worth while to transcribe (Histoire du Peuple d'Israel, tom. ii. chap. i., v.) A word may here be said as to the ascription to him by the Biblical tradition of the gift of song. (See above, vol. i. p. 104.) Vatke, relying on Amos vi. 5, 6, says that the Davidic muse had scarcely the predominant religious tendency which a later age presupposed. And Robertson Smith goes the length of saying: "It is very curious that the book of Amos represents David as the chosen model of the *dilettanti* nobles of Ephraim, who lay stretched on beds of ivory, anointed with the choicest perfumes, and mingling music with their cups in the familiar manner of oriental luxury" (O. T. in the Jewish Church, p. 205). It is "very curious," certainly, that a learned professor should make such an assertion, for Amos does no such thing. All that the prophet says about David in this connection is, that the nobles in question "devise for themselves instruments of music like David." To make the comparison extend to the whole passage is monstrous. The prophet tells the luxurious nobles that they are enjoying everything *that is best* themselves, but "are not grieved for the affliction of Joseph"; and if there is any inference to be drawn as to David's musical attainments, it is this, that his instruments had the fame of being the *ne plus ultra* of their kind. There may be—probably there is—irony in the prophet's words, as one might describe as a Solomon a person who made great pretence to wisdom. When Isaiah utters a woe upon those who "are mighty to drink wine, and men of strength to mingle strong drink" (Isa. v. 22), he does not mean that all athletes are drunkards. The view of Amos in regard to the position of David in history is found in chap. ix. 11.

Note XIX. vol. i. p. 289.—From the form of the question in Amos v. 25, and the emphatic position of the word "sacrifices" in the original, it may be concluded that the prophet expected a negative answer to the question, "Did ye offer sacrifices to me in the wilderness forty years, O house of Israel?" But this being admitted, the difficulties of the passage only begin. Did he mean to refer to the desert period as a good time, and imply—It was not sacrifice that constituted the good feature of Israel's behaviour then? Or did he mean to say that even in the desert they were a rebellious corrupt people, or a people under displeasure to such an extent that sacrifice would not have been accepted from them? Both Amos (ii. 10) and Hosea (ix. 10, xi. 1 ff.) refer to the time of the desert as one of favour shown by Jahaveh; but this is not inconsistent with the view that they were even then a rebellious and backsliding people, as even these prophets, as well as the historical writers, indicate. It may be, as Bredenkamp maintains, that the forty years is given as a round number to indicate the greater part of the period—viz., thirty-eight years—when the people were under chastisement (see Deut. ix. 7 ff.; Josh. v. 6), and excluding the two years spent about Sinai, when the legal system is represented as having been organised. Apart from this, however, the difficulties of the passage in the present connection begin at v. 26. For whereas some writers (as Daumer and Kuenen) see a reference to the past, and make the prophet declare that this idolatrous worship was practised in the desert, others (as Robertson Smith, König, Schrader, &c.) take the reference to be to the future, "So shall ye take up (viz., on the road to exile) the stake (or column) of your king, and the pedestal of your images," &c. (see Queen's Printer's Bible). Bredenkamp (Gesetz u. Propheten, p. 83 ff., who takes v. 26 to refer to the *past*) discusses the passage at some length. See also Robertson Smith, Prophets, pp. 140, 399; Wellhausen, Hist., p. 56; König, Hauptprobleme, p. 9. As to the idolatrous objects named, see Schrader, Cuneiform Inscriptions, Eng. tr., vol. ii. p. 141 f. Why is it, by the way, that Amos should be considered such an authority on the stars in this passage, and yet not be allowed to be the author of passages that speak of them in connection with Jahaveh's greatness? (Amos v. 8).

Note XX. vol. i. p. 293.—Daumer, of course, makes a great deal of all these cases (pp. 26 ff.), arguing that the expression "before the Lord" denotes a formal religious act or ceremony of worship. It may be conceded that the expression has a religious reference —*i.e.*, that it was under a strong religious impulse that Samuel slew Agag, and that David thought he was performing a "religious duty," as we say, in giving up Saul's descendants to what was no doubt a cruel and unmerited fate. All this, however, is far from proving that human sacrifice was part of the recognised worship. That the sacredness of human life was not so great in the age of David and Samuel as to outweigh what was regarded as a sacred obligation or blood claim on the other side, need not surprise any one who believes in a progressive education in morality. When (not so long ago) men were hanged in this country for sheep-stealing, it was done in obedience to what

were regarded as the sacred demands of justice. See Mozley's
'Ruling Ideas in Early Ages.'

Note XXI. vol. ii. p. 41.—The distinction between monotheism
and monolatry is one that it is easy for us to draw. At the same
time, the important point in this discussion is whether the Israelites worshipped only one God, and what was the character
they assigned to Him. It is quite probable that it never occurred to them to ask themselves what precisely were the gods
of the nations around them; and, as is shown in the text, had
they put such a question, they would very probably have been
at a loss for an answer. We must not look in the Old Testament for what it does not profess to give. Max Müller speaks
of a primitive intuition of God which he calls henotheism;
which in itself is neither monotheistic nor polytheistic, though
it might become either, according to the expression which it
took in the languages of men (Selected Essays, vol. ii. p. 412 f.)
His well-known explanation of the monotheistic turn of the
Semitic races is that their languages enabled those using them
to keep in memory the predicative or appellative sense of words,
so that they did not run into *nomina*, which were confounded
with *numina*. But the question always recurs, Whence this
peculiar build of language, if not from the mind of those forming and employing it? So that the problem why the Semitic
race (or a part of them) *thought* in this peculiar way, is no
nearer solution on a merely philological basis. (Compare
above, vol. i. p. 211.)

Note XXII. vol. ii. pp. 53, 82.—Stade also, though he speaks
of an intimate relation between Jahaveh and Israel as subsist-
ing from Mosaic times, yet maintains that the designation of
this relation as a covenant cannot be proved anterior to the
seventh century (Gesch., i. p. 507). The Hebrew word for covenant (כרית) is no doubt etymologically connected with a verb
(כרר) to cut, and in its derivation, and in the usual connection with the verb כרת (to cut), there is clear reference to sacrificial rites in connection with its ratification. (See Gen. xv. and
Delitzsch's Comment.) Robertson Smith has pointed out the

old Arab usages in this matter (Kinship and Marriage, p. 47 ff.;
Religion of the Semites, 296 ff.) He says, however, very appos-
itely, that "a nation like Israel is not a natural unity like a
clan, and Jehovah, as the national God, was, from the time of
Moses downward, no mere natural clan god, but the god of a
confederation, so that here the idea of a covenant religion is
entirely justified." He thus seems to take the original sense of
the word as συνθήκη, with a reciprocal sense. Others, less
properly, give it the sense of διαθήκη, from the idea of decision, determination, and then institution. Though this is not to
be maintained, and though the obligations resting upon God,
as one party to the covenant, may not be brought into the foreground, as being understood, yet we cannot conceive of a covenant without obligations, in the form of commands, resting on
man. Even Jeremiah's new covenant implies a law (Jer. xxxi.
33). See Bredenkamp, Gesetz und Propheten, p. 22, and his
reff.

Note XXIII. vol. ii. p. 57.—It seems to be generally taken
for granted, without proof, that the early Israelites knew little of
the great outside world. Robertson Smith, *e. g.*, says of the
times of Amos, "We are led to suppose that the very name of
Assyria was unknown to the mass of the Hebrews" (Prophets,
p. 91). He admits, however, that Amos himself knew with surprising exactness the history and geography of all the nations
with whom the Hebrews had any converse; but instead of
taking one man as the type of many, as he does in the case of
Micah the image-maker in the book of Judges, he supposes
that Amos had been a great traveller (ibid., p. 128 f.) For my
part, I do not see any reason to think that Amos, who tells us
plainly what his manner of life was, differed in this particular
from the average man of his time. When the Franco-Prussian
war was raging in Europe, there were numbers of Druze peasants in Lebanon, who had never been on a boat, inquiring
eagerly day by day for news of the campaign, and following
closely the fortunes of the combatants. Palestine was not so
large a country, nor its people in those times so dull, that the
great Phœnician trade could be carried on about their borders

without their having some knowledge of the great world. Jeroboam was not the only adventurer that went from Palestine to Egypt, nor was Jonah the only Jewish youth that ran away to sea. It has generally been taken for granted that it was only after the advance westward of the Assyrian power about the eighth century that Israel came to know of the great Eastern world (Knobel, Die Bücher Numeri, &c., p. 579); but are we to believe that a people who traced the origin of Abraham to the East supposed that all that region had disappeared, or ceased to talk about it? The tenacity with which old traditions cling to the oriental mind is illustrated by the fact that the inhabitants of Syria at the present day speak of the Russians as *Muskôbi* or Muscovites, a recollection of the period when Moscow was the capital (although the name Russia is known to old writers). And I would offer the conjecture for whatever it may be worth, that the name of Babel (for Babylon) retained similarly its hold on the Israelite memory as a designation of the great Eastern country, in which the supremacy oscillated between Babylon and Assyria. Schrader tells us (Cuneiform Inscriptions, on Genesis xxxvi. 31) that the name Israel does not occur in the Inscriptions as a general name for the Israelites, nor does it appear, as a rule, as the name of the northern kingdom, the designation of which is usually " land of the house of Omri. " This fact is full of suggestiveness as to the way in which " sources " may be used.

Note XXIV. vol. ii. pp. 80 and 117.—One of those general statements made without reflection on its foundation or significance, is that the Israelites who left Egypt at the exodus were a horde of slaves. We must, no doubt, accept it as the best evidence of their servitude there that the national consciousness of a people otherwise proud of their freedom, retained so vivid a recollection of their hard bondage and of the "high hand" by which they were delivered. Stade's off-hand dictum that if any Hebrew clan ever sojourned in Egypt no one knows its name, is (not to speak of the difficulty of finding traces of the Hyksos themselves in Egypt) opposed to the whole testimony of the nation, and, besides, leaves no room for the development of the pre-prophetic ideas which he himself is so fond of tracing. But if we admit that the sojourn of the people in Egypt was a historical fact, we must consider what it implies. The things that make the deepest impression on the memory are not necessarily those that make the most lasting impression on character. Although their life was at one time made "bitter in mortar and in bricks, and in all manner of service in the field," we are not to suppose that this went on from generation to generation. Even during the time of this hard service it is probable, judging by the customs of forced labour in the East, and hints in the Hebrew narrative, that they were far from being, as perhaps the popular conception represents them, an unorganised gang of slaves. They would be arranged and drawn for labour by their families and under their own chief or heads (Exod. v. 14 ff.) And we know not what amount of organisation they had reached, or what experience of ordinary life they had gained during a residence of several generations in a country like Egypt. The Egyptian *fellahîn* in the time of Mehemet Ali were probably as much oppressed as the ancient Israelites. Yet, with an army of such men, forced into the ranks, and fed on black bread and onions, Ibrahim Pasha drove the Turks from Syria. "The History of Israel," says Delitzsch (Introd. to his Commentary on Genesis), "does not begin with the condition of an ignorant, rude, and undisciplined horde, but with the transition to a nation of a race which had come to maturity amidst the most abundant means and examples of culture." He points out also the influence of the legalism and multiformity of Egyptian national and private life as seen in the laws of the Pentateuch; and dates from the sojourn in Egypt the first impulse to literary activity among the Hebrews. I do not know that there is anything incredible in the supposition that the book of the Covenant may be the codification of law and custom that prevailed even in Egypt (The Kingdom of all Israel, by James Sime, 1883, chap. v. This is a book that no doubt will be considered wild by critics, but is deserving of attention for the intelligent and honest effort to treat the Old Testament by the same rules of historical research as have "been applied in verifying the literature of Greece and Rome").

Note XXV. vol. ii. p. 89.—There is another passage in Hosea which may be referred to in this connection, not so much because of the positive evidence which it furnishes, as because it has been explained away by those who maintain that at the time of that prophet the Levitical aspect of the law is scarcely perceivable. In Hosea iv. 4 we read, "Thy people are as they that strive with the priest;" and advocates of the early existence of the Deuteronomic Code see in it a reference to Deut. xvii. 12, where it is said, "The man that doeth presumptuously is not hearkening unto the priest, . . . even that man shall die." On the other hand, the advocates of the late production of the Levitical Code, and of the lateness of the priestly authority generally, seek to explain the passage as if it contained a false or corrupt reading. I think that the explanation given by them of the expression, "As they that strive with the priest," is very frigid and weak; and I am prepared to defend the reading on purely grammatical and literary grounds. The construction of the particle *kaph* (meaning *like*) with a participle is found in Hosea in so marked a manner that it may be said to be an *usus loquendi* of that prophet. Thus in one passage (v. 10) he says, "The princes of Judah are like them that remove the landmark;" and in another place (xi. 4), "I was to them as they that take off the yoke on their jaws;" and in another passage (vi. 9), "Like the waylayers of men." Cf. also the expression, "Like the dew that early goeth away" (vi. 4). Such a usage as this, I think, guarantees the reading when there is no external evidence against it, and the expression, moreover, read as it stands, fits the context better than the reading proposed. See Robertson Smith's discussion of the passage, Prophets, p. 405 f.

Note XXVI. vol. ii. p. 132.—Not only is it the case that the dates of the "sources" are variously given by various critics, and that two at least of the sources (J and E) present a hitherto insoluble problem, but it is plain that critics like Dillmann and Nöldeke have come to very different conclusions as to the development of the history from the school of Wellhausen and Kuenen. Quite recently, too, we have had Klostermann putting forward a revolutionary view as to the original documents (Neue Kirkl. Zeitschr., i. 618 ff., 693 ff. Compare Presbyterian and Reformed Review, April 1891). And not to speak of the small school represented by M. Vernes, the articles of Halévy appearing in the ' Revue des Etudes Juives ' show that he is far from accepting the current conclusions of criticism. If it should come to be accepted—as the discoveries of archæology and the failures of criticism seem to indicate that it will—that literary activity was much older and more common in Israel than is now admitted, we shall probably the better understand how, side by side with the growth and modification of religious observances, there went on a rewriting and modification of books; which is, on all points of view, a more likely thing than the supposition of literature produced in the mass for certain specific temporary purposes. As to the dating very far apart of documents that now lie side by side, the critics themselves see no incongruity in two contemporaneous prophets, Amos and Hosea, the one saying nothing against the calves, and the other making them the very root of Israel's sin (R. Smith, Prophets, p. 175). Nay, they find in the person of Jeremiah two tendencies on this subject of law that are quite contradictory (see chap. xvii. p. 451). I will venture to add that the mode of composition, and transition from one style to another seen frequently in oriental authors, should be a warning not to push the '' separation of sources '' too far. Lane incidentally (Modern Egyptians, 5th ed., vol. i. p. 271 f.) furnishes an example, which could be paralleled by quotations from almost any Arabic author. He gives a long passage taken down to the dictation of his informant, and relating a vision of the prophet which was given to one Mohammed el-Bahaee to settle a difficult matter of tradition. The narrator first relates his vision, apparently in fullest detail, till he '' awoke from sleep joyful and happy.'' He then goes on to tell how he visited his teacher to report the occurrence, and in this relation brings in quite a new set of details that were not hinted at in the first narrative. The two accounts show so much variety that they could easily be ascribed to different writers, and it would be very easy to make out that the latter is very much later than the former. But, indeed, the Koran itself, uniform as it is above

most Arab works, exhibits quite a number of styles and not a
few divergent tendencies.

Note XXVII. vol. ii. p. 157.—A few words may here be said on
the view of Wellhausen and his school that "the kingdom which
bore the name of Israel was actually in point of fact in the olden
time the proper Israel, and Judah was merely a kind of append-
age to it" (Hist. of Israel, p. 188). Robertson Smith of course re-
peats the statement, even to the corroborative proof of the cedar
of Lebanon overshadowing the thistle that grows at its foot (2
Kings xiv. 9; Prophets, pp. 93, 137). The remark might be allowed to pass if it referred merely to political importance, for
the northern kingdom was larger and nearer to the great powers
that moulded history in those days. Yet happy is the people
that has no history. The dynastic changes and internal troubles
of the northern kingdom are in strange contrast with the long
quiet reigns of the southern kingdom; and from this point of
view the sweeping statement of Wellhausen is *a priori* improbable—viz., that "religiously the relative importance of the two
corresponded pretty nearly to what it was politically and historically." Israel, he says, "was the cradle of prophecy; Samuel,
Elijah, and Elisha exercised their activity there. What contemporary figure from Judah is there to place alongside of these?"
Why, Samuel belongs to the undivided kingdom, a proof, even
if we had not stronger ones, that the cradle of prophecy is not
to be located on geographical considerations. And who were
Nathan and Gad; and where did Amos come from? Isaiah
himself cannot be a sudden apparition in Judah. The quiet of
the little southern state, the prestige of Jerusalem, the disposition to rest on the past, all speak for Jerusalem as the centre of
religious life, and for the Davidic house as, in religious regard,
something quite different from the northern kingdom. Palestine is not so large, nor were the boundaries of the two kingdoms
so firmly set by nature, that the mere distance of a few miles
could make much difference in the social and religious condition
of the people. Yet the tone of the northern prophets, who seem
to have had before them a worship full of idolatry, differs so
much from that of the prophets of the south, who reprove the

people for too much attention to forms, that we must recognise a difference in the religious associations and standing of the two kingdoms.

Note XXVIII. vol. ii. p. 181.—In Cheyne's Jeremiah, His Life and Times, pp. 69-86, the English reader will find in an accessible and comprehensive form a statement of the main critical positions in regard to the date and authorship of Deuteronomy. It does not fall within the scope of the present work to enter into critical questions as to the composition of books, and I have stated my reasons for believing that the Biblical theory of the history is not inconsistent with the supposition of a late date for the book of Deuteronomy. A good many of the statements of Professor Cheyne are, I think, quite controvertible; but I can only refer briefly to one or two points bearing on the theory of the history. For instance, he does not seem to take any account of the possibility of one in Moses' position foreseeing (in the ordinary and literal sense or the word) what was most likely to happen after the occupation of Canaan. And when he tells us that the author of Deuteronomy "is full of allusions to circumstances which did not exist till long after Moses" (p. 71), and, guided by such allusions, brings the date later and later down till he reaches the age of Manasseh or Josiah, he somewhat invalidates his own argument by adding that, after the promulgation of Deuteronomy, "even very near Jerusalem the reformation was but slight" (p. 73). For it is always open to the objector to argue that, if breaches of the law are found after the solemn national adoption of it, the earlier "circumstances" alluded to are no proof that, at the time of their occurrence, such a law had not been promulgated. What I particularly dispute, however, is the statement that the fundamental idea of the holy people is Isaiah's, and that "it was that great prophet's function to transfer the conception of holiness from the physical to the moral sphere" (p. 73). Such a statement, even with the qualification added to it that "others had laboured in the same direction," is to my mind altogether inadequate, in view of the writings of Amos and Hosea, the book of the Covenant, and anything that can at all be ascribed to Moses himself. Whether the word be there or not, the idea of a people *separated* from other nations in belief and practice, and constituted as a people on an ethical basis, is fundamental and Mosaic; and it is only on such a supposition that it can be asserted with any proper significance that Deuteronomy is in spirit Mosaic. But, indeed, is it not conceivable that this Deuteronomic spirit was a thing of development and growth, having its germ in the Mosaic religion, and, instead of appearing for the first time in one late age, coming to maturity in the course of the history? In other words, instead of saying that Deuteronomy speaks as its authors supposed Moses would have spoken had he been alive, and that it abolished things which Moses might have tolerated in his own day, but would have condemned had he lived later (p. 78 f.), I think we get a more reasonable view of the matter if we suppose that it is the final expression, in the light of history, of views that had been germinating in the minds of good men from the days of Moses, the exposition of principles so firmly rooted in their minds that the writers in all sincerity regarded them as Mosaic. It is one thing to ascribe to early times an institution which exists and has long existed, or an idea or tone of thought which is well defined and deeply rooted; it is not so easy to conceive of this being done with institutions newly set up, or ideas for the first time formulated. This distinction would, I think, help materially to explain the success of Josiah's reformation, as it would also remove the necessity for the ascription of any fraud or delusion, or even illusion, to those who were its prominent agents. I believe it would also explain the Deuteronomic colouring, as it is called, which is found in other books. Cheyne speaks of "the school of writers formed upon the book of Deuteronomy—a school which includes historians, poets, and prophets, and without which the Old Testament would be deprived of some of its most valued pages" (p. 68). It is not so very obvious how a school could be formed upon a book. A book issuing from a school is at least as conceivable; and the fact that the school embraced "historians, poets, and prophets," would lead us to suppose that it was of more gradual growth, under influences wider and more fundamental than a book. Even if we explain the school by the existence of the book, the book itself has to be accounted for, with characteristics sufficient to give rise to a school.

Note XXIX. vol. ii. p. 187.—The linguistic comparison of the various books or sources lies quite beyond the subject which I set before myself; and I have already indicated my doubts whether this kind of argument goes very far to determine the actual dates of the compositions, much less to determine the order of historical events. The student will find the linguistic peculiarities of the Hexateuch fully stated in Dillmann's Commentaries on those books, and in his summary statement, 'Ueber die Composition des Hexateuch' at the close of the series. Delitzsch's new Commentary on Genesis also takes note of them; and of course, in Kuenen's Hexateuch, they are produced in detail. A special work on the subject is Ryssel's 'De Elohistæ Pentateuchici Sermone' (1878), which is criticised by Kayser in 'Jahrb. für Prot. Theol.,' 1881. Riehm treated the subject also in 'Stud. u. Krit.,' 1872, and is criticised by Wellhausen in Bleek's 'Einleitung,' 4te Aufl., p. 173 ff. There is a discussion by Klostermann of the relation of Ezekiel to the law of holiness (Levit. xviii.-xxvi.) in 'Zeitschr. für luth. Theol.,' 1877. Strack gives a brief statement of a conservative view in Zöckler's 'Handbuch' (1883). vol. i. p. 138 ff.; and Giesebrecht has an important discussion of the subject (Die Sprachgebrauch des hexat. Elohisten) in Stade's Zeitschr. für Alttest. Wissensch.,' 1881. Ryssel, who has been much criticised, concludes that it cannot be asserted that the Elohist is later in date than the exile. Bredenkamp, while laying less stress on the linguistic argument, comes also to the conclusion that no part of the Elohistic Torah was produced in the period of the language succeeding Malachi; and he points out, in particular, the contrasts it presents to the language of Ezekiel (Gesetz. u. Proph. , p. 17). F. E. König, to whom I have acknowledged my indebtedness in these pages, has a special treatise, 'De criticæ sacræ argumento e linguæ legibus repetito ' (1879); and he gives also a very comprehensive statement of the whole question as to the order and relation of the various documents in his 'Offenbarungsbegriff des Alten Testaments ' (1882), vol. ii. p. 321 ff. He declares himself an

adherent of the view of Reuss and Graf that the Priestly Code
is later than Ezekiel; yet he strenuously asserts that the historical order, law and prophets, is to be maintained, and says that
the Grafian hypothesis does not involve a denial of this order.
His own position is that Moses received a veritably supernatural
revelation, that through him God brought Israel in a miraculous
manner out of Egypt, and concluded a covenant with Israel at
Sinai, where the foundations were laid of Israel's ordinances for
religion, morals, worship, and daily life (p. 333). As to the extent to which König differs from the prevailing school, it may
be mentioned that he defends the Mosaic origin of the tabernacle (ibid.), and holds that the absence of mention of the
Great Day of Atonement in Nehemiah is no proof that the law
relating to that institution was not then known (p. 331). The
laws relating to worship which he regards as belonging to the
original Mosaic legislation are, besides the prohibition of images
and the Sabbath law (which are in the Decalogue itself): the
erection of altars wherever God recorded His name, along with
which, however, the tent or tabernacle as chief sanctuary; a
priestly tribe of Levi, with high priest at its head; offerings of
animals and fruits, as burnt-offerings and thank-offerings; the
Sabbath; new moon; three collective festivals, &c. (p. 347). It
is but just to a careful worker like König to present this enumera-
tion (and the " &c. " is added by himself); for the conclusion involved in regard to the history and the credibility of the documents differs widely from that of most of the critical writers
whose views we have considered. It might be suggested that if
König is willing to believe in the antiquity of some institutions in
regard to which the history is silent, he might have been content
to accept the statements of the priestly writers as to others. At
all events, if all the institutions he mentions are Mosaic, it is
evident that an equally ancient terminology and diction must
have existed (in priestly circles at least) in regard to them. But,
as I have already indicated, 1 cannot profess to have arrived at
any certainty on such matters, and therefore do not hazard conjecture on the subject.

Note XXX. vol. ii. p. 189.—One or two instances of this style of proof may be given—it is evident that it may be carried to any length: (*a*) The cities of refuge are not of early institution, but the law in regard to them arose out of the old Bamoth. That is to say, an altar used to be a place of asylum, but when a multiplicity of altars was abolished something had to come in their place. (See Well., Hist., pp. 161-163.) Places thus set apart formed the germ of the idea of Levitical cities, and the compilers of the Priestly Code went on in their usual way to trace them back to Moses, imagining a condition of things neither known nor workable in their own days. (*b*) In Deut. there are references to the monarchy, but none in the Priestly Code. The conclusion that used to be drawn was that the Priestly Code was older than the monarchy. On Wellhausen's theory, however, that the historical sphere of the Priestly Code is one " created by itself out of its own legal premises " (p. 39), the silence as to a king is explicable by the fact that it belongs to a time when the monarchy had disappeared, and the high priest was the chief magistrate. The so-called theocracy of the pre-monarchical period is just, in short, a reading backward into history of the hierocracy of post-exilian times—p. 148 ff. (*c*) According to Exod. xxx. the expenses of the Temple worship are met directly out of the poll-tax levied from the community, which can only be explained by the fact that at that time there had ceased to be any sovereign—p. 80. (*b*) " One might perhaps hazard the conjecture that if in the wilderness legislation of the [Levitical] Code there is no trace of agriculture being regarded as the basis of life, which it still is in Deut. and even in the kernel of Levit. xvii.-xxvi., this also is a proof that the Code belongs to a very recent rather than to a very early period, when agriculture was *no longer* rather than *not yet*. With the Babylonian captivity the Jews lost their fixed seats, and so became a trading people"—p. 108.

Note XXXI. vol. i. p. 224.—I have purposely avoided making any reference to the book of Joel, although much might be said in favour of its pre-exilic and early date. I will not say that it is on account of their theory of the late origin of the Priestly Code that most of the modern critics relegate this book to post-exilic times, or even that the theory in question, taken strictly, requires this. Yet, seeing that the date of the book is so much disputed, and that so much, if anything at all, would have to be said on the subject, I prefer to leave it altogether out of account, as I have practically done in regard to the Psalter.

Note XXXII. vol. ii. p. 227.—It may be thought that I have given more importance than their views demand to the small school represented by M. Vernes, and also that the extreme positions of Daumer and Ghillany are not worthy of consideration at the present time. It is, however, to be noted that many of the views of these older writers are put forth by modern critics, and on the same grounds; and it is but fair to M. Vernes to say that his chief objection to the prevailing school is that their method is *insufficient.* He professes to carry out to their legitimate conclusion the principles on which they proceed; and if, as it seems to me, the critical "circles" to which Wellhausen refers (Hist., p. 9) are concentric, we are entitled to look at the operation of central principles. It may not be agreeable to the prevailing school to be called traditionalists; yet M. Vernes has some right to ask, if the recollection of the period immediately preceding Saul and David has almost completely disappeared, how any one can be justified in going back centuries beyond that dim period, and talking of migrations of pre-Abrahamic peoples and suchlike matters which are shrouded in impenetrable darkness (Résultats, &c., p. 42 f.) So it seems to me he is only carrying out the principles of the prevailing school when he points out that the (so-called) pre-exilic prophets have the exile, the restoration, and the spread of religion among the heathen so clearly in their view, that the books must have been written after these events had happened or become possible (p. 213 ff.) Scepticism must always be prepared to meet scepticism; and when critics triumphantly tell us that Amos declares that the Israelites did not sacrifice in the wilderness, and Jeremiah informs us distinctly that God never commanded sacrifice, and therefore the controversy as to the early legislation on that subject is ended, it is always open to the objector to ask what information Amos or Jeremiah had about times so remote that was not possessed by their contemporaries. Again, Daumer claims to be consistent and thorough; for he not only proves the *original* fire and Moloch worship of Israel from the same texts that Kuenen relies upon, but concludes, from a passage of similar tenor in Jeremiah (xlvi. 10; comp. Isa. xxxiv. 6 ff.), that this was to the *last* a recognised legal service (Feuer und Molochdienst, p. 25). Not without reason M. Vernes says (Pref., p. iii), "If erudition is an excellent and indispensable thing, it cannot take the place of method." Prof. Briggs tells us that "higher criticism is exact and thorough in its methods" (Bib. Study, p. 194). I can perceive the thoroughness; the exactness is not so apparent.

INDEX.

THE MODERN PRINTING COMPANY, NEW YORK.